THE
LINEAGE
OF THE
CODES
OF
LIGHT

by the same author

THE LINEAGE OF THE CODES OF LIGHT

Jessie E. Ayani

HEART OF THE SUN
1998

Published by Heart of the Sun, PO Box 495, Mount Shasta, CA 96067
First Edition
First Printing 1998
Second Printing 2001
Third Printing 2005
Ayani, Jessie E.
The Lineage of the Codes of Light / Jessie E. Ayani – 1st Heart of the Sun Edition
ISBN# 0-9648763-1-0
1. Shamanism 2. Women's Studies 3. Myth & Legend 4. Spirituality
5. Enlightenment

Cover Art:
"Invitation" by Francene Hart
P.O. Box 900, Honaunau, HI 96726
hartart@haii.net www.francenehart.com
Cover Design:
Silverlining Designs, Leanne Krause
P. O. Box 1346, Talent, OR 97540
www.silverlining-designs.com leanne@mind.net
Editing & Typesetting:
Heart of the Sun

Published by
Heart of the Sun
P.O. Box 495, Mount Shasta, CA 96067
info@heartofthesun.com
http://www.heartofthesun.com

*To the souls of the blessed lineage
who have held and raised
consciousness on the Earth.
To the Brotherhood of Magi who
have shared this mission as
guardians of the lineage.
Above all, to Sananda, the
ascended Jesus, who inspired and
guided this work.*

THANKS

The author wishes to thank the following for their heart-felt participation in bringing this book into being: all the women in Minnesota who have stayed with the work for years. We have reawakened the Sisterhood of the Sun together and it has been a wonderful journey. Special thanks to Neddy Thompson for proof reading the manuscript, encouragement and warm friendship. Thanks to Richard Shulman for critical reading and support, Pan Brian Paine for the original editorial assistance, Molly Hansen for final proofreading of this printing, and Leanne Krause at Silverlining Designs for the cover layout. I am grateful to Francene Hart whose watercolor painting, *Invitation*, spoke so deeply to this lineage of women. It is a particular privilege to live and write on Mount Shasta where the ascended frequencies lend a unique support to this work.

For that, I am most grateful.

JEA

Contents

*

This book is fiction . . .

. . . unless, of course, it isn't!

Leah

The circle of women drew closer as twilight blanketed them in the depth of its mystery. Candles flickered on the altar illuminating the radiant face of Sananda, the ascended Jesus, who was flanked by his mother and his beloved Mary Magdalen. Carefully placed between vases of spring flowers were photos of luminous women and children from the Andes, like flowers themselves in their brightly colored sweaters and embroidered hats. Curling smoke from spicy incense rose in the dimming light as the group of twelve turned their attention to Leah who sat cross-legged in front of the altar.

Leah was in her late fifties. Though she looked like a young woman, the wisdom emanating from her left no one to doubt her crone status. She held a light in the blueness of her eyes that was both soft and deep, and she was wearing a flowing dress of purple and black with a gold image of the Sun emblazoned upon the chest. Her skin was soft and fair and her shoulder-length blonde hair fell across her cheeks as the shadows lengthened. Minutes before, her eyes had been filled with the last rays of the setting Sun as it came through the window opposite on its way to the horizon. Leah was filled with the Sun. It radiated from her every cell and warmed all those who gathered around her.

These twelve women were not strangers to Leah. She had been gently guiding their spiritual work for five years. They had grown in their wisdom to the point where she no longer needed to guide them overtly but through the gentle movement of energy, opening doors to higher levels of consciousness and inviting them to enter. It was very subtle work as all of these women led circles of their own across the country, each coming into their fullness under Leah's gentle guidance. Many similar circles around the world had been guided by her as a teacher of teachers, but this was the first to form from the many students she had gathered around her during the initial phases of her teaching. These twelve women had been tested by the path and had endured. They had strength and softness, spiritedness and tranquillity, laughter and silence. As different as twelve women could be, they had over time, developed a cohesiveness that allowed them to act as one and fully support each other's work. A level of mastery had been achieved that was about to open the next door for them.

Leah understood the risk she was taking this evening. She was about to activate a deep remembrance at the soul level for each of these women. Some of them were more than ready to incorporate the incoming energies, but others would struggle with core beliefs and archetypal patterns before integrating fully. A risk had to be taken because it was the innate timing of the Planetary Ascension Program that was directing her, and she knew her students could support each other. Part of her mission was to activate these women who would, in turn, facilitate the activation of others. She was fulfilling her part in the Divine Plan for the Earth and humanity. Her sense of sacred timing, resulting from her own training, pulled the energy together at this time of the setting Sun, the hour of power, to open the door to a new level of consciousness.

Leah picked up a blood red velvet bag and spread an array of crystals on a black velvet cloth before her. Moving to the center of the circle, she arranged six clear quartz points into the shape of a Star of David about two feet in diameter across the points. Using her intent and the energy of her own lightbody, she connected the filaments of light emanating from the star with the endless filaments comprising the universe.

In a rich, low voice, she spoke. "My beloveds, I ask each of you to connect your filaments of light with this grid. Choose a point of the star and send the filaments from your hearts, your wombs and your third eyes to that point. With the filaments of our intent, we enter the universal grid of consciousness." Then Leah took from the black cloth six small points of rose quartz crystal. She placed them as a second star, inside the first. "With this star we connect our grid with the Christ-consciousness grid that holds the planet in readiness for ascension. Let us open our hearts to the soft pink light of our beloved Sananda as he guides our journey into the realms of higher consciousness."

Next, Leah formed a third star from pointed amethyst crystals and placed it within the rose quartz star, invoking the alchemical energies of beloved St Germain and all the ascended masters who continually guide planetary ascension and the consciousness of mankind. With the completion of the tri-form Star of David, Leah brought to the center of the circle another, larger green velvet bag. From it she took small pictures of Jesus and Mary Magdalen and placed them in the center of the grid. Again she withdrew a photo of a beautiful young Peruvian woman, and her child and set it in a specific spot in the grid. Finally, from this bag, she removed a statue of Merlin with his long white beard and magical staff. This she placed in an empty area of the grid, invoking the powers of the lineage of great magicians, the Brotherhood of the Magi, who have always worked the Earth grids. She asked that each member of the group's intent be pure.

From a heavy purple velvet bag lying beside her, Leah carefully removed an enormous generator quartz crystal. This she placed in the center of the grid as a transmitter to activate and increase energy. The women inched forward, bringing forth small votive candles to the circle and lighting them. They sat in stillness with Leah for a few moments as the last rays of the sun released radiant energy from the peak of the beloved mountain, which rose like a temple to the east of their sanctuary.

Leah closed her eyes and scanned the filaments in the room. The interlocking light of the women and their triple connection to the grid raised the star from the floor creating the true dimensions of a double star tetrahedron, the merkaba. This merkaba was connected to the endless filaments of light that are the background substance of the universe. Seeing that they were locked into the universal grid and the Christ-consciousness grid, Leah used her subtle power and intent to open a door for these women and the merkaba immediately expanded to include them all. At the same time the higher aspects of themselves, their lightbodies, connected to them from their fourth dimensional awareness and the darkness behind them became filled with the spirits of those who had carried the truth throughout time.

Without further hesitation, Leah opened her eyes and began. "My beloved sisters, we've been together for many years working in this circle. You have come with me to Peru to meet and work with the shamans there, and you have embraced the light of Sananda as I have brought his truth forth in my own work. Because something inside you feels deeply connected to all that we have done, you have opened yourselves to the teachings without question. It is a journey, our journey, but there is so much more to it than you might have imagined. This night I invite you to walk with me through yet another doorway of consciousness. Are you ready?"

All the women gave a strong affirmative as they straightened their backs and took deep breaths. They knew this was to be a night to absorb, if not fully understand, all that Leah would say. A sigh escaped Leah as a pulse of the divine vibration moved through her, an energetic affirmation that all was in readiness. Her eyes glowed as she continued.

"There are many ways in which I could gift this to you, my sisters. What I am called to do is to tell you a story. The telling of this story will stir within you a deep remembrance of your own soul mission, though it may not be understood for some time to come. It has many layers. Partly built from my own remembrances, research of my mother's bloodline and past-life healings - these have been woven together like a fine *tejido* by the revelations of the shamans, my work on the inner plane, and the translation of recently revealed documents pertaining to the life of Jesus. There are many events in our lives that serve to open our codes of knowingness. We allow light to enter us and the cryptic packets of energy that awaken us burst open. What has happened to me over time is the revelation of my identity. It has taken me years to accept it, to complete the weaving, and then to know what to do with it. The story I tell you this night has never been told in its entirety before now. Most of it is known only as bits and pieces of a puzzle by individuals who have held certain keys for me. When the last piece came into place, I was catapulted into a cosmic awareness of my being and my whole existence suddenly made sense.

"I choose to tell you this story not because it is the history of my blood and soul, but because it is the universal story of the children of God. It is no more unique than your own story and will awaken that within you. You are women bearing codes of light in the genes of your souls. It is time you knew who you were. We have this retreat time together to continue our inner work, to play and pray on the mountain, and to awaken within us the codes of our true lineage. Each day we will meet at this most sacred time of the setting Sun and continue the story until it is complete."

The women rubbed away the goose flesh provoked by Leah's passionate statement about their own codes of light. Though they knew her well as their guide, Leah seldom spoke of her own experience to them. She chose often to work in metaphor, to de-personalize her teaching. It was the shaman's way to subdue the ego and work with subtle energy. They had been privy to several divinatory coca leaf readings with the shamans in Peru but those were only pieces of an identity Leah herself obviously found unbelievable. The circle heaved a collective sigh and gave her their full attention. The room was completely dark now except for the altar and the circle of candles around the grid. Light flickered off the metallic sun on Leah's dress as she anchored her higher self within her heart and allowed the words to flow from that higher awareness. In this way, personality and ego were not involved in the discourse, the energy and intent were pure, and only truth could be spoken.

Taking a deep breath, Leah began: "I have found that we are much more than meets the eye. Yes, we are souls who have experienced a multitude of lifetimes. Yes, we are women who are individuals but also part of the collective feminine consciousness. Yes, we are part of a collective of human consciousness. But we are more than that. We are part of the consciousness of God and we are being called to bring that forth on the Earth right now. I want to tell you the story of how I came to know this about myself and therefore how I know this about you.

"As you know, I have a deep connection with the beloved people of Peru. I have often wondered why I am so connected, and they to me. I have often wondered why they know so much about me and honor me in the way they do. As I came to understand the profundity of my bloodline I understood my Peruvian connection even less. Until the last piece of the puzzle was put in place, it was a mystery to me. Now I will weave for you the story of my bloodline which has been revealed to me as I have healed it in all layers of my being. I will then confide to you the story of my soul lineage which often intertwined with this bloodline, but more often was called to serve in different cultures around the world, most notably in Peru.

"My mother's mother was named Jesse. She crossed over while I was in my mother's womb. All clairvoyant people who have encountered me have seen her standing behind me. She has been my guide and protectress, and I have always been conscious of her to some degree. She has known the mission of my soul and has, with my higher self, steered my life when this conscious part of me was too caught up in mind or emotion to see my own way. We all have this protection. It is the unseen part of us that makes books fall off shelves into our arms when we need to read them.

It opens doors and shoves us in when we're not paying attention.

"Well, Jesse has had motivation beyond keeping me out of trouble in this life. She has been the guardian of the bloodline as it has been carried on through my genetics. You must understand that cryptic packets of light can be encoded into the DNA and passed through the bloodline via chosen individuals. Scientists call this 'junk' DNA but it is far from junk. This DNA, on the higher consciousness level, serves to stabilize planetary consciousness through genetic material planted here by what we will call creator gods. Certain bloodlines have carried this material because it facilitates the evolution of consciousness at the level of the physical and etheric body. We could say that it invites in change and stabilizes it on the planet. It isn't the source of the inspiration, rather it's champion, in metaphorical terms. So Jesse has been assisting me in bringing in concepts from our lineage and anchoring them in this reality.

"Jesse's name was no mistake. It was a cryptic message, an encodement to let me know that I sprang from the tree of Jesse, from the House of David. A few years ago, this would have been unbelievable to me because I left the Catholic Church in my early twenties quite convinced that they had the story all wrong. What I have learned is that they have contrived their own story to serve their own needs, not unlike every conqueror who seeks to control his subjects. What we have been taught as history has precious little truth in it. Now there is much evidence as to the continuation of the lineage of the House of David. The genealogies of my mother's family drift in and out of the royal houses of Europe which held this blood. I have been to France and walked in the footsteps of my ancestors, and what they have had to tell me is astounding.

"I have heard the ancient voices in Egypt and followed them to the Holy Land. I have traced this bloodline on all levels through all time. It holds the key to the identity of many on the Earth right now and, by the same token, it holds the mystery of our destiny. You will see in the telling how the bloodline and soul lineage touched each other when new consciousness was being seeded on the Earth. You will see the soul lineage vanish and reappear in other civilizations when the forces of darkness overtook the bloodline. The telling of history has been complicated by the lies of those who sought the power. The lineage will become clear to you during this retreat and you will have the opportunity to recognize that it is yours as well as mine.

"Let me give you some background information about both

[14]

the soul lineage and the bloodline. Our story will begin in ancient Egypt, long before the dynasties and long before the deluge that changed the landscape as well as the population. However, the soul lineage began millions of years ago on the Earth when the first human genetics were introduced. There have been many, many races of man on the Earth, some of them achieving technological wizardry quite beyond our comprehension. Some have been dreadful failures, genetic dead-ends. Most of these seedings have been engineered by the Siriuns, our dedicated solar system guardians, but some have been from other star systems. The dog star, the brightest star in the heavens, is the home of sixth dimensional beings whose soul mission in the universe is to heal separation. These Siriun Akhus, Shining Ones or star people, are intimately associated with the Akhus of Orion, particularly the brighter stars of Orion's belt, El and An. It was in An that our galaxy came to know separation - that many souls lost God-consciousness. Some souls who continued to hold their connection with the Divine settled on Sirius. Colonization on the Earth took place eons later and there have been a few battles here as well, but the Siriun mission has prevailed and we are, with planetary ascension, moving one step closer to the heart of God.

"The soul lineage has been continually recoded to hold the frequency intended at any particular time. As you will see, the Siriuns, legendary gods in many cultural myths, have taken many forms upon the Earth, sometimes incarnating into the human birth experience and, especially in the old times, manifesting a body to facilitate the Mission. The Mission, again, is healing separation. The souls of this Siriun-based lineage were recruited from many star systems, all souls dedicated to this Mission, all souls with the deepest yearning for God. They incarnated repeatedly, usually in the typical unconscious way of humans, into the lineage's enclaves on Earth. They were guided by their elders into consciousness and, as a general rule, achieved enlightenment. Many of the lineage has been lost to the cycles of human death and rebirth. Because this is a free will planet we can move forward or in reverse. Many experience conscious death and then ascend, and a few have ascended taking their bodies with them.

"We will follow this lineage from the era of ancient Egypt called Zep Tepi, *the First Times*, to the present. These pioneering souls carried the codes of light into a lineage of women. Many of them experienced other incarnations when it was not their turn to incarnate in the lineage. In these lives, which were challenging experiences in the human dimension, the codes lay dormant and

[15]

other experiences led to soul growth. There are men who have these codes in their light body DNA but it cannot be activated from the male body. Why is this true? It has to do with the concept of balance. The Siriuns are androgynous beings because they mastered their polarities long ago. On Earth we are still deeply invested in duality where there exist masculine and feminine principles. The masculine principle has everything to do with action, doing. The feminine principle is just the opposite. It is about being, non-doing, dreaming the future and holding consciousness. You know a great deal about these principles, so it should come as no surprise to you that something like codes of light, which hold consciousness on the planet, are not about doing.

"Women who hold the codes of light are not the least bit attached to them either. They cannot be. Oh, many men and women have personal codes, gifts that they will personally come into as they anchor their light. Some women are holding key codes that are personally beneficial as well as energetic gifts to the Earth. In this lineage I am speaking of planetary codes, codes that are activated for the elevation of human consciousness. They are energetic, difficult to name and certainly impossible to possess. Do you see, then, the depth of commitment in those souls who have carried these codes?"

The group responded, slightly dazed, and Leah dove in a little deeper. "I am also speaking of goddess codes, immensely important energetic impulses that integrate consciousness opportunities on Earth with the galaxy, even the universe. These do not get activated very often, as you will see, and are not carried by all souls in the lineage. We will meet some women whose missions were so great that they incarnated as six or twelve souls of the lineage merged. The group carrying the codes of light is large and contains several subgroups who have evolved to monadic consciousness on Earth. This means that they have moved past individuation, past soul awareness and into a more universal, more inclusive concept of soul. We will meet some of the women representing these monads. It is only in separation, remember, that we would have this concept of individuation at the soul level as well as the personality level. Monadic incarnations occurred at pivotal times during this particular genetic experiment which the Siriuns called the Ascension Activation Program.

"We need to address one more important point about the codes of light and that is their opening and activation. This ties in directly with the bloodline. Men have carried the keys that open the codes of light, contributing the action component to the program.

For this particular project, they were men of the bloodline of the House of David as we have come to know it. Indigenous shamans have also carried the ability to open the codes as did the magi of old. There has been a major seeding into the indigenous cultures of South America as a fail safe for the program. We will have much to learn of this later. As for the House of David, it did not begin with Adam. It began when the first Siriun Ascension Activation Program emissaries alighted on this planet to seed the genes that would be found as a hybridization in Adam. It was the first impulse on the planet of the Grail legacy, the codes of kingly service to the people and the Earth. Many bloodlines were spawned but this particular bloodline became the vehicle for the keys to planetary ascension. It was necessary to re-introduce the genes from time to time as the keys, carried in the physical and etheric DNA, mutated and the bloodline, which was human after all, fell into very unconscious behavior. Let us remember that the codes of light are carried in the light body DNA as a soul commitment and are not subject to incarnate mutation. We will see several occasions when the bloodline was thoroughly reconstituted by a Siriun emissary, a god-incarnate.

"During the latter stages of my story, you will become aware that we have now entered a period in which the Mission has broadened and is being carried out simultaneously in three dimensions - the third, this reality, the fourth or astral, and the fifth, soul reality or the first ascended state. Eventually, the fifth dimension is where Earth is headed - a state where negativity does not exist and the predominating frequency is divine love and enlightenment. It is a masterful plan being executed by many both on and off the planet. Many humans who have mastered certain aspects of their soul growth are carrying personal and key codes at this time and the soul lineage of the codes of light has incarnated *en masse*. Since the time of Jesus, the genes of the bloodline, which harbor the ability to open the codes, have been disseminated everywhere. These genetic keys lay dormant in the blood of so many men who are completely unconscious of the gift they carry. Do you see what is happening? It is the fruition of the program. We are poised on the brink of planetary ascension. Everything is in place for us. All we have to do is wake up and remember who we are. All we have to do is step out of the density of this three dimensional illusion and embrace Divine Love."

Sparks seemed to fly out of Leah's eyes and her passion was not lost to her close-knit circle of apprentices. "All we have to do is remember that we are God, that we are not separate from the creative force of the universe.

"I know you remember the times I have talked to you about the filaments of light. How could you not remember my obsession," she laughed. "Well, one more time isn't going to hurt." Everyone was laughing now for they had heard of the filaments hundreds of times, though none had seen them yet. "These filaments are the matrix of the universe. They are in everything and they connect everything. This was the most profound teaching of the shamans for me. We interact with this matrix from a place in our fourth dimensional or astral body which Don Juan, the Shaman who taught Carlos Casteñeda, called the assemblage point. It is where our reality is assembled or perceived. He also taught that these filaments are another name for intent. It is intent that moves the cogs of the universe - that shapes reality. If our filaments emanate out into the collective unconscious, our reality and limitations are gleaned from that resource and we are locked into the collective behaviors that are not going to serve us now. If we shift our perception, shift our assemblage point, and align our filaments with Divine Love, that becomes our new reality. It sounds simple but it is generally a lot of hard work shifting beliefs and patterns to accept a new reality. Every once in a while we receive a jolt and a shift is accomplished in the wink of an eye, but usually such shifts are incremental and painstakingly conscious. I hope that you are able to let go of old ways of thinking and receive the jolt of new perception as this story unfolds. It means leaving the old ways behind, without attachment to them, and it means incorporating filaments of higher frequency into your energetic body. It is time for all of you to move into your mastery and before you know it, your students will be doing the same.

"Well, that should suffice as background information for my story which is really ten different stories. Most of the lives touched upon will be those of pivotal importance to the program but some will just be touching journeys of remarkable women. I will introduce each woman to you, then allow her to speak through me. We will, in each case, be privy to their story as they fulfill a tradition of the codes of light - one woman activating the codes of the next in the lineage before she departs the Earth. The codes are activated, another way of saying consciousness of them is passed, as they tell their story, just as I am telling you part of mine." Leah's eyes twinkled as she let that one sink in.

Julia put her hand to her heart. "Leah, does that mean you are preparing to leave?"

"No, my dear Julia, I am not leaving yet. I am sparking an

unusual variation in the lineage - expansion. You will see in one story that the lineage split into two lineages as a fail-safe, and further down the time line it is shifted to those who will keep it safe while our culture entered the darkness. RIght now, we have this soul lineage incarnating *en masse*. Do you think that I don't know who you are, all of you? There are many more of you all around the world. I will keep pushing you into mastery because opening codes is not enough. The Divine Plan activates and releases them when the carrier reaches the code frequency. It means continually uplifting your consciousness, doing your spiritual work. When the filaments of these codes of light are released, they will interact with the Christ Consciousness grid that surrounds the Earth. This grid has already irrevocably interlocked with the telluric grid within the Earth. Earth is moving into the fifth dimension and mankind is lagging behind. The codes of conscious ascension need to be opened, activated and released to complete the Mission. Then the frequency of that consciousness has to be held by those capable of holding it, those walking in mastery. What I am doing is turning that responsibility over to you. New codes are begging to be opened within me and I need to turn my attention to the attainment of their frequency. In other words, I have to get to work on myself!"

The whole group laughed at Leah's last remark and the matter-of-fact way she stated it. She joined them, then asked if they had any questions or if there was any additional background information they felt they might need. Katy cleared her throat and ventured forth with a question.

"Leah, why do we not know of that very ancient time in Egypt? Is it because of the flood?"

"That's an interesting question, Katy," Leah replied. "That time in Earth's history can be referred to as the Sothic period since Sothis is Greek for Sirius. It was a golden age of peace, harmony and great achievement. The truth is we do know about it but the Egyptologist are not willing to accept the facts because they would have to revamp all of their theories. There are political, cultural and religious reasons why people in power do not want history to be rewritten. This is the sort of thing that happened when it did get written, which is why it isn't accurate. It is, on all levels, the devilish work of human egos that separate us from the truth. It is the ego which separates us from God as well. When the timing of the Divine Plan demands the truth, all will be revealed, Katy. There will be undeniable proof of the creator gods, the seedings, the lost races and more. When all of that is revealed, it will be a time of unparalleled cooperative scholarship and all of the egos will be abandoned to it. It will be so extraordinarily exciting."

The women felt a rush of energy move through them and recognized that their truth had been spoken. "Leah, can a woman know she is carrying planetary codes of light?" asked Pat.

Leah spoke softly to the circle. "When her consciousness has been raised to the frequency of the codes, she will know it. Since this system operates outside the ego, she will have shifted her assemblage point to universal consciousness. She will know what every Earth master knows and have no attachment to it. Knowing that one carries the codes while still in the ego's field of perception makes the work of detachment a little more challenging. Those women of the lineage who were skillfully trained from childhood to hold consciousness were never attached to ego. Those of us who are flying by the seat of our pants, so to speak, are having to detach from ego through exercises in hypervigilance, that acute state of awareness wherein every word and deed is monitored to assure that it serves a higher purpose than ego gratification. This progresses into higher states of consciousness where small transgressions bring stupendous lessons until we just finally get the assemblage point in the right place. If the knowledge that you hold codes of light feeds your ego, you may not be able to hold the frequency for them to open. When they open, it is beyond your control to activate them or release them. They really don't belong to you. You are acting as a carrier. You may or may not feel it happen. Sometimes it is earthshaking and sometimes it is very subtle. It is best to detach from any idea of importance or possession with respect to the codes. Allow all of this to unfold in your soul space, that universe where personality does not have so much power. We have worked a lot with ego in this group and I dare say that your students have put each of yours to the test."

With that they burst into peels of laughter, each one of them recognizing the personal honing that spiritual teaching provided. Leah was their veteran, their role model and she had been through it all. She rose to her knees, hands on her slender hips and closed her eyes for a moment to silence the group. She took a deep breath, released it and said "It feels right to take a break now, have a little snack, and then Sananda is encouraging us to continue since we have established a very receptive energy field. We will begin our journey in ancient Egypt where this current seeding started. What do you say, my darlings?"

"Yes!" they cried in unison rushing to hug her, rushing to share their love with her and receive the loving power of her heart.

Mir-An-Da

Leah speaks

"As I've already mentioned, ancient times in Egypt were referred to as Zep Tepi, *the First Times*, the times when the 'gods' ruled the Earth. It was a very long time ago, an era ending before 10,500 BC when Earth moved into the precessional age of Leo and the great deluge cleansed her of vast negative energies that would have destroyed her. Before the arrival of the 'gods' and Zep Tepi, two tribes, one dark-skinned and the other olive-skinned, inhabited the land known as Egypt. They were remnants of previous human seedings. Each practiced religious rites and honored gods of their lineage but their beliefs had become distorted through the ages because their initiates had succumbed to earthly pleasures and the desire for power. With the loss of the great primordial teachings of their ancestral spirits they were reduced to simple agrarian lives, each occupying their own shores of a great lake where now the Nile runs. This was a time when all of Egypt was fertile, rains fell plentifully, and the landscape was a paradise.

"Our story begins as a gentle young woman, Shaleb, of the olive-skinned, dark-haired Murite tribe who lived on the east side of the lake, quite unexpectedly found her womb swelling with child. Her husband, Peth, had a very poor memory and Shaleb never spoke to him of the impossibility of this pregnancy. The child was conceived during the time of harvest when both she and Peth were far too exhausted for love-making. Shaleb held her thoughts and fears within even as she held the child within. During her sixth month of pregnancy, she began having dreams of the most beautiful girl-child she had ever seen. This fair-skinned and golden-haired child was always sitting in a shady spot along the lake with a handsome white dog. She brought to Shaleb feelings of love and purity.

"These dreams continued every night and Shaleb began to long for sleep just to be with the child. Soon the little girl began to speak to her in her dreams, telling Shaleb that her name was Mir-An-Da, daughter of the stars, and that she came from the brightest star in the heavens, Sirius. She had a great Mission to perform on the Earth and it was her desire to be born of an earthly mother. Some vastly mysterious part of Shaleb had apparently agreed to bring Mir-An-Da forth. When she had released her monthly egg, it had been fertilized with genetic material from Sirius. This was where the creator gods orchestrated this new genetic intervention on Earth. Shaleb's head was spinning - she understood little of Mir-An-Da's words but knew that something quite extraordinary was about to happen to her. There was no doubt she could feel this, and she asked Mir-An-Da to make the way easy.

"Mir-An-Da began preparing Shaleb for her birthing and child-rearing. During the ninth month of the pregnancy she began speaking directly to Shaleb in her conscious waking state - it was like a clear voice in her head. At the same time Shaleb began to dream less and less of Mir-An-Da and the young child moved into the dream space of Peth, who having never remembered dreaming before, was astounded and immediately began sharing these dreams with Shaleb. She burst into tears of relief that she could now speak to her husband about the impending birth and she secretly thanked Mir-An-Da for this gift of making her way easier.

"The child's voice within her head coached her to prepare herbs for teas and poultices to ease the pain of childbirth, and with very little effort, Shaleb brought forth a baby who embodied the wisdom of the stars and Divine Love. Mir-An-Da looked like no one around, and least of all her parents. Her skin was a creamy white and her golden hair was softly curled. What was most astonishing about her features were her eyes of the deepest, clearest blue, the color of her star. So unusual was her inner radiance that village gossip spared Shaleb and Peth, and gravitated toward the concept of a gift from the gods, perhaps a messenger from their gods of long ago. From the day she was born, Mir-An-Da worked with the unconscious minds of this tribe to establish her presence upon the Earth. As her energy merged with that of the villagers, they became more reverent and loving in their everyday lives.

"Mir-An-Da was born conscious of her Mission and her origins. Until she could speak to her mother directly, she continued to steer her upbringing through the voice in her mother's consciousness. When she was a young girl, she began touching people's wounds or places of pain, healing them immediately with the love she radiated. It did not take long for her reputation to spread, and the dark-skinned people from the west crossed the Nile to meet this child and be in her company. They too felt she might be a messenger from their gods and began to revere her and incorporate her simple love and peace into their lives. She grew in beauty, grace and wisdom during her childhood to become a maiden of great power.

"Hers is a story of feminine wisdom, but also of balance and true mastery. She was the sister bride and soul twin of Aman-Ra, a Siriun creator god made manifest, who ruled with her for thousands of years. They and their golden-haired offspring were of much taller stature than the tribes around them. Their legendary reign, the golden age of Egypt, spawned the myths of Isis and Osiris and saw the building of the lion monument and initiatory temples which stand as messengers from those ancient times. In the context of Earth history, theirs was a recent genetic seeding but one of vast importance to planetary ascension for it brought the codes of light for Christ Consciousness, the Grail legacy, upon Earth.

"Let me travel back in soul memory to the time when Mir-An-Da and Aman-Ra were preparing to leave Earth, their Mission complete at last. Even as Aman-Ra was preparing his high initiates for his departure, Mir-An-Da was completing the passage of the codes of light to her daughter Mai-An who, with her brother/ husband Amen-Se, would rule the lands in their stead. Mother and daughter sat together before the eternal flame in the temple of the feminine at Annu (Heliopolis). Mai-An, a reflection of her parents, was already several hundred years old but appeared as a young woman before her mother. She carried pure Siriun genes and, with Amen-Se, would further the lineage of the gods upon the Earth.

'Mir-An-Da led Mai-An to the women's temple, and dismissed the guardians of the inner chamber, ushering her daughter within. Following behind them was a magnificent white dog with great pointed ears who never left Mir-An-Da's side. This she-dog, Te-An, appeared one day when she was a child, and like her own immortal being, had lived these millennia to act as her guardian. She knew that immediately after her departure, Te-An would walk off to the west and disappear, her mission also completed. As they entered the sacred chamber, the Sun was low in the western sky. The circular room was the highest in the temple complex. Its windows were made of elegant pieces of colored glass held in place with copper, not unlike our stained glass. Sacred symbols of the stars and Earth elements comprised the designs. In short it was a chamber where Earth and sky met. The ceiling was dark blue painted with glittering silver constellations. Sirius, known to those of the Sothic age as Ak-An lay on the eastern horizon of this sky dome. Its name referred to its role in the galaxy as the doorway to An, the middle star in the belt of Orion, which is the galactic stargate, the portal to the outer galaxy. The floor was fashioned of colored stone chips, like mosaic, but much smoother. Within its design, was a copper inlaid Star of David, its six points almost touching the circular walls.

"Mir-An-Da took from a shelf on the wall six small clay oil lamps and set one at each point. Then she reached into the pockets of her robes and withdrew six large sapphires that were cut into pointed wands. She set one in front of each oil lamp, their points directed toward the center of the star. Mai-An carefully watched her, and felt the energy move within the room when her mother activated the grid with her intent. Mir-An-Da deftly opened the west facing window to allow the Sun's light to bathe them and then moved to the center of the room, within the hexagonal space of the star, to the throne of the high priestess.

"Mai-An's eyes glowed in the light as her mother seated herself in the regal chair before her own soft cushion. Te-An curled up at her mistress's feet, ears alert but eyes closed. Mir-An-Da wore the black robes of the high priestess, embroidered with golden stars and lined with soft golden cloth. Her ageless face shone with an unearthly radiance and was framed by wavy golden hair. She wore the crown of a queen, studded with sapphires symbolic of her blue star, Ak-An, and bearing a halo of golden stars, each one attached by gold filaments to its points. This temple had been established by her, and she had trained all the women who were dedicated to the feminine principle. She felt not a single regret at the completion of this Earth Mission. She could feel herself move out of, then back into, this reality. Mai-An noticed this, and knew her mother's readiness."

Leah shifted her body and closed her eyes. Taking several deep breaths, she allowed the energy of Mir-An-Da to begin moving through her - to come alive within her. When she felt connected at her core, she allowed the words to commence.

[24]

Mir-An-Da speaks

"My beloved daughter," she began, her soft blue eyes embracing Mai-An with her soul light, "tomorrow Annu (the Sun) will reach its most northern place in the heavens. As it rises, our Ak-An will rise with it. It is time for your father and me to return to Ak-An, for our present Mission is complete. Before dawn tomorrow morning, we will arise and board the royal barge which will take us across the lake to the great lion temple of Aman-Ra. We will cleanse ourselves in the temple baths and rub our bodies with the sacred oils of transmutation in preparation for the journey. Leaving our earthly garments behind for you and Amen-Se, we will walk the sacred pathway to the great lion king monument which lies facing the dawn in stony silence. Your father had this monument carved from the rock outcropping that already bore the appearance of a lion. It will rest here for eons, a stoic reminder to the adept of the starry origins of humankind. Long after we Akhus (star beings) leave the Earth to allow the new seed to develop, the great lion will see its starry counterpart rising with the dawn at the midpoint of Annu's journey to the north, and the Earth will enter a time of trial.

"Tomorrow we will take our places, naked before the heart of this great beast, and face the east. We will watch Ak-An rise before Annu. Then, between the time that the first ray of Annu strikes us and the full rising of the disc, we will transmute these earthly forms using Annu's energy and be returned to the sixth dimension. You will do likewise when your time is finished here, which will be much shorter than mine. We have trained both you and your brother in the transmuting rituals and you have been working with Annu's energy for decades. I cannot stress enough the importance of this practice. If you cannot transmute your earth bodies you will be trapped in the cycle of human reincarnation - the very thing we have come to transcend. I know that you and Amen-Se will have no problem with your ascension. This will not be so in the future for the kings and queens many generations hence, but I will speak of the prophecies when I am drawing this transmission to a close.

"I have two stories to tell you, one of the past and one of the future. It is my hope that they will spark within you your own Mission on this planet now that I pass my robes and crown to you. I have trained you well to serve these people and know that neither you nor Amen-Se will ever misuse the power you now inherit. You understand that you are not of this world, but are here only to serve the evolution of consciousness on this planet, and in particular those aspects of consciousness carried in the blood and light codes brought by your father and myself. It is most important that you remember who you are and why you have come here. You were not born in full consciousness, Mai-An. You came forth as the humans do but with completely new genes that your father and I introduced here. You have had many brothers and sisters who took the new genes into marriages with the old. They journeyed to many lands carrying this genetic material along with the teachings of our star system. In time, these new genes and truths will prevail and we will be able to complete the next step of the larger Mission on this planet, her ascension into the fifth dimensional universe, the place of the soul. But wait, I jump into the future already," she laughed, "let me begin with my own remembrance.

"I was called before the High Council in the Great White Lodge on Ak-An. The Akhus there are sixth dimensional beings working on their own ascension into the seventh dimension. They have long been involved with seeding genes on the Earth and have assumed the particular duty of guiding the evolution of this solar system and aspects of the galaxy, a process that was set in motion eons ago. I had been involved in countless missions for them, usually bearing different aspects of consciousness within the feminine polarity. What the council was proposing to me this time was somewhat different. It was becoming more and more difficult for their souls to incarnate on Earth and remain pure. These Akhus were either unable to withstand the heavy frequencies of the human field and had to leave, or they would succumb to them and become entrapped in the cycles of human death and reincarnation.

"The High Council had developed a new strategy for the evolution of human consciousness and wished to enlist the services of myself and your father, the beloved male half of my soul. Sitting before them, we listened to their plan. We were to remain on Earth longer than in any previous experiment, to allow the full implanting of all that we were to carry. It was to be the principle seeding for the fifth dimensional shift, although other fail-safe seedings would be carried out. Thousands of years is a long time for humans to consider living but that is only because they are locked into the patterns of death and rebirth. For us, as you know, that is meaningless. Looking at all possible futures, it seemed the plan might work. We agreed to come to Earth as part of a large soul group working on behalf of the planet, and now the part of the plan involving us has been completed. You will

[26]

understand as I continue my story. Now your part is about to begin - this you will also know before we have finished.

"I was asked to come forth as a human child, to be birthed from the womb of a Murite woman who lived in this place we are now calling Annu, in honor of the great solar disc. The Murites were the remnant of an earlier seeding from the planet Nibiru. There were few Murites, the tribe having suffered much from famine in the lands to the east where they originated, but they were fairly pure genetic stock. The Akhus of Ak-An were most interested in this geographical location for the preservation of certain truths during millennia of Earth change and conflict that have yet to come. This Murite woman, Shaleb, was uncomplicated and very receptive to guidance regarding my birth and upbringing. Her husband, Peth, was less intelligent than Shaleb but supportive in every way. I had cleared them with the High Council after scanning their Akashic records. I then fertilized her egg through interdimensional genetic manipulation and inactivated her Murite genes to accommodate the pure strain being introduced from Ak-An. This is not always necessary but, in this case, it was important to introduce a high level of purity. As you know from your own experience, Mai-An, this sort of genetic intervention is not difficult. Sometimes, however, it does not conform to cultural patterns of impregnation. One has to be mindful of that. In my case, it was not a serious transgression as my earth father had a very poor memory of his procreative efforts. In your case, of course, it was part of the program.

"Shaleb, my mother was the sweetest, most loving woman, and she did not, in the least, resent my directives. I was fully aware of the codes that I was carrying and, above all, kept that knowledge from my parents and the villagers. My personal codes began opening at an early age, indeed some were opened in utero to facilitate telepathic and dreamtime communications with my mother. It was my vision to open the filaments of light so that I could see blocks in the energetic bodies of those around me as well as their dreadfully dull auras. I began moving their energy and healing physical and emotional wounds. When I was no more than five years old, I was sought out as a healer. My parents had additional children after I was born and it was easy to see them in the womb. The day my mother almost lost my little brother is still clear in my memory. We were sitting in the garden preparing vegetables when I glanced at her worried face. She was attuned to something, and I looked within her womb to see the little one suffocating with the cord around his neck. Without a thought to

[27]

her reaction, I rushed to her and reached through her belly to unwrap the cord. She felt nothing as I used a higher energy form of myself to do it, but she was shocked. These were natural skills, personal codes, for me that I had awakened in many previous Earth Missions. When my little human brother, Chad, grew up he became one of your father's greatest students and then an important astronomer here in Annu.

"The chosen genes soon had me towering over the villagers and looking quite spectacular, I am sure. Oh, I laugh to think of it now for the stature of the people has greatly increased with the success of the breeding program. All of this golden hair on a fair-skinned giant was quite phenomenal. People were quick to love, however, and it did not matter. Soon the dark-skinned nomadic tribes farming the west side of the lake were coming for healings, or perhaps just to see the fair giant. I took them into my heart readily for they were also open, loving people and I do not see separation. All is an extension of myself and I am an extension of Prime Creator! That is the absolute truth, Mai-An. Well, soon it was common to see both tribes in the others' village and some trading took place. These were primitive people who had few useful farming tools, yet there was some sharing of ideas and refashioning of tools which made life a little easier for them. It was a simple life and as I grew older, mother, with her hands full of little ones, gave me the task of cooking, while the rest of the time was my own. I loved cooking for it was a way to work with energy and alchemy. My whole family was being energized with love and wisdom every time they ate. I spent as much time as I could with the Earth, accustoming myself to her frequency. Sitting in the water, I learned of her power. Standing in the wind, I listened to his messages about the weather, and with my cooking I observed the transformative power of fire. These were my friends, but also the four important anchoring devas of the Earthwalk, and I was here to walk the Earth.

"Now you see that I had an unusual childhood by human standards. I helped my mother, healed ailing people by seeing and moving their energy, and allied myself with the great devas of nature to secure their support for the program. When I was fourteen I could feel the pulse of the feminine stirring within me. I told Mother that I would soon begin to bleed and I would need her help with my initiation. Within the tribal custom, there was a symbolic celebration for a girl, to ensure that everyone, particularly the young men, knew she was of age. I agreed to that celebration after my first bleeding, but I had something more meaningful in mind for myself and for all women who would follow me. Mother took me to the traders' booths at the market and I found a woman selling crystals. I picked a long wand of clear quartz and negotiated a healing in exchange for it. At another booth, I found precious oils, aromatic herbs and resins from the east, and again traded my healing work for them. At home, I first added some of the spices and herbs to the oil, then put all my treasures out of sight, high up in my room, until my time was at hand.

"I could feel the fullness of the blood within me and knew that the next full Moon would bring it forth. The night before the full Moon, my mother and six other women who also mothered young girls, gathered at my request in a cave overlooking the lake. I had brought my crystal and some feathers from great eagles who flew overhead. Little oil lamps surrounded the group, their flames flickering against the cave walls. There were ancient drawings depicting people hunting and flying in the sky, memories of previous seedings. It was quite magical and the women stepped out of their everyday lives and assumed the role of priestesses, even though there were none left in their culture. I brought forth the oil, now ripe with its fragrance even as I was ripe with my womanness, and set to burning the aromatic resins in small earthen bowls. The aroma allowed the women to transcend even further and become as one energy. Then I let my robes fall away and stood before them in my nakedness, my ripeness.

At this point I began telepathically to guide them as I lay, face up, on a mat before them. They surrounded me and began to stroke me with the feathers. I could feel my energy moving, like the eagles on the wind, and soon became aroused as they stroked my breasts and between my legs. Then I had them take up the oil in their hands and massage my body with it. We were moving as one in a group consciousness that had nothing to do with everyday reality. It was a magical trance. They thought nothing of it as I directed them to massage my pleasure spot, bringing me into waves of bliss, then moving away, allowing me to cool. This was repeated time after time. When I could stand it no longer and orgasm was upon me, I had my mother ease the crystal wand within me and break my shield of virginity as I came into the feeling of union with God. My spirit took flight and my body moaned in release as climax and blood came together. They allowed me to fly, to treasure my bliss, until I came back to rest in my body. Holding the spell we'd cast, they took me into their arms and bathed me with the spring water seeping from the cave walls. They softened me again with the fragrant oils, and we all curled up as one to sleep away the night.

"This ritual awakened a memory in the women and they felt arousal of their womanness in a vastly different way. They began to perform the same initiatory ritual for their girl children as they came into fullness. This was the first of many gifts I would give to heighten the sexual practices of these people. Their own traditions had become completely empty, making them eager to incorporate what I offered. Since I began to bleed the next day, I showed them how to collect the blood using small pieces of sponge brought from the sea. Mixing it with water until it was many times diluted, I used the blood to water the plants in our fields. This gift transferred a portion of the feminine mystery to the food, which was subsequently ingested by men and women alike. In this way the men began to integrate some of their feminine nature and the entire village sweetened with the practice.

"It was at this time of initiation that I truly made my commitment to the Earthwalk, allowing myself to have a human form and enjoy it. As you know from your own ceremony it is vitally important for Akhus to anchor their form for the duration of each Mission. Unless one is to work with the people as an apparition, this calling requires full participation. After the ritual a community celebration was held to honor my coming of age. Since I towered well above all the village boys they were more than shy toward me. In fact, I was so strange that they were fearful in spite of the love and radiance flowing from me, or perhaps because of it. The ritual and the coming of my blood had awakened a powerful sexuality in me so I must have aroused untold feelings in these young men. However, I put them at ease by announcing that I would marry no one of the village, but awaited a very special man who would be coming from the east. The exercise of my keen intuition had gradually opened my third eye to full oracular powers which I used sparingly to assist the soul growth of others. Generally I used these in metaphor or suggestion, not in proclamation, but that day I proclaimed. It is odd for me to think back on those times before your father came and wonder that I didn't feel alone or abandoned. I believe my dreamtime was spent with him on Ak-An until the High Council was convinced that I could hold my own without separation. I have never felt lonely on Earth, but now I feel the crack between the worlds opening and am anxious to walk through it."

*

The light was rapidly fading as the sun neared the horizon. Mir-An-Da gazed out of the window into the blazing ball of fire and prayed for purification and transmutation when next it should meet her eyes. She and Mai-An watched together as Annu sank into her resting place for this last night. They embraced each other for a long time, then circled away to light the oil lamps within the temple. The light was reflected from the sapphires in Mir-An-Da's crown and those within her eyes. Stars of the temple dome twinkled as their celestial twins began to appear in the darkening sky. The polished granite walls with copper inlay became warm with the lamp glow. Voices of the priestesses in evening chant rose up to their chamber, provoking smiles of appreciation for the beauty of it all. When, once again, they were seated before each other, Mir-An-Da squeezed the hand of Mai-An and breathed deeply.

*

"My dear one, the story of your father's arrival in the village is legendary, so humor me while I give you my rendition of it. He manifested his human form completely clothed in a grove of olive trees east of the village of Annu. Tall, golden-haired and radiant, there was no doubting that he was the fulfillment of my adolescent prophecy that day he strode into the village. His long hair caught the glint of Annu's light as did the solid gold breastplate of Annu that hung from his neck and covered his heart. It was your father's advent that prompted the renaming of the village, for he was truly a ray of Annu. His blue eyes were riveting to all who dared look into them. Aman-Ra was magnificent, one of the better forms he had ever manifested, at least to my recollection. Striding with uncanny precision through the village he reached our little house near the lake. Bypassing my good parents, he found me with Te-An sitting upon a big flat rock, my crystals laid out before me. Te-An immediately recognized him and bounded towards him wagging her tail wildly and prancing like a wolf.

"I took one look at him standing before me, truly a god made manifest, and jumped from my stone into his arms. We laughed and cried and danced and sang. Twin souls uniting accept whatever form they happen to be in and this was very human. I was nearly sixteen years old, by village standards an aging woman. His timing could not have been better for all concerned, especially my mother and father. They loved him. My younger brothers and sisters crawled all over him and he thoroughly enjoyed them. When

[31]

the two of us were together everything intensified for us and for everyone around us. The villagers were quite overwhelmed. We knew that before long we would tell them who we really were, but in that early time there was innocence, bliss and Divine Love to hold us in their embrace. It was truly Divine, Mai-An.

"We married of course, but not for several years. Aman-Ra and I have such a pure and high love for each other that we would have been quite content to be brother and sister only. However, part of the program called for the seeding of the genes through our offspring so we did eventually marry. By that time, Aman-Ra had established himself as a knowledgeable teacher in the community though not in any organized way. He slept in one of the caves by the lake where we spent most nights in each other's arms, gazing at the stars. As might be expected, the wedding ceremony was another ritual gift to the people whose custom was to publicly state their intentions and then have a big feast. Anticipating Aman-Ra's arrival, I had asked my dear friend who sold herbs in the market to acquire a special herb and oil for me. The herb, spikenard, grew high in the mountains of the far east, and the oil, squeezed from nuts, had no impurities, and was of the highest grade. This aromatic oil had been aging on the ledge above my bed for three years in a delicate jar of soft stone. I brought it to the ceremony, with my crystals, flowers, baskets of freshly baked bread and, of course, Te-An who never left my side. Some of the flowers were put in jugs of water, while the women tore the petals from others and filled baskets with them. Aman-Ra brought two rings of gold with sapphires embedded in mine and rubies blazing from his - and wine to share with the villagers. He had fashioned the rings himself from some gold he had produced by alchemical transformation. Aman-Ra had many gifts to bring to the people. The sapphires and rubies he simply manifested from thin air. Your father was quite a magician.

" Annu was a village of simple dwellings without a single temple in those times. Since my temple had been the Earth, we held the ceremony in the grove of olive trees where Aman-Ra had manifested himself. It was springtime and the fields were blooming with wildflowers and flax. Breezes blew through the olive trees and birds sang cheerfully. The entire village and many people from the west side of the lake came to the wedding, laying down their field tools to celebrate with us. I had used my crystals to set the star grid within the grove to connect the energies of our intent with the Great White Lodge on Ak-An. We appeared dressed in new white linen robes that I had woven myself and embroidered with colorful flowers much like those in the meadows around us. It was not an elaborate ceremony but we called upon the devas of the four directions, Earth Mother, and the boundless energies of Prime Creator to bless our union and make it fruitful. We silently prayed for the success of our Mission and the entire Ascension Activation Program. The blessings of the High Council and of all Akhus committed to the program were bestowed upon us. We really felt supported from above and below as the villagers took us into their hearts. I could see the reasoning behind my being born of them, for it made our way easy. Exchanging rings, we spoke our vows aloud. Within the vows were words and energies to awaken the people to new ways of thinking about Prime Creator and the universe. There were no codes to open or activate within the blood or souls of these people. That was what we had come to integrate. Many generations would pass before the crystalline blood codes of a higher consciousness would become operative through the offspring of your brothers and sisters, Mai-An. The codes of light must remain within the pure blood until a future time when the new genetic lineage is strong enough to accommodate the incarnation of our Akhus.

"When we had finished speaking our vows, I took up the tiny alabaster jar containing my precious oil of spikenard and your father knelt before me. Holding the jar over his head, with the strength of my hand I broke it open and allowed the exotically fragrant oil to drip upon the great vortex at his crown. I then used both of my hands to move the oil through his golden hair, annointing the head of my beloved twin soul. My womb stirred with this sealing of our commitment to each other and the Mission. It was a royal marriage, the first in a lineage, and the people fell silent with respect. Aman-Ra rose and poured the first cup of wine. Holding it before me, he spoke of the wine as the blood within my womb space. He announced to one and all that my womb would bring forth the new leaders, kings upon the Earth, whose lives would serve the people and the land. I drank the red wine from the smooth stone cup and passed it back to Aman-Ra who did likewise. We embraced, the people cheered, throwing flower petals before and over us as we walked, holding hands, to the feast table. Breaking the bread, each feeding the other a morsel, we then invited our guests to share the food and wine. It was a joyous day for everyone. When the feast was over, the Murite villagers led us to the top of a knoll where they had built our first home. I was overwhelmed with gratitude for the depth of their acceptance. Here we could look upon the whole village and sit upon our doorstep to watch the rising of Annu. It was a simple place but it felt like a palace - the very spot where the palace sits today, Mai-An.

"The words of truth we had spoken in our vows did have an impact, since a few of the village men and women came to us after the wedding wanting to know more. Aman-Ra invited them to take a day of rest from the fields after every six days of working and join him in our gardens for regular teachings. At first a few people came, but in time, more and more villagers and a few of the dark-skinned people from the west side of the lake gathered in our garden. We designated this Annu's day, a day of rest. Teaching them the concept of One Supreme Being, what I have always called Prime Creator, we gave it a name in their dialect, a coded word of power, and the name was God (translation). God, we said, is the sum total of all that is, all of the energy in the universe, and everything in the universe is energy. The frequency or vibration of God emanates a feeling of vast love saturating our beings. When we experience God within us we project this love to ourselves and to others. If we block the feeling with something like fear, that is what we receive and give out and it is not pleasant - it alienates us from God. This made sense to them. It sounds quite simple but, in fact, this is the highest philosophical teaching, a key to the program, because it knows no separation. We are one with all things.

"More and more people began to show up in our garden. We introduced the idea of a dualistic world, the feminine and masculine. Each could be honored in its own way but eventually the conception of God would call for the union of the two in balance. Aman-Ra and I have assumed these earthly bodies as man and wife but when we are not in density, in matter, we are in union with our male and female, appearing androgynous. This was too difficult a concept for them to understand so we asked them to begin looking at whether things were masculine or feminine, including different aspects of themselves. They loved to participate in this way.

"The lessons continued, but we moved outside the garden to the hillside behind our house. I was ready to begin working with the plant beings in the garden space and could not have scores of people tromping around there. They were curious about my garden but it was some time before I invited people in, and then only a few women who had more receptive auras. Te-An and my little sisters were there to help me all the time, for they knew that plants were beings of light from our work together in nature. The villagers helped me build a low wall of stone around the garden, which was many times larger than our dwelling. I buried crystals in the sacred star and the garden took the same form. In the center was a second grid of crystals, above ground, with which I worked daily, moving the energies as needed. I would put new seeds in the center to activate them and the products of the garden were placed there after harvest or processing to be reactivated according to my intention. The devas of the wooded hillside used to sneak down to see what I was up to. I welcomed their advice, but mostly listened to the plant devas themselves, for every plant has a spirit guide. They let me know where to put the plants and who wanted to live and grow next to whom. At first it was chaos, much like the creation of the universe, but in the end everyone was happy and growing robustly.

"I experimented by putting some plants together whose devas indicated they would not be happy, and their auras diminished to almost nothing. In my lifetimes everywhere, I have always had a great love for experimentation. During the first season I had flax growing more sturdily than any village farmer could boast, flowers with breathtaking fragrant blooms, vegetables with a wonderful flavor and medicinal plants of great potency. I wouldn't let the villagers in my garden, but they spent a fair amount of time observing it from the other side of the wall. Everything of an organic nature was thrown into a corner to rot, and soaked with water occasionally. This, added to various manures from village animals, made a fine spring cover which fed the soil well. In the cooler months I planted grains which I tilled under after harvest, their roots and stalks bringing more air element to the soil.

"My helpers could not yet speak to the plants, but they followed instructions and used what they were learning in their own gardens. Nothing was secret once the proof was in my hands. When I was sure of my results, I brought small groups of farmers into the garden and spoke with them about the compatibility of certain plants. I did not broach the subject of auras and devas but hinted that there were elementals and spirits in nature that could work for them. The next season saw them planting in new ways, and I was introducing new plants from seeds that my trader friends had brought with them from far away lands. Once the compatabilities were worked out, I left the gardening to my apprentices and concentrated on listening to the herbal plants in order to understand their powers of healing. I then mixed compatible cultivated and wild plants into vibrational healing remedies for the physical and etheric wounds of the people who came to me for healing. Here began an entire system of herbal healing that took me years to develop and understand. Later, I experimented with vibrations, working with flowers, pure water and the sun, creating frequencies to move energy in more subtle ways through the self, and the emotional, mental and spiritual bodies. This was one of the most productive and joyful tasks I have performed here on Earth. These remedies are in the archives of the healing school and at a designated time in the future, which we will discuss later, are to be spirited away with other documents to hiding places so they will not perish.

"While I was working with the small garden, your father took on the task of improving agricultural methods. He helped the men develop more efficient tools and, after studying plant compatibilities, taught them to rotate their crops and develop two different but compatible plants at the same time. The results showed that both crops grew more robustly. This is an incredibly fertile part of the Earth, but the land does not automatically remain that way. If harvests are continually gathered without regenerating the soil or letting it rest, it will not cooperate with the growing. This had happened many times to the Murites who, as nomads, would just move to another place. Here we wished to establish something permanent and your father's work was vital to that stability. Without stability we would not have been able to fulfill the Mission, which called for a center of learning and high culture.

"Attracted by the quality of my linen and the elegant patterns that I wove into, or embroidered onto my cloth, the women began asking how to do this. I decided to teach them, showing how to grow stronger flax for the thread and then how to color it with dyes made from different plants. Practicing these arts resulted in enlivening their appearance, and gave them a stronger sense of artistry and freedom of personal expression. Everyone was having fun, and there was a great sense of brotherhood and sisterhood amongst us. You might ask what your father and I were doing in our private life, and I can tell you that the villagers were becoming a little concerned that I was not pregnant. Years had passed, almost eight to be exact, and where were our golden-haired children? To tell you the truth, Aman-Ra and I hadn't had intercourse yet, not out of lack of love to be sure. We had so much love for each other and so much God energy, that we merely needed to touch each other with intent to be in the bliss of orgasm. This might have gone on indefinitely had not the High Council sent a very clear directive to procreate. That was, after all, vital to the Mission. I understood from my healing practice the rather mindless and brutal way the people sometimes went about intercourse, so I took on yet another research project. It makes me laugh to think of it now. Your father is very good natured, so he supported me in every way. Though he has little interest in research himself, he wholeheartedly enjoyed participating in this project!

"After enduring the initial energetic shock of intimacy, which severely taxed our nervous systems, we experimented with our bodies fully and freely. We found that, with discipline and attention, pleasure could be sustained indefinitely while both our bodies and hearts were deeply connected. My mastery of Earth forces led to the discovery of an ecstatic energy that could be pulled up from the Earth through our bodies. I called it *kun-ta*, energy of the Earth. Since we were fully in our light bodies, this energy met and mixed with our *ak-ta*, star energy, and was a consecration of the Earth and the sky to the Prime Creator. It was sexual expression on a Divine level. I allowed conception at the dark of the Moon during the month of lowest Sun for eleven years, bringing forth eleven boys. Different herbs had been prepared, and I studied natural breathing techniques that helped with the birthing process. The women assisting me incorporated these into their midwifery practices. Our boys were destined for your father's part of the Mission, which would begin in its fullness when they were of the age of higher learning, a concept unheard of in Annu. Your father took over their studies when they reached fourteen years of age. He taught each of them mastery in a skill for which they had shown great talent.

"We raised an astronomer who also learned navigation and time-keeping; an architect who used sacred symbology and form in buildings; an artist who was both artisan and fine artist; one who developed a universal language and a system of recording it, using descriptive glyphs carved in stone or written upon prepared papyrus with organic dyes; a philosopher; one who performed sacred ritual; another who developed a system of counting by working with the magic of numbers; and a purely practical son who loved the administration of agriculture and economics, and developed a monetary system. This revolutionized trading since not every merchant needed or could use twelve chickens a day. These sons were set to work incorporating their skills into society. At the same time, they were encouraged to marry Murite women and begin infusing the bloodline.

"It was not hard for these handsome giants to find wives, especially since your father and I had seen to their sexual education. Your brothers chose strong and intelligent women to mother their offspring, and those selected were grateful for this unique opportunity. Of the next three boys, one was trained in the art of construction with stone masonry to build the architectural projects designed by our second son. Another learned the physics of the natural world, including mastery of the weather. The last son worked with alchemy and the magic of the natural elements, using transmutation. Over time, all became masters of their crafts. Aman-Ra directed them to establish craft brotherhoods and apprentice their own sons of mixed blood in them. These brotherhoods became the backbone of the community, training young and old alike to contribute skills to the whole. The village of Annu began changing its face, as many grand and beautiful stone buildings with narrow paved streets, and graceful courtyards took the place of mud houses and litter strewn dirt trails. At the same time education was offered to the people as our grandchildren became teachers. It was a magical transformation to watch from our vantage point, but for the villagers it was not so noticeable. They were engaged in their cycles of death and reincarnation, and we were not even aging. Our sons' wives would die of old age so they would have to re-marry. Because we persisted, we were, in time, able to predominate genetically. But I am jumping ahead in my tale, Mai-An, do forgive me."

*

Night was descending, prompting Mir-An-Da to draw a shimmering silver- black cape around her shoulders. Mai-An wrapped herself in a blanket, still sitting on a cushion at her mother's knees. Te-An stretched and yawned, then after changing position, fell back to sleep. Mai-An, drawing water from a pitcher left for them by the guardian priestesses, offered a cup to her mother. Mir-An-Da drank slowly after energizing the water with her hands. Mai-An also drank, then replaced the cups and pitcher, anxious as she was for her mother to continue, and more than ready to take on her responsibility.

*

"Ten years after my last boy was born, I began birthing my daughters, each conceived during the dark Moon when the Sun was at its highest. In choosing these times, I brought the most feminine energy into my boys and the most masculine into my girls, so that balancing polarities would be easy for them. I

[38]

conceived and brought forth eleven girls. As I raised them everything that was my life became theirs - the garden, the healing herbs, the work with nature, Earth's power, spirits and devas, and the alchemy of cooking and weaving. We shared our dreams every day and learned to interpret them. Their psychic powers were opened and they worked with the Akhus. They began seeing energy fields and using healing techniques including massage of the muscles. All experienced their puberty rites even as Aman-Ra officiated at their brothers' and they began teaching the village children and young people as they came of age. When they were older I taught them the sexual arts and the deeper magic of moving energy within, without and with the universe. They each mastered the understanding of Earth elements and the spirits of nature, and Mother Earth embraced them with her love. Among the building projects that your father directed was the temple of the priestesses that I had requested. We had built our spacious home to accommodate all the children, but only you and Amen-Se, who were not yet conceived, would remain with us and inherit the dynasty of Ak-An. Your eleven sisters were trained as priestesses to be masters of healing, medicine, alchemy, weaving and sexual magic. Your brothers were sent out to breed with the Murites and their sons were sent to your sisters to learn the arts of sexual magic as part of their coming of age ritual. Their future wives were treated with honor and respect and found pleasure in their marriages with our grandsons. Children born of the temple teachings were raised within the temple by the priestesses. Eventually the boys were sent to be trained under your brothers, and the girls became temple priestesses. Do you see the logic of bringing the mixed genetic strain back to purity in order to strengthen it?"

Mai-An nodded, and her mother continued. "As the young girls grew up, they served for a time as sexual priestesses for boys of mixed blood at their coming of age. Many of them stayed in the temple all their lives, but many married and raised families of their own. By that time there were enough Murite-Akhu mixed bloods that they could have a reasonably long life together. None of our children have lived as long as we have. It was not part of the program. Some have now already incarnated within the bloodline to assist you and Amen-Se. You were both born last, twins within my womb, twin souls in the land of the Akhus, conceived on the new Moon at the time when Annu rose with the stars of the lion just two hundred years ago. Your future heirs will be conceived in this way. They will live even shorter lives than yours, and this is meant to be. You and Amen-Se were born too late to even know your brothers and sisters, but you can appreciate them through the legacy they have left behind.

"This brings me to a very important change that took place in the Murite people. After we had conceived these twenty-two children and your father, with your brothers' skilled assistance, had masterfully erected the temple as well as our dwelling, their attitude towards us was different. Neither I nor your father had aged a day beyond twenty. Twenty-two children would have put the strongest of their women in the grave. They were growing old and dying, and we had hardly begun our Mission. It was clear to these people that we were more than gifts from the stars, we were from the stars. Rather than denying it, we had seized the opportunity to teach them about the stars, the galaxy, the universe, and their Earth from the perspective of the Akhu. We told them of the previous seedings and the roots of their race, which they appreciated hearing about. They began to seek out the new strain of genes for the marriages of their own sons and daughters, wishing them long lives and well developed intellects. Also they began regarding Aman-Ra and myself as well as our sons and daughters as royalty. We were on a Mission to heal separation so we discouraged forms of adoration and hierarchy that did not serve our purpose. However, as generations passed, it became quite evident that we were here to stay, and the village, which was by now a city with complex economics and government, depended upon us for our wisdom and its growth.

"Most of the citizens were of mixed blood, some with high percentages of Akhu genes, and were well educated or skilled in a craft. The remaining Murite population was happy to provide food for the city and prospered as farmers living in the countryside. It was a unanimous decision to elect us their leaders. As king and queen we ruled always with the needs of the community and the Earth as our highest priorities, apart from the mission itself. Your brother, the artisan, made this lovely crown which I find somewhat burdensome. I trust that you will wear it with grace, Mai-An. You and Amen-Se were reared and still live in our lovely dwelling upon the knoll. It will be yours tomorrow. You have both been schooled in the arts of kingly and queenly service and I see no need to remind you of them. Make them your highest priority while you bring forth the next generation of pure genes and you will not fail the Mission.

"Your tasks for the future, like the present, are plentiful and difficult. Whereas your father and I have the gift of innovation and experimentation, you and Amen-Se will take what we have begun and go deeper into the magic of it all. For example, I have deduced the healing powers of plants and flowers and left records of our findings for you. You will work from the perspective of the body's structure and energy. How is the tissue affected? Learning the inner workings of the body, you will develop a system of medicine that can remove unwanted tissue and repair it when damaged. This is just as important as moving energy with herbs or with your own energy, but more difficult perhaps. You will not damage the afflicted one at all, as when I intervened with my brother, Chad, while he was in utero. It was not my Mission to develop this science, it is yours. You will continue teaching the arts of sexual intimacy and the mysteries of the blood to all the young women called to temple life. Some will remain as priestesses and others will marry. In many instances you will be training the queens and priestesses of distant lands.

"I have taught you and Amen-Se the magic of working with your second body, your double. You will take this beyond our work, and learn to transport to distant sites while your physical body remains here in trance state. These practices will help maintain your interdimensionality. It was difficult for your siblings to do this. I have used the practice to assist some of your father's projects in other lands and you may need to do the same. You will, as high priestess, train another in the art of prophecy. She will be one who shows the gift. The temple should never be without its oracle. You have watched me teach women to prophesy, to use the full power of their feminine gifts. Do not let them forget, Mai-An. It is vital to the future and the preservation of the codes of light. The codes come through our soul lineage and will incarnate with the future high priestess of the temple. It is of utmost importance that each code carrier knows and is confident of the next in the lineage. She will wear the disc of Annu between the brows and within the heart of her etheric body. The principle duty of the high priestess is to train the next in the lineage. In so doing, she will reach her own enlightenment and show the way to the next in line. The codes will be passed, which is to say, the lineage will be spoken as we speak it now, when the high priestess is ready to die. Her life is to be protected above the king's! The bloodline will survive and populate the Earth, but the codes of light come through one single lineage of women. Do you understand, Mai-An?"

*

The Priestesses of Annu

Mai-An shuddered at the severity of her mother's words and nodded her head quickly. She drew the blanket more tightly around her, holding it at her throat. Her soft eyes looked like blue pools of water as tears welled up within them. Mir-An-Da was uncompromising in her posture and the intensity of her unearthly stare. Mai-An felt light blazing within her, first in her womb, and then in her heart, and then everywhere. She threw off the blanket, burning with fire, and rushed to the window for air. Flushed and panting, she returned to her mother, standing before her holding her heart. To Mir-An-Da she looked like a star at its birth. White light shot from her center far beyond the temple walls. It pulsated and quivered as if announcing a great event. She smiled. Falling on her knees, Mai-An placed her head on Mir-An-Da's lap. The codes of light were fully activated. Mir-An-Da breathed a release at this culmination of her work. She stroked Mai-An's hair and kissed her crown. Mai-An, still breathless, looked at her mother and felt the power of her magic. She wondered how she could ever measure up to this god-being incarnate. When breathing normally, she smiled and Mir-An-Da eased her back onto her cushion.

*

"It is time to speak of the distant future, Mai-An. Your father sits now with his council of twelve, the grand masters of the brotherhoods and Amen-Se. He is instructing each as I am instructing you. Our blood contains crystalline codes, the codes of consciousness from the Akhus. These codes will be spread around the Earth in due time. You know that some of your brothers were sent to far away lands before your were born, as emissaries of the Akhus. They seeded the genes into certain populations so that the crystalline codes would begin spreading in these places. Three of your brothers went on very long journeys, one to the east in the land of high mountain peaks, and the other two to the west, beyond the ocean. Both went first to a very advanced civilization on a great island in the western ocean. Here the red-skinned pyramid builders received them well, and they were assisted in the next part of their journey even further west to lands where both red and bronze-skinned people lived. Starting at the northern edge of these lands, Sha-Ma walked across the entire continent to the other ocean. Many of the inhabitants were colonists from the island, but some had come from other islands to their west. In many places the two groups of colonists had interbred. Sha-Ma continued his journey south into a warmer climate and then easterly into a tropical paradise. As the grand master of stone building, he was quite moved by the pyramids he had examined earlier on his journey. He had found several tribes in the northern lands who built pyramids from the soil, but in the tropics he found many grand pyramid temples built of stone. Like his brothers, he taught the people about the one God and how we are all part of that God. Thus he taught union with God. He had a wonderful journey and was so committed to his mission that I used my double to check up on him. Both bronze- and red-skinned people honored him as a god and he had no trouble introducing the genes into their tribes. The red lineages had previously been seeded by the Pleiadians. On the other hand, the bronze-skinned people were mixed bloods whose ancestors had lived on an island, now submerged, in the western ocean. Its name was Mu, the Motherland. This was a very old seeding from Ak-An, although not the first on this planet. Everyone flourished on the continent of Mu which had the longest Golden Age of any of Earth's civilizations. Its history and hidden teachings have been placed in safe but secret chambers within some of the mountains of the world. They will be revealed in the future at an appropriate time.

"The second brother, Mak-Ma, took a more southerly route and wandered through jungles, then over the mountains until he came to a great lake on a high plain bordered by snowy mountains. Here he met people who seemed to be expecting him, and called him Wiracocha, the great white god. They treated him as a king and he seeded many women with the new genes. He taught them to build beautiful cities in the mountains, how to cut stone with sound and move huge cut stones into place with energy, just as we have done here. Teaching them about the Akhus, he guided them to communicate with them through the spirits of the mountains. Mak-Ma showed the people how to observe the heavens, and chart cycles of time on Earth. He taught them of Ak-An which they called Chaska in their language. Like his brother, he also taught them how to use the power of Annu to increase the light of their energetic bodies. He told them of the one God, that Annu could represent that God as a source of energy, but Annu was not God. They gave Annu the name Inti. It's really quite beautiful isn't it? He stayed with these people until leaders among them reached enlightenment, and then he came home. Like Sha-Ma, he told the people he would return far into the future, when the world would see many changes.

"Other brothers went north to the coast beyond the inland

[43]

sea, and one of them went north and east to some beautiful islands and peninsulas in the northern seas. When all had returned there was a council meeting and everyone heard the reports. It was decided that some lands were favorable for the establishment of colonies, and small groups of young adventurous people with a high percentage of the Akhu blood volunteered to travel out as colonists. They were sent to the great island in the western ocean, the mountainous land far to the east, a beautiful land between two rivers not so far to the east and north, and the north shores of the inland sea. In the future, Mai-An, the seedings they created will survive and mix with the remnants of old seedings from other stars, and thereby move the crystalline blood codes around the Earth. This, as you will see, will not be enough to assure success of the program, but it is a start. People will begin holding some light in their energetic bodies. There will be additional seedings on the Earth far into the future and you, Amen-Se, your children and their lineage will still be producing pure Ak-An genes for some time to come.

"Now, Mai-An, listen carefully. You must pass this information on through the lineage of the codes of light and the pure bloodline. When the great lion monument, which sits facing the dawn across the lake, gazes upon the constellation of the lion at the time of equal days when the people of Annu come north, the Earth will change forever. This does happen at long but regular intervals. However, there have been so few survivors that no one has documented it and, needless to say, all the teachings and advances of civilization were lost. People forget about the Akhus and the one God when all their energy has to be focussed on survival. They feel God is the cause of destruction and harm when, in fact, their own thought forms and behavior precipitate these events. We cannot stress enough in our teaching that reality is created by our thoughts. That is why we have a Golden Age here in our lands. Our thoughts have always been of harmony and union.

"Well Mai-An, the High Council of the Great Lodge of Light has no intention of aborting a program that is meant to span one full cycle of the constellations. Yes, the Earth and her people will falter and become ignorant many times over, but this program will come to completion on schedule. It will not seem possible, but it will. Our astronomers, as brilliant as the stars they chart and follow, will know exactly when the time is at hand. At this time of the lion, there will come a great flood and change of climate. Ice will melt far to the north and Earth herself will quake and split open. The great island civilization of the red-skinned men, which was seeded so long ago by our Pleiadian brothers will perish beneath the sea. The energy of this civilization will turn on itself before long. They will perish from the misuse of power. Before that time comes, your father will have taken over the body of a young man in our colony there. This colony is under strict regulations to keep the blood pure and you will replenish it with more colonists from time to time as we have, sending part of the previous population back to our lands.

"This young man, whose name will be Thoth, will suddenly show amazing abilities as a record keeper, and will begin to record, in our glyphs, the history of the island civilization, including the cause of its demise. He will document all their sciences including the building of pyramids which are unique receptors and transmitters of cosmic energy. At that time, perhaps a thousand years before the deluge and sinking of the island, Thoth will make his way back to our lands with the colonists and all his records. Here he will be a great teacher and scribe, and will start schools to teach the Akhus' mysteries to the adepts, those who have light and are seeking to know. It is not to be exclusive that he does this, but to preserve and enrich the magic, to give it more power. For this he will need adepts with much light. He will also be a gentle teacher to all people, and together with the rulers of our lineage, will strive for equality and harmony in his service. It is the only way an Akhu can be at peace with himself.

"Thoth will supervise the construction of three pyramids to the east of the lion monument. Within the construction will be every secret teaching of both cultures and the stars. The monuments themselves will be a map of the heavens at the time of the lion. Aman-Ra and I came to Ak-An through the stargate of An and then through El. These are two stars of three in the belt of the man who stands above Ak-An in the sky. All these things will be a reminder to intelligent people far in the future - that Earth is but a reflection of the heavens. Like Ak-An and the belt in the heavens, the great city of Annu will be aligned with these three great pyramids. Even further into the future, when the Akhus and the lineage of the codes of light incarnate in great numbers, it will remind the incarnated Akhus that they come from the stars. This will happen at the completion of the program when the lion in the heavens moves halfway around the circle of the sky and the water-bearer rises in the east at the dawn of equal days. At this time, the Akhus will return as incarnated beings, and the records which Thoth will hide within the hundreds of chambers inside the pyramids will again be discovered.

The Priestesses of Annu

"Thoth will also become a great advisor to our lineage at that time. The pure Akhu blood will still run in their veins, but natural mutation will have shortened their lives considerably, and also their ability to reach the High Council. Thoth will reawaken them so that they may prepare for the changes happening to Earth. He will advise the building of boats and the duplicating of all records in the archives to ensure their survival. Everything of highest importance, the records of our civilization, the teachings, and all the advances made by the brotherhoods will have been secured. Aman-Ra has many secret chambers deep beneath the lion monument. He has used these for initiation, and his priests, alchemists and magicians will continue to use them. All the documents relevant to our reign and to the program have been hidden in one of these water and air-tight chambers. Included are accurate predictions of the future that will provide proof of the advanced nature of our culture and the astronomical calculations dating it. This chamber has already been sealed. Others are reserved for future records of the brotherhoods.

"The bloodline will survive, Mai-An, but it will not be the same. The Golden Age that we have initiated will end at that time. Yes, there will still be Akhu blood on the throne, but in time, it will weaken with mutation and with the temptation of power. The codes of service to the people will have been lost. Kings will follow rituals of transmutation for which they do not have the light. Records will be somewhat distorted and those who study our civilization in the distant future will be misled. However, when the record chambers of your father are discovered, and that will not happen until such time as it can be received in the light, there will be no doubt that many human beings came from the stars. The more arrogant intellectuals will be humbled when they realise the age and origins of humanity.

"There will be many of our culture who survive the deluge and the earth changes, but the beautiful city of Annu will be in ruins, much of it swept away by the force of the waters. The time will have come for something new. At the south reaches of our lands, the Brotherhood of Architecture and Sacred Symbols has a beautiful initiatory temple which lies along the river that empties into our lake. In distant times this temple will be an enigma for, like the great lion complex and the pyramids with their hidden treasures, it will survive the deluge. The brotherhoods will carry on, but their power and integrity will weaken over time. Astronomers of Annu will become well known for the precision of their calculations and their findings will spark a great science.

[46]

Architects and stoneworkers will continue building many more pyramids ordered by future kings and queens. They will take their secrets and techniques into the future and erect monuments to cosmic truths in the east and north, but eventually forget the meanings. The magicians and alchemists will become even more powerful but will be forced to work in secrecy. They, also, will disappear. This is not a tragedy, Mai-An, it is a part of the history of Earth's cycles. Everything will fade away, except the codes of light. They will not falter or weaken. At times they may appear to die, but rest assured, they will be alive somewhere on Earth or in the higher planes.

"After the flood, Mai-An, this lush and bountiful land will become a desert. It will appear as nothing but sand. Our lake will recede and become a river that floods every year to provide soil for the crops. It will be much warmer than now and the magnetic field, the polarity of Earth, will shift. The dawning of the next Golden Age will not happen here, but far across the sea where your brother walked and talked with the red men. Our civilization's remains will become a memorial to the last golden age, but will be confused with later kings and queens and times that were anything but golden save for the egotistical adornments. People of the Earth will become more unconscious. They will not see the lessons of the demise of those who abused power. Centuries will be spent fighting with each other - imagine, brother to brother, for most will carry our seed. Their civilizations will be based upon the thought form of separation. They will forget there is one God and worship many gods, or worship materiality instead. Only the brotherhoods and the lineage of the codes of light will carry the truth of the one God forward. The bloodline will slip in and out of truth. Believers in one God will say theirs is the only God, not recognizing the similarities,but only the differences in their beliefs. Millions of people will be slaughtered because of this unconscious ignorance. Yet, what we do now is not in vain, my daughter, because your father has taken care of these aspects of the future.

"Now, let us talk about the women. The priestesses of the lineage will hold the energy for the Golden Age. The high priestesses, those who hold the codes of light for the planet, will continue to bring new consciousness onto the Earth. Each will pass her responsibility on to the next woman who bears the disc of Annu upon her third eye and within her heart. As time passes, this consciousness will spread and elevate that of many. Women are patient. They are willing to be silent and still. They can energetically imagine the future and bring it into reality for they are dreamers. The codes of light are in good hands. Women will uphold the one God and use Annu as a symbol of God. They will recognize that there is both masculine and feminine in God, in everything, and they will honor this. In the future, many other sects of priestesses who do not uphold these principles will appear. This will be a test for women to maintain their power when men alone seem to carry it. Some sects will react against the feminine in anger and lose their power accordingly. They will fight amongst themselves and betray one another. Remember the balance, Mai-An.

"Work with the devas, the nature spirits and the elements of the Earth, for these forces are powerful and can be great allies. We are here to assist the Earth and to be assisted by her. The priestesses know they must uphold the sacredness of the sexual act. This is a service to the happiness of all women as well as men, and to the success of all marriages. If they fall into abusive patterns around sexuality, their power will be lost. Nurture the ability of women to heal, and see that the development of medicine and healing stays primarily within their hands, for they more naturally work with their feelings as well as their minds. As the queen and high priestess, you must uphold the legacy of service to the people - equality, harmony and abundance. You are greater than no other on Earth, Mai-An. There is equal power in your humility as there is in your wisdom. The lineage of light will be of service to the bloodline for it will bring forth future incarnations to purify and strengthen it. There will be times for the lineage when sabotage might be the best way to be of service. The High Council and all the beloved Akhus will ceaselessly serve those who incarnate into this program. Ask for help every day. Guide the culture in the mastering of energy. This is at the core of every brotherhood and sisterhood. You are masters and will continue to be! Above all, my precious one, guard well the codes of light, but do not hold onto them when it is their time of release. Be content to have been of service."

Mir-An-Da grasped her daughters shoulder and sighed. "Oh, Mai-An, I will soon depart this planet. I love it well but long for a respite. My love for you will be as eagles' wings, constantly embracing you from the inner planes. Now, it is late and you must have your sleep, for tomorrow you will become both a queen and a wife."

*

[48]

Mai-An fell into her mother's lap again, weeping from both joy and sadness. Mir-An-Da soothed her, stroking her golden hair. When Mai-An became quiet, she drew a small wax-sealed jar from her deep pockets. She gave the jar of spikenard oil to Mai-An who blushed and kissed her mother's hand. Mir-An-Da passed the golden sapphire ring to her daughter as well, even as Aman-Ra was passing his ruby ring to Amen-Se. She gathered the sapphires from the points of the stars on the floor and handed them to Mai-An. Extinguishing the lamps, they walked silently home. Mai-An went to her quarters to rest and Mir-An-Da watched the Moon from her garden. She was soon joined by Aman-Ra, returning from his council meeting. They held hands for some time, their eyes resting upon Ak-An. When finally they retired, they took joy in their earthly bodies for the last time. Their bliss would always be with them as they merged with the filaments of the universe.

The next morning, well before dawn, Aman-Ra, Mir-An-Da with Te-An, Amen-Se and Mai-An walked together to the lake. The royal barge awaited them, oil lamps glowing in the darkness. It was the summer solstice in the age of Libra, the bringer of balance. Aman-Ra and Mir-An-Da said farewell to their children. Placing their crowns upon the heads of their successors, they boarded the barge, Te-An accompanying them. It took them silently to the western shores of the lake below the great lion. A guardian accompanied them to the royal temple where they cleansed themselves in the baths, and rubbed all the sacred herbs of transmutation into their skin, which began to emit a soft glow of light. They left their robes with the guardian who returned with them to the opposite shore. Amen-Se and Mai-An held their parents' robes as Aman-Ra and Mir-An-Da walked naked along the causeway to the great lion. Climbing to the altar between its paws, and holding hands, they turned to face the east where the brilliant light of Ak-An could be seen on the horizon. Te-An sat as their guardian at the edge of the monument's base, her pointed ears scanning the sacred space in the growing light. The first rays of the Sun reached over the horizon to fall upon the face of the great lion. Aman-Ra and Mir-An-Da breathed deeply, down to their toes. When the Sun hit their crown chakras they began to vibrate and shimmer with light. As they became engulfed in this light the vibration increased and their cells started transforming into light quanta. The brilliance was blinding to their children across the lake, as if the heart of the lion were on fire. When the Sun was fully risen, the light shot out in all directions like fireworks, and Aman-Ra and Mir-An-Da disappeared.

The Priestesses of Annu

Te-An could be seen running towards the forest behind the great lion, like a wolf returning at last to her pack. Reaching the edge of the forest she became as a shooting star, her spirit self leaping through form into essence, her journey complete.

Leah Speaks

There was hushed silence within the circle of women. They felt at one with Mir-An-Da and were all swept away by the power of her transmutation. Leah moved the energy in the circle, gradually drawing everyone back into this reality.

"It is late my friends and sleep is quickly coming upon me. However, I would like to draw a few threads of Mir-An-Da's life together with some legends and myths that have followed her. She was the daughter of the stars, but keep in mind that she was as real as you and I. She walked the Earth for a long time and her myth was firmly established in all the cultures that were seeded from her work. Without question, she was Isis and Aman-Ra was Osiris. She also spawned the archetypes of the Mother Goddess found in later sub-cultures, namely Ishtar, Astarte and so forth. She and Aman-Ra began a bloodline that continued and seeded the dynasties of the pharaohs - the very early post-deluge kings being pure Akhus. The nature of the genes allowed the marriage of brother and sister, indeed demanded it, to maintain purity. These were Siriun star beings after all, master geneticists. Their sacred city of the Sun became known to the Greeks as Heliopolis. Another great center of culture was established at what we now call Memphis. The landscape changed drastically with the polar shift, destruction of Atlantis, and end of the ice age. However, some of the original temples, the Valley Temple at Giza and the Osireion at Abydos, remain as enigmatic reminders of that Golden Age.

"Mir-An-Da was right to warn Mai-An of the importance of balance for she could see the future. She foresaw her elevation to goddess and the pagan cult of goddess worship that would result. It split up Egypt as it would many cultures thereafter. The conflict held dissonant energies that plagued the bloodline down to the present time but it did not, for one single moment, enter the matrix of the codes of light.

"The sons of Mir-An-Da and Aman-Ra walked the Earth as great white gods. They live on in the legends of native peoples throughout the Americas. Many colonies brought the bloodline into proximity with pre-existing populations. Most were starseedings from the Pleiades, the Emissaries of Light who seeded the indigenous cultures upon Earth. The Siriuns and Pleiadians have collaborated in earth consciousness projects in our distant past. The Pleiadians, who have not been active on Earth for thousands of years, recently returned to guide reincarnated souls from Atlantis to the light. Atlantis, one of their seeding projects, ended in tragedy from the misuse of power. As the Pleiadians moved into their future a possible reality manifested for them. It saw reincarnated Atlanteans misusing power again at the end of this millennium. They returned with the blessings and assistance of the Siriuns to correct this glitch. I cannot tell you if they have succeeded, but their influence is waning and that may be a good sign.

"The last thing on my mind is something that Mir-An-Da did not discuss with Mai-An because Mai-An did not carry the goddess codes. Mir-An-Da brought a very important energy to the planet, one that would be pulsed rarely but effectively in future generations of the codes of light. In keeping with the Siriun Mission, Mir-An-Da's life opened, activated and released the thought form of union with God into the energetic field of the Earth. She knew she was God. She knew the name of God and the name was she. That thought form pulsed the collective unconscious which had similar remnant thought forms from previous seedings. These had dwindled to ideas about the gods and an afterlife. Certain Pleiadian sub-cultures retained a purity about God being in all things, but the collective was deep in separation. The seed thought of God-union was planted with Mir-An-Da and, as we will see, it was reinforced twice more within the lineage of light. Each time it would bring the thought of union forth into the consciousness of more and more incarnated beings. This thought form has guided and nourished all Akhus, Shining Ones, star beings, who are now incarnate. Mir-An-Da or Isis, was the first Black Madonna. She opened her personal codes and, with the help of Aman-Ra, her key and planetary codes, but the goddess codes of the Black Madonna, she who knows the name of God, were opened and activated by the Siriun High Council from the Great White Lodge on Ak-An. Even though she did not speak of them, she was fully aware that she carried them. Mir-An-Da and her beloved twin soul, Aman-Ra, were servants of mankind as well as creator gods. They were so far beyond the need for individuation that they each incarnated as a group soul. The quintessential Grail couple, they embodied an ideal that would survive numerous setbacks to bring forth the return of the Golden Age."

[51]

Leah looked around the group, meeting each woman's eyes. "Let us take the essence of Mir-An-Da silently to our beds and bring our thoughts and dreamtime experiences to a discussion after morning meditation." The women nodded agreement, each lost in her own thoughts and feelings. Leah left the grid in place for the next evening along with two long burning church candles on either side of Sananda. Silently, she thanked him for his guidance and support, and asked to be welcomed to his ashram in the astral during her sleep to prepare her for the day to come. In bringing forth Mir-An-Da's story, there had been many cryptic encodements, many opportunities for codes to open in the women and in herself. She asked that anything activated within her be released for the highest good of the planet, then wandered off to her room, her consciousness barely in her body.

Lilith

Leah speaks

The next morning, the women had a lively discussion about Mir-An-Da and the gifts she had brought to Earth. They each felt a different piece of Mir-An-Da within them. It seemed pointless to argue about the age of the great monuments in Egypt; whether they were built before or after the deluge or whether Atlantis really existed, for all of this would be resolved when the records were found. All would be discovered when humans were ready to accept it and not a moment before, because the High Council would not allow the destruction of these records at this stage of the program. Leah was adamant about the need for integrity and impeccability with respect to present and future investigations of record chambers. "The chambers, sealed by high magicians who created the energetic fields, could not be penetrated by humans of low density and ill-intent." she said. "At the time of Christ, some chambers of lesser importance containing records of the post-deluge mystery schools were opened and the records were transferred to Alexandria where they were later torched by religious fanatics. This will not happen to the legacy of the Golden Age."

She spoke with a determination that left no doubt of the lineage moving through her. Then she suggested they spend the afternoon on the mountain, cleansing and preparing themselves for the evening. They hiked to a secluded sacred spring and took turns lowering themselves into an ice cold pool of pristine water. Allowing the sun's warmth to dry and energize them, they followed a shamanic trance journey within the mountain to work with the ascended masters, then returned, rejuvenated, to the retreat center. That evening, when the Sun was low in the sky, the women gathered again in their sacred space looking out on the mountain. Candles and incense were lit and a dark-haired beauty named Ellia led the group in meditation as Leah prepared herself for the work. Sitting in her room before the altar, she prayed for guidance and clarity. She spoke with Sananda who assured her that all was unfolding as it should. Entering the room as the women sat in silence, she took her seat in the circle, the altar behind her and the grid before her. Without one word of a social nature, she began.

"I do not want to get bogged down in the details of the disintegration of the lineage in Egypt. The Divine lineage of kings continued after the deluge until 3000 BC. Then they began losing consciousness, diluting the blood and distorting the teachings. Through the misuse of power, they lost the Grail code legacy that had been gifted to them by Aman-Ra and Mir-An-Da. The magi withdrew, taking with them the secrets of king-making - the inter-dimensional pathway to the Investiture of Divine Rule carried out before the High Council. Of course, the High Council knew that this was inevitable. The days of the Ahkus in Egypt were drawing to a close but that was irrelevant to the High Council for the pure seed, in the persons of the first born son and daughter of Amen-Se and Mai-An, had been sent to the lush colony that lay between the two rivers to the east and north (Mesopotamia or Sumer) before the deluge. All the colonies were forewarned to build seaworthy vessels to insure that many would survive the cleansing. From this particular colony, we have the story of Noah and the ark, but there were many vessels and many survivors. The High Council would not put the future of the program in the hands of one man, even if the royal blood did flow in his veins. When the flood waters subsided, the survivors found themselves in many different places, but some found their way back to that fertile valley between two rivers which had hardly changed their courses. This part of the world was some distance from the Atlantic where the major submergence and subsequent tidal waves were experienced. The concomitant melting of the polar ice brought more water into this area creating more fertility and a yearly flooding of the delta. It was a paradise.

"The bloodline continued here in the city of Ur. By the middle of the second millennium BC, it had weakened and unconscious behavior was prevalent. Changes had been made in dynastic inheritance to favor the first born male, and the culture had slipped into competitiveness with its neighbors. The Golden Age was, by that time, a mere legend. This spurred the community, and many others dotting the landscape of the middle east, to become more patriarchal. Women's temples were still respected and they were sought out for healing, but the queens had little power even though many were brought from diluted strains of the bloodline in other cities or countries on the pretext of giving more power to the throne. Patriarchy was already established and few women of power were left. Indeed, most found it wise to keep their wisdom alive in secrecy to maintain its purity. Sacred sexual practices were being dishonored in many places, with priests advocating sacred prostitution instead. Sadly this was only the beginning. Where were the codes of light at this time? They were safely tucked away in the luminous genes of a warrior woman who lived in the middle of the second millennium BC. She was the high priestess of a strict sect of traditional women who lived beneath Mount Sinai on the Red Sea. Her name was Lilith and her Mission was of supreme importance.

"We meet Lilith at the closing of her Earthwalk. Her Mission completed, she sits with Sarah, born with the solar disc upon her etheric brow and heart. Lilith looks the crone, her life force spent upholding her integrity within the imbalanced patriarchal energies. Had it not been mandatory for her to pass the lineage through the telling of her story, she would have preferred to die without saying a word. In her later years she had lost the edge of her warrior nature, but many of the codes she released were directly connected to her ability to stand in her truth when no one else had the slightest idea what the truth was. Now her hair was white and long, pulled up atop her head, twisted and held with a long fork of gold. Her brown eyes were still sharp and quick in the furrowed face of age. Well into her nineties, she was a fragile gem hidden within the black robes of her calling. She was not born into the bloodline. In fact this whole sect of priestesses left Jericho, one of the colonies of old, not long after Lilith joined them. Their oracles could see the desecration of the women's temples coming. Rather than fleeing at the last minute, they had chosen to retreat into solitude a hundred years ahead of time. They understood well their commitment to the codes of light and the need to protect the lineage.

"This group of women was quite close to a sect of magi whose dwellings were but a stone's throw away. They were descendants of the original brotherhood of magicians ordained by Aman-Ra. They were the magi who had sealed the chambers of the pyra-

[55]

mids and who held the secrets of king-making. They had retreated from Egypt long before to maintain the purity of their work. There were lesser magi still working for the pharaohs, but none with a fraction of the power that these men possessed. Sarah, now forty, was born to Ruth, the temple oracle. She was conceived during the sacred sexual awakening of her father, Jacob, at his coming of age. Jacob subsequently married the daughter of one of the magi and had a large family in their community. Sarah often visited her father who had become one of the most powerful of magi in the community. He shared his wisdom freely with her and she was doubly prepared to assume her responsibilities. A handsome woman, she had birthed three children in the temple. Her hair was deep auburn and her eyes a lively green. One could see the trace of Akhu blood she carried through her father. Temple born, she was skilled in the medicinal arts as well as prophecy. Lilith felt she was an excellent successor for the lineage.

"Lilith scanned the temple room of the eternal flame. Sarah had laid down the grid and prepared the lamps as requested. Fragrant resins burned upon the altar which held the flame, the Divine light, in a graceful golden oil lamp. Golden images of Mir-An-Da and Aman-Ra were placed in wall niches, relics of the past held within the lineage. Behind the altar was a radiant solar disc of pure transmuted gold, also from the ancient temples of Annu. The room was round and the ceiling rose in a small dome which was painted deep blue with silver stars, much like the temple in Annu. Oil sconces hung at intervals on adobe-whitened walls. On the stone floor was the gold inlaid symbol of the six pointed star where Sarah placed the sapphires at Lilith's direction. Lilith sat in a pillowed chair, her back propped up and her bare feet flat upon the floor connected to Earth Mother. Across from her in a lower chair, her body held naturally straight like a splendid noble cedar tree, sat Sarah, whose soft eyes were focused intently upon Lilith. The sun shone in the window opposite Lilith, gathering the first orange glow of its descent. Gazing upon it brought a smile to her face and fire to her eyes. She sighed, sipped from a cup of medicinal tea that Sarah had prepared to assist with the holding of the energy of the lineage, then shifted her gaze to Sarah.

Lilith speaks

"My dear Sarah, I call forth all the life force left within me to take you through your passage this night. You know the history of the codes of light from the many times you have sat before me and my outward story is also familiar. I have completed my work upon

Earth, but how I have done it is for you alone to know. The dominance of the patriarchs and their dismissal of Earth Mother, I have fought with every ounce of my flesh, the quickness of my mind, and all the filaments of my subtle bodies. It was not for me to stop them, this I have always known, for this situation was inevitable. What is more, it will continue and become a menace equal to the ten plagues of Egypt, Sarah. The feminine will be feared, punished and dismissed for almost forty-five centuries. The codes of light will be hunted down and nearly extinguished - millions of women being murdered in the process - but it will not succeed. All things pass in time, Sarah, even the imbalances of the patriarchs, but the codes of light will remain in the pure state of their inception, until Earth ascends.

"The codes of light were first brought to Earth by the children of the stars. These Shining Ones continue to incarnate, lifting the consciousness of Earth, teaching the celestial truths of Prime Creator, coaxing humanity along toward higher consciousness. It does not always look as if they are succeeding, I know, but the vibration has continually shifted upward. We are moving toward a cleansing of Earth, but before humanity is ready for the resulting upliftment of consciousness, certain dramas need to be played out. Humans will navigate in dangerous waters, moving toward the greatest possible separation from God. Divine union of male and female is the balance, but goddess cults will continue to grow in strength to counter the patriarchy. Patriarchs will claim one god and declare him to be male. What an absurdity. There will be continuous fighting between this 'god' and the goddess cults, both little more than heathen worship. It cannot be stopped, Sarah. It must be played out. There will be great messengers both in the lineage of light and the bloodline of Mir-An-Da and eventually they will prevail. At last there will be peace, balance, and light upon this planet. For this reason you and I are here tonight. I have seeded within the crystalline grid of the Earth, the energies of strength, perseverance and fortitude for all women coming after me. I have delivered to the collective consciousness of humanity, the thought form of union, that we are all part of one God, one energetic creative force that motivates the universe. We are not separate from our star beings. We are not separate from all that we oppose. It is all One. We are all God. This is, you will agree, an advanced thought form for the present situation on Earth, but it seemed even more obscure when Mir-An-Da first introduced it into the present seeding. I have merely reinforced it, to make it more substantial.

[57]

The Priestesses of Annu

"Now, tradition asks me to begin at the beginning, to tell you of my life. Forgive me if I leave out some details - it was not as long a life as Mir-An-Da's but truly long enough. I was born not far from here, in Jericho, to educated parents who dealt in the trading of cloth. It was most unusual to have an educated mother. She was the daughter of a city administrator who trained her well in the keeping of accounts. My father was a scholar particularly interested in the history and cultures of the far east. He often traveled in search of elegant cloth which fed his desire to learn more of other lands. Being very successful merchants, they could afford a large family, yet chose to have only five children and rear them well. I was the youngest daughter and third child. My older sister, Abida, whom I adored, was mainly responsible for raising me. We spent hour after hour together, she teaching me everything as she learned it herself, discovering that I had an amazing capacity to memorize as well as an uncanny ability to know her thoughts. My personal codes were opening and I was to a certain extent conscious of it.

"When Abida was ready for her puberty rites, her raising, my mother decided to take her to the priestesses at the temple of Annu. Abida insisted that I, three years her junior, be allowed to accompany her and our mother. Permission was granted and my whole being began whirling in anticipation of this event. I was far more excited than my sister. Mother chose this specific temple because the traditional rites of sacred sexuality were practiced there, while other temples were being drawn into servicing men's desires. Also, the priestesses were highly educated and skilled in the medical arts. She felt them to be honorable and little inclined to ungodly practices such as she and my father abhorred. I was quite careful when I picked my parents from spirit world, Sarah!

"The day came for Abida's initiation. She was dressed in pure white linen and I wore a black robe and cloak as a symbol of invisibility to respect her day. With the other young women who were participating in the rites, she first entered the temple of the eternal flame, a room much like this one, but far larger, at least to my young eyes. The initiates stood in a half circle before the altar, their mothers behind them. I was on a stone platform which afforded a little girl a good view, near the side of the room. The young women were first cleansed with the smoke of frankincense and brushed with palm fronds, then they received teachings of the blood mysteries from the high priestess. She was a powerful middle-aged woman named Leah whose strong voice, bright eyes and lustrous skin impressed me. Though dressed in black as I was, she was by no means invisible. When the formal teachings were completed, the young women repeated vows to honor their own sexuality whatever their role would be in the world, and to bring forth girl children who would do the same. I realized that my mother had been here when she was a young girl and that she was fulfilling her vows to Abida.

"At that point in the ceremony, the mothers withdrew and the girls were led to private rooms where the priestesses of the temple would invoke their sexuality and bring them into womanhood with the sacred crystal. The mothers were to return for them the next day. As I saw Abida being led away from me, the little girl within me reacted spontaneously, feeling the separation, and I ran to her calling her name. It was as if I had appeared from nowhere, coming from the invisible to embarrassing visibility. The high priestess stepped into my path and I stopped as if hitting a wall. 'Who have we here?' she laughed. I can still hear her words echoing in my head just as they did in the temple. Abida disappeared through a doorway and I felt Mother rushing up behind me. Leah held out her hand to stop my mother and stood back, arms folded, to take a good look at me. She asked me my name and I stated it clearly. Smiling, she introduced herself, taking my hands in her own. My response was to bow before her, but she lifted my chin and called my mother forward. She told her that I bore the golden disc of the Sun between my brows and upon the heart of my etheric body. I belonged to the temple for I was marked to follow in Leah's footsteps. Mother bowed before her, kissing her hands, for this was a great privilege. My mind was racing toward the consequences, leaving my family and especially Abida. Leah seemed to read my thoughts and turning back to me, told me to come to see her once each week, at a time to be arranged by the timekeeper with my mother. When I was ready for my raising, just three years hence, I would remain at the temple. Then she told me she had been looking for me, expecting me, and was very happy that I had rushed forward, for whatever reason, in my black robes of destiny, to become visible to her. My compulsiveness was no less than a push from my soul for Leah was holding the lineage of the codes of light."

*

The Sun was sitting just above the horizon and Lilith stopped, turning her gaze to the west. Sarah rose and stood alongside the window as they watched the descent of Annu in silence. As the

[59]

last ray of the Sun entered Lilith's eyes, she closed them, holding the energy she'd received within, consuming it, allowing it to feed her. When she could feel it shooting out of her hands and feet, she drew it back into her center and opened her eyes. She looked at Sarah, observing the expansion of the solar discs in her etheric field. Her entire filamentous field was radiating in response to the solar energy she had absorbed. This was why Annu was revered, not as a god, but as a giver of life, of sustenance for the filamentous light body. Annu was one of the keys to ascension. This she knew, for even as she sat within the shell of an old human body, her light body was preparing her way home to the stars. Sarah walked silently around the room lighting the oil lamps, her long braid brushing the floor each time she touched her small torch, a spark of the eternal flame, to each lamp wick. Her light body danced above her with the torch, the eternal flame and the light from the lamps. It was a choreography of spirit. Smiling at Lilith who brushed a tear from her wrinkled cheek, Sarah returned to her chair. Lilith wondered if all the passages over the preceding millennia had been as touching, as beautiful. She suspected they had. A shiver of bliss moved through her and brought her back to focus on her task.

*

"I began my work with Leah soon after Abida's initiation. Abida shared her experience with me and I tingled with excitement to know that my own was just three years away. My studies with Leah were decidedly more mundane, but interesting nonetheless. She set about augmenting my schooling by teaching me additional languages especially the Egyptian and Hebrew dialects. The former would assist me in the study of the mysteries as handed down from the brotherhoods and Divine lineage of kings and queens. Why she demanded the latter of me was a mystery to me until after my 'raising' into womanhood. We delved into astronomy, the magic of numerals, sacred shapes and symbols, as well as practical areas of learning such as plant medicines and healing. It was all very exciting for I had a quick and active mind. This education fed me, much as Annu does now.

"I continued my normal studies with my sibling for which Father brought tutors to our home. We were disciplined, but in a loving and joyful way. My family has always been very dear to me, even when I was far away or deep in the training of the sisterhood. Abida planned to marry near the time of my 'raising' so we would both leave home, going our separate ways together. I believe this made things easier for us. My rite of passage was, and still is, a treasure to me. Mother gave me away with dignity and honor for she was a strong woman and, quite frankly, it was a great honor to have a daughter chosen by the high priestess to follow this path. After the priestesses had brought me into full womanhood and had spent the night telling me appropriate stories of love, they took me to an austere little room that was to be my home. Though the temple was glorious and every consideration was taken to provide the best for the healing arts, the priestesses lived quite simply. My room had a window overlooking an enclosed garden with an olive tree growing alongside. I was happy to have a simple room with little to care for, sure that life would be filled with leisure time, books and artistic pursuits. You laugh, Sarah, for you know from your own experience that temple life is not for lazy women.

"I was put to work in the kitchen the very next day. No doubt it was the first test of many. From the kitchen I went to the garden, growing some of the food we ate. Because I was clever and had closely watched my father mending things, I was given the task of fixing whatever was broken. In addition, I had my studies, much as before I had joined the sisters. Two years passed before I was allowed to scrub the temple floor or wipe the dust from the altar. At that same time, I began receiving instructions from Leah to prepare me for my calling. These were teachings of the lineage explaining the cosmos, the one God, the power of women, and the dangers of the ways of the world. It was an awakening for me to understand how men used fear to control people. Early on, I learned that fear enslaves and love frees. I have always lived my life without fear. For this reason, I have appeared as an enigma to the world. Learning not to react, Sarah, I have never intentionally put others in a state of fear. It is the power I have gained in this life.

"While learning the mysteries I became interested in energy. Opening to my capacity to 'see', I was aware of the light filaments. I watched light! I watched people interact, and the light that dipped in and out of their filamentous networks. There would be flares of red light when someone projected anger, and a white pink light came with love. My own filaments reached out to link with a network of universal filaments, especially when I was in meditation. How I perceived the world was changing very rapidly with this gift. When I finally confided my observations to Leah, she moved me out of the kitchen and into the studio to begin drawing the geometry I saw. Realizing that I had been intending this in my meditation for several months, I could see there was a connection between my intent and that which came to pass. It was profound for me to realize that I could create my own reality. I have been doing so ever since!

"As I began to understand energy more deeply, it occurred to me that people who have the gift of prophecy are somehow able to step outside time and follow the universal filaments into the future, or they draw the future to them from that network, for all things are contained in the universal filaments. I experimented with this theory and was soon predicting future events. One of my greatest gifts, my most treasured personal code, is this ability to understand life, the energetic part of life, and my capacity to investigate things intelligently. I understand that Mir-An-Da loved to experiment as well, and many have suggested that part of her soul is in mine. It may be so, Sarah! I will know soon enough, won't I? Well, Leah had a prodigy on her hands and she made no secret of the fact that I taught her about energy. She, on the other hand, taught me about people and I was astounded to hear some of the violent and senseless things they did. I had led a sheltered life in a good home in a city that had seen plenty of violence but not in my short life. Surely I could see that coming to Jericho and to the temple. Leah listened as I warned her of this. Then she told me bone-chilling stories of human events. I would feel the emotions involved and try to find the basis for the particular conduct. It was a little game I played, until I realized that fear was at the root of all unloving behavior. It might look like lust for power, for example, but it was really fear, fear of loss, fear of death, fear of not being someone important. Becoming skilled in the art of human observation, I could see the laws of karma at work on the grand scale. After a time, I begged Leah to tell me some love-filled stories - stories about the golden era of the past. Finally she assented.

"When I was sixteen years old, an owl began sitting in the olive tree outside my room. It was not a chance occurrence for she came every night. I began to mind-talk to this bird who confided to me that she could give me additional sight. She would demonstrate this by rotating her head full circle, a feat that was both outrageous and fascinating. Assuring her that I didn't want to use my neck in quite that way, she just stared at me. My elbows were propped up on the window ledge, and I was looking up at her when she flew straight down to land in front of me. She stared even harder. I asked if I could stroke her, and she consented. I think it helped ease her frustration with me for I had obviously missed the point. Finally she spoke again and told me to call on her power the next time I was seeking to understand someone. Even though this seemed very strange, I agreed to it. She told me her name was Seline - I was to call on Seline! I told no one of this encounter but kept it in the back of my mind. Seline routinely visited my wide mud-brick window ledge at sundown and it wasn't long before the first opportunity came to call on her for help.

"Abida came to visit me one day. I had not seen her in over a year for she had moved to the north of Jericho. She was obviously troubled, and had brought her youngest child, a boy, who was just turning two years of age. Wrapped in swaddling, she held him in her lap, while we shared the years' events from each of our lives. I thought it curious that she did not put young Zeb down upon the grass to play and finally asked her why. Her eyes welled up with tears and I reached for her hand, asking what was wrong. Unwrapping the cloth, she showed me Zeb's legs, as scrawny as a baby bird's. Her healers had told her that he was not going to walk, his muscles were withered from bad seed. Bursting into tears, she held him close. I was near tears myself for he was a sweet young boy and quite handsome in every other way. My mind began racing through the remedies and treatments of the priestesses, anything that I could offer. There were some oils that she could rub into his muscles daily, but nothing else came to mind.

"I was about to tell her that I would fetch one of the healers when Seline flew into the tree above us making quite a fuss and knocking leaves down on our heads. I asked Abida to wait while I searched my inner knowing for help. Closing my eyes, I silently called Seline. Suddenly, there appeared before my inner eye scenes from another place and time. I saw a gentle old man with a walking stick leading a young woman by the hand. He tapped every stone that came in her way with his stick and she learned to walk around them. He peeled fruits for her, letting her smell the morsels before putting them in her mouth. He appeared to be training her. I looked more closely at this young woman and saw that her eyes had no sight. As this truth was delivered to me, I knew that she was Abida and that the old man was the little boy Zeb. Seline had opened the door for me to Abida's Akashic records. Here was the part of the human story that was deeper than the energy exchanges of interaction. This was the soul's history, the playing out of karma, and it offered complete understanding of an otherwise incomprehensible tragedy.

"I shared what I had seen with Abida who looked at me startled. She felt the truth of my words and owned it. Looking at Zeb, she understood the love he had given her in that life, the patience, the tenderness and the time. Holding her son to her with new understanding, she vowed that he would have every opportunity in this life and all her love. We spoke of many other things, family and friends, then I led her to the healers who gave her oils, herbal remedies and essences for Zeb. That night Seline sat upon my sill making strange little throat noises. I had no idea what she was up to until she began rotating her head around full circle. Then she came back to center and made the noises again. I realized that she was laughing at me for being so slow to understand the gift that she brought to my life. The gift she was offering was the ability to see completely, in all directions, through time, into the records of any soul. As soon as I understood what she was trying to tell me, she became as still as a statue and it was I who laughed. She was imitating my stoic reaction to her dramatic display. Seline has been my companion ever since. I was not gifted with the plant medicines as the healers of our temple were, but it became recognized that I was connected to the magical power of this bird, and when I was older many people were sent to me to heal the unresolved issues of their souls. This was a gift to be used with the utmost integrity to help others with their personal growth. Zeb did eventually gain some strength in his legs and learned to walk with crutches. Whenever I saw him, he would ask to see Seline, and she would sit where he could watch her, while I ran energy into his legs. He was, as the old man he had been, gentle and loving.

*

At that moment, the owl alighted gently on the sill of the opened window. Sarah laughed and Lilith snapped her fingers. Seline, with one beat of her wings, flew behind Lilith and perched on the chair back at her right shoulder. Sarah, who was not unfamiliar with Seline, did not flutter an eyelash. Lilith was pleased with Sarah's training. She would be a fine high priestess and in time her codes would be released and she would come truly into her purpose. The brilliant colors of the sunset had faded to pale pink and lavender, the lamps and eternal flame in the room becoming the predominant source of light. A young priestess brought a fresh cup of hot tea for Lilith who sipped it slowly as she continued.

*

"One day, near the end of my sixteenth year, Leah asked me to sit with her in the garden. I could tell she had something important to tell me by the crispness of her demeanor. She asked me to stand before her. I could not imagine what she was looking for that she would not have seen a thousand times. I had long, softly waved, burnt red hair, was of medium height, and was amply proportioned as a woman. My eyes spoke more the power of my mind than any feminine mystery. My idle thoughts were reading Leah's mind of course and I knew she was assessing my person. Since I could read her thoughts, I asked her to reveal her plan, but was not prepared for what she had to say. I knew I had work to do in the world but assumed I would be stepping into her shoes when the time came. That was not to be the case.

"Pulling me down beside her, Leah said that my Mission was unfolding. She mentioned for the first time the Siriun High Council under whose command the carriers of the codes of light were bound. She suggested that I begin contacting them in meditation to establish my autonomy with them. Asking if I were going away, she replied that I was, and that everything I would experience was part of my training and essential to releasing the codes I carried. So fearless was I that I was ready to jump on a donkey and leave immediately. Calming myself, I asked where I was being sent and with what purpose. Leah explained that the bloodline of Aman-Ra was in peril. The lineage of kings was losing its conscious connection to the one God and to the mysteries. Many practices had become blatantly heathen and certainly all the mindful rituals were being abandoned. I was to journey to Ur, in Sumeria. There I was to marry the young Hebrew king who had just come to the throne. I would become queen to these people, use my mastery of energy, many of my codes and all my intelligence and wit to reverse the energies that were building. Reaching out through the universal filaments, I could see the future. Confronting Leah, I shared the impossibility of the Mission. The bloodline was locked in patriarchal belief systems that would reinforce male leadership for thousands of years. She urged me to look past the illusion of this reality and watch the energy. I was to plant seeds, not reap a harvest. Speeding out on the filaments again, moving far into the future, I could see the opportunity for balance. It seemed an impossibly long time to wait for balance, especially for a warrior like myself, but she assured me that the High Council would not let it fail.

The Priestesses of Annu

"A man named Petra had been sent ahead of me to establish residence in the city of Ur. He was a Hebrew who had lived in Jericho. A man I had never met, but knew of as a trader who had brought spices from the east to the temple. He worked the trade routes from Jericho to the far east and was well known from Jericho to Ur. Petra would live in Ur as a silent guardian. When I felt my work was finished (Leah had never expected me to stay forever), I was to find him in the marketplace and he would see to my safe return. With the unfolding of her plan, my sense of adventure was building. I would be accompanied by two magi from the Red Sea who were traveling that way on business. Leah had been in communication with their community on the northern shore of the Red Sea. She was planning to relocate the temple in that area beneath Mount Horeb, having heeded my warnings about Jericho.

"Everything around me was changing. I boldly asked what she knew of this young king and she looked a little distressed. Apparently he was hot-tempered and headstrong, much like a bull. Adam, as he was called, was, if anything, crude in manner and somewhat unkempt in appearance. He was quite fond of military strategy. I raised my hand and asked her to say no more. It seemed reasonably certain that this young man had not been trained in sacred sexual practices and had little respect for women. What he and his family wanted, of course, was an heir to the throne. I knew from my studies that the Hebrews were still observing a form of dynastic marriage established by Aman-Ra and Mir-An-Da. It was a form that favored the male energy with conception at the height of the summer Sun and birth during the month of the warrior. Because of this law, I would be obliged to have intercourse with my husband only one month of the year. If I failed to produce an heir within nine months, the process would begin again. The marriage was not fully recognized until an heir was produced. This tribe had always maintained a high percent of pure Akhu blood and from what I knew their priestesses had not been forced into prostitution. I learned from Leah that I was to work, on behalf of the sisterhood, with the high priestess in Ur to rejuvenate the mysteries in the temple. When I asked Leah how I came to their attention, she told me that my father knew these people well and was highly respected by them. The royal family wished to have a queen of considerable intelligence, skill and who was dedicated to the one God. It was not explained to them that my concept of the one God was not that of a patriarch. At the time I thought of this new part of my life as a great adventure and a learning experience. If I had traveled the filaments into the future I could have seen the design of the High Council, but I chose to live it a day at a time.

"I was reunited with my family for some days before my departure. Father bought beautiful cloth for a wedding dress and Mother helped the priestesses with the sewing. In the temple, I had been wearing the dark blue robes of a novice. As queen, I would wear fine clothes of many colors in public, but would prefer my robes of sisterhood when I could be alone. I chose to travel in them as well, and on the eve of my departure Leah brought me a gift, the purple robes of the vowed sisters. Protesting that I had not made my formal commitment to the sisterhood, she smiled and assured me that my Mission was commitment enough. In addition, I had the support of the Siriun High Council for this Mission, which indicated to her that I was moving into the time of code activation and release. She would not hold me back in any way. On the other hand, when I felt my Mission was complete, I would find her on the shores of the Red Sea near the dwellings of the magi. I breathed a sigh of relief that I was not expected to remain in Ur my whole life and thanked her for those words.

"That night Seline came to my window assuring me that the palace in Ur from whence she had just returned had a beautiful garden with many good roosting trees. I was greatly relieved to have the company and wisdom of this great friend for I knew she would help me in my position as queen. Resting uneasily that night, I was up before dawn for meditation, breakfast, and to make my final preparations. The new robes felt heavier as did the responsibility, but I loved the color purple which was especially striking with my red hair. I was seventeen years old, it was springtime, and I was on my way to become a queen. Bidding farewell to my little room and my little life, I picked up the two bags and met Leah at the temple gate. One of my guides took the bags and strapped them to a donkey. We would both ride and walk the great distance to Ur so I was given sturdy footwear and a purple hooded cape to protect me from the elements. Leah introduced me to Mek and Esrom, the two magi who would be my guides and guardians. Mek, who had taken my bags, was most handsome in face and body. He had the magus' beard and turbaned head, but long curls of golden hair hung to his shoulders. His eyes were blue and piercing, his manner gentle but forthright. Esrom was older than Mek and much quieter. He seemed to be always in a meditative pose and was a very wise man. His graying hair and beard contrasted sharply with a rather youthful countenance. I reminded myself that these were magicians and what I was perceiving in this reality could be totally fabricated. It seemed this should be an interesting journey. Embracing Leah and several of my sisters, I took the reins of my beast. We walked through Jericho, stopping to bid farewell to my family before leaving the city by the north gate. Mounting our donkeys outside the city wall and leaving the lush oasis behind us, we rode north into the desert.

"The journey was long, hot and dusty but the company was good and the innkeepers along the way quite gracious. We rode to Damascus where we rested a few days, bathed and ate well. The more time I spent with Mek, the more I liked him. He was twenty-three and not yet married. I wished for all the world that I could trade him for what awaited me in Ur. Neither of the magi knew Adam but they did know the city of Ur and praised it highly for the intelligence of its citizens and the variety of its pursuits. It was the major Hebrew community and the original colony established by the son of Aman-Ra. There were many smaller communities between Ur and Egypt owing to the many migrations of people between the two places. Ur was a prominent trading city and I was sure to see my father from time to time as he went there to purchase silk and find cloth from the east.

"From Damascus we followed the river north through Elba and then to Haran. This was the common route to the fertile valley lying between the Tigris and Euphrates rivers. Ur lay south of Babylon on the south side of the Euphrates which we followed the rest of the way. I can't even tell you the length of our journey. In some ways it seemed an eternity and in others so short that I was saddened at its conclusion. Esrom had become a second father for me and Mek was my warrior guardian. When we slept beneath the stars, Seline was always close at hand. If we stayed at inns or within spiritual sanctuaries she always kept a respectable distance, but I knew she was there. Esrom and Mek did not speak much about their work as magi and I, in turn, spoke little about the life of a priestess. We were good traveling companions, content simply to be present with one another and maintain some mystery about our Missions. Arriving in Ur, I was delivered to the temple by my two guardians after being shown the booths of the traders including the particular one who would be able to contact Petra for me. When I said my farewells to my two guides, Esrom encouraged me to stand in my truth to detach from any outcome for I was on a Mission. I thanked him and gave him a hug. Mek squeezed me beneath my cloak playfully and I laughed. I kissed his cheek and told him I knew I would see him again. He smiled, saying that he too knew as much and, focusing his intense blue eyes upon me, declared he would await my return to the south. I blushed, sharing his feelings. It was not the most desirable way to enter an arranged marriage. Slowly I retreated through the gates of the temple to the awaiting priestesses, my eyes fixed upon that mysterious young man. With laughing eyes, Mek placed my bags inside the gates and closed them behind him. Sarah, in the months that were to come, that last image of Mek kept me from losing my senses and Esrom's words constantly supported what I knew to be my truth.

"The marriage was to take place in a month's time. I was to become acquainted with the customs of the Hebrews by attending a number of social events and temple services. The priestesses were very kind to me and anxious to learn anything they could since I was the first priestess to visit them from outside their tribe. In a light and social way, I introduced them to some of the differences in our ways of living and invited them to share their ideas with me. I did not overtly teach them for that would have been usurping their high priestess's power, but I told stories of my experiences, and wove into them enlightening information about sacred sexuality, working with crystal energy, the healing power of plants and the Earth elements. Both our temples originated at Annu in ancient Egypt with Mir-An-Da, but theirs had come under the influence of other tribes and eastern culture owing to their position along the trade routes. The stories I told circulated within the temple and caught the ear of the high priestess with whom I had only had a brief formal audience upon my arrival. She was a slight woman, but one of great strength. With sparkling eyes, she had brilliant luminous filaments emanating from her heart. Her name was Jerushah.

"One day Jerushah came to me and asked me to sit with her in a secluded spot in the lush temple gardens. She asked many questions about the mystery teachings, our temple customs and the history of our order from ancient times. Knowing that their temple had strayed somewhat from its original intention, she was not sure when it had happened but felt it was in more recent times. I shared with her some of the mindless, even decadent practices that had become part of temple life in other regions and how closely we guarded our truth and freedom. She had also heard of these reports and would fight vigorously to uphold the truth in Ur, but revealed that the priests were being given great power over the people's beliefs. The feminine aspect of God was being transformed into a fertility goddess for the crops - one who

[69]

would appeal to Mother Earth for abundant food. This was a ploy to remove the feminine from religious practices which were becoming entangled in politics and power. It was the grossest form of separation - similar to the deterioration of the teachings happening everywhere else as nations developed and men warred with one another. I could see there was no way to bring the Golden Age back at this time, and knew in my heart that this dominance by men would grow into powerful systems of government with fear as their greatest weapon.

"Jerushah and I agreed that the priestesses were the only women in positions of respect apart from the queen whose shoes I was there to fill. We made a commitment to uphold the truth of the dualistic nature of God which also existed in each of us. There was no need to create complications. God was in all of us - we were God. But this was the advent of the time of the ram, a time predicted by the astrologers of old to be one of patriarchal dominion. When I followed the filaments into the future, I saw this dominion extending much further than that, perhaps through the age of the fish. The images that came to me were horrifying. I knew that a certain strength of truth needed to become part of a woman's core essence for the feminine to survive the future. These visions filled me with rage, Sarah. I asked more questions of Jerushah, particularly about the priests and their intentions. They seemed entangled in the government of Ur, their prophets were advising the king and their power was growing. I, once again, sped out on the filaments into the future and saw the power of the priests and the temples of the men. They began holding the people in fear and separating them from God. I was outraged. God was in all things, yet these priests declared they were Divine channels and the only way to reach God was through them. Their sabotage occurred gradually, over centuries, so that people would become less and less conscious of this manipulation.

"Jerushah could see my rage building and put her hand out to calm me. I asked her to bear with me a moment longer and called on Seline. She flew from her place of hiding to the tree above our heads. Asking for her help, I opened my vision to the whole truth behind the future and witnessed a great battle of light in the void of the universe. The conflict between love and fear was very close to the level of Source - the Heart of God. This was allowed because God allows all expression. The beings involved in this great battle began to feel separation from each other and thus from God. Stars exploded and eventually everything was quiet. Before this great battle, there was only love. After it, there was love, fear and separation. From fear there emerged many negative feelings and yet they were all part of God.

"I expressed some confusion and found myself before a circle of Akhus who announced themselves as the Siriun High Council. The first thing they told me was that my immediate personal task would be to transform my rage into tranquillity, or I would be of no use to them at all. I stood humbled before them. They explained that the great battle of An, where separation first took form in the universe, had created a polarity. It was not that one was good and one was evil. There were only losers in that battle. Now all beings passing through the Stargate of An entered a world in which separation existed. Realization of God within the world of separation was the highest achievement of the soul. All souls in the universe were sent by God at one time or another through the stargate to reap the benefits of this opportunity. So, in this separation, God had designed a way to become an even greater energetic force. God is in all things, even the least obvious. The Siriun Mission to heal separation, to bring the two forces of An together in love, is accomplished by bringing those two forces together in wholeness within each soul. This is the path of return to the heart of God. Thus, the battle of An was a metaphor for the battle within each of us. It is the battle between individuation, personality and our Godself which knows no individuation. Individuation occurs everywhere in the universe, but Earth is uniquely coupled with free will. Earth is the ultimate test of the soul, the densest of vibrations. The soul can advance greatly through Earthwalks, but it can also become trapped in illusion.

"The High Council dismissed me and I returned to the garden with Jerushah who was holding the energy of the space for me. We talked of my visions of the future and what we could do to strengthen the feminine aspect of God amongst her people. We agreed to meet once each week in the queen's garden to continue our work together. I asked if I could be excused and she graciously accommodated me. Seeking the solitude of my quarters (Seline flying after me to her place of hiding outside my window), I prayed, begging God to forgive me for my rage and to help me find peace within myself. It was a request I would make quite often while in Ur, but a state of being I would not realize until much later in my life. I have not discussed the battle or my appearance before the council with anyone until now, Sarah, although I repeat it to you as clearly as if it had happened this morning. With and without Seline's help, I have been back to the council many times, and I will show you secret ways of the high priestess that will assist you to find your way there also. It is essential that you be able to access the High Council in the future when you have the need to do so."

*

Lilith needed to move around and asked Sarah to take her out on the adjacent rooftop to see the night sky. They walked together to the doorway and Sarah helped her down the one step to the roof of the sewing room below. Night was fully upon them and the stars twinkled above the sea. Lilith fixed her gaze on Ak-An and felt a charge of energy run up her spine, much as a traveler feels a burst of energy when he spots his destination. Something in her quickened and she grabbed Sarah's arm, recognizing it as the call home. After telling Sarah that her time was close at hand - that they must finish the passage soon - she looked out over the community of the magi and unleashed a loud cackle. Then pulling Sarah's face down to her own, she told her that they needed to make quick work of her ill-fated marriage and get to the good part of her life. Sarah laughed as well for the stories of Lilith and Mek were well-known. Leading Lilith back into the temple room, she seated her comfortably in her chair, once again. Seline had never moved. She also knew that time was running out for she could feel it in every quill, every muscle, every bone within her. It was through her association with Seline that Lilith had developed the owl's gift of understanding the natural world.

*

"After that experience in the garden with Jerushah, she and I spent time together daily until my wedding. I gave her most of the teachings and practices that she needed to reorganize their temple during that time. After my marriage our meetings were more in the nature of discussions about the fate of nations, spirituality, and women. She brought me undistorted news of the world - something I could not get from Adam. I first met my husband at a social gathering just before our wedding. His family wanted to meet me and discuss my preferences for food, wine and musicians for the wedding feast. I had been in Ur for weeks before this contact. Adam's father had died unexpectedly the year before and Adam had assumed the throne immediately without a queen. His mother, Ruth, had been filling the woman's role at the same time as she was grieving her husband's death. The family accounts of the dead king, Judah, portrayed him as an honorable and kind-hearted man and yet I knew that it was he who gave much power to the priesthood through his own indifference. The priests were well represented at the gathering as were Adam's political associates.

"I was introduced to Adam who was a solidly built dark-haired young man of twenty. Though he lacked social skills, he excelled in storytelling and seemed quite pleased to entertain his friends. I spoke to him briefly about my life in the south and the journey to Ur. He knew of my father and gave him praise for my education in Hebrew. Letting him know that my father had me tutored in many subjects, I told him that Hebrew was not one of them. To Leah I gave credit where it was deserved. Testing me in other areas of academic pursuits, he found me to be more knowledgeable than himself. To counter this realization he turned to political topics on which I would have liked to challenge him, but pretended disinterest, knowing full well that I needed to protect my place in the palace and not risk imprisonment. Eventually I was drawn back to the women but found him staring at me in a curious way more than once. I knew full well that he was appraising me sexually and I quickly threw up a force field of invisibility around myself. He looked bewildered, then turned away to his friends. Such was our first encounter.

"The wedding was celebrated by the entire community and I knew how every foreign bride felt whose marriage was arranged for reasons other than love. My dress was beautiful and held the love of my father, my mother, and all the women who had worked so hard to make it. Adam's younger sister was so enthralled with it that I agreed to give it to her when her own time of marriage came. I received a delicate golden crown as part of the ceremony and learned that our kingdom was, for the most part, in attendance. It consisted of Ur and the surrounding countryside where crops were grown. Our northern border was the river which gave access to the sea. Life was good, there was plenty to eat, and the people were quite happy in their ignorance. They did not see the subtle shifting of power and, of course, they could not see the future.

"It was not yet the month of dynastic intercourse so I was spared that aspect of our relationship after the wedding. We were taken to the palace where I was led to the queen's quarters. You can imagine my relief to know that they were not shared with Adam at other than approved times. My quarters were quite large. The bedroom had a big comfortable bed and stove for winter heat.

The Priestesses of Annu

There was a sitting room, a library filled with books, and a beautiful bathing pool as well as the complete privacy of a walled garden where Seline had already installed herself. Adam and I dined together in the evenings and were expected to spend some social time together. We spent those times in what was to be our usual form of communication - sparring. I don't believe he liked me any more than I liked him. It became clear that the only expectation he had of me was the birth of a male heir. To that he was committed. In time, I found he had many women to choose from each night for sexual companionship, and was not lacking in the youthful energy to spend his seed. The chances were quite good that he already had children in many wombs.

"I was permitted to chose the women who would serve me in the palace. Naturally I filled all the positions with priestesses that Jerushah sent to me. Their quarters were connected to mine in such a way that Adam could not get to them, so I was certain of their safety. My days were spent in conversation with these young women, teaching them my skills, stimulating their minds, and allowing them to entertain and educate me. I treasured the days when Jerushah visited, spending long afternoons with her in the garden. She was my source of information from the outside world, and my dear friend.

"Occasionally I would take three or four of my servants and venture out into the market. I loved to look through the traders' stalls, especially those with interesting things from the east, and I was free to purchase whatever I wanted, often buying cloth and elegant trimmings for dresses. Also I was moved to buy crystals and objects of natural power. Many such items, I had brought with me from the south, so I was making quite a collection. I kept them in the library where I began using them to move energy in the kingdom. My pure intent was to bring this tribe to a place of strength wherein the bloodline could receive greater impulses of consciousness. I could see that it would eventually force them to leave Ur and become nomads, searching for the precise place to bring through the light. I knew they would find that place one day very close to Ur and that the light would come through. These intentions I received directly from the High Council.

"I was given a certain amount of money every week - money that only held value in Ur. Having no real needs, I gave most of it to Jerushah, asking that she use it to care for the poor. Before long I was secretly funding a program which brought healing care to the needy and food and shelter to those who had none. The women's temple gained much respect and the love of the people.

"Each night I took time to assess my Mission and what was expected of me next. I also dreamed of Mek and wondered how it would come to pass that I would be freed from my sumptuous prison to be with him. I could not imagine it. When the month of dynastic intercourse came, I was required to receive Adam in my bed whenever he desired. I am not certain that he ever desired me. I perceived myself more as an object of conquest. Love was never a factor in our relationship. Though the women's temple had not yet fallen into the hands of the patriarchy as a source of sexual pleasure, it had lost its way where sacred sexuality was concerned. The community was not supporting it as a means to initiate and educate boys at their raisings, and the priestesses had also discouraged it as the boys became crude and demanding. Adam was no different than the other young men in terms of his lack of skill and sensitivity. The only difference was that he was the king and he could do as he pleased, paying no heed to my requests. On the nights when he didn't come to maul and molest me, I prayed to know my purpose. When he did come, I left my body and flew to the stars to avoid his vulgar, brutish ways. Everyday I took plant medicines that would prevent conception. Our only discussion about sexuality occurred on our first night together when I did not bleed. I took the opportunity to educate him as to the life of a priestess and the initiatory ritual, adding a few remarks about the boys' raisings as well. He shrugged it off and fell asleep.

"Adam was not a stupid man. He was very intelligent but failed to see the obvious. He had spent no time at all studying human behavior, the nature of man, and I had devoted my whole (admittedly short) life to it. Strategy, mathematics, and sport interested him, but in an abstract way that did not involve other people. He did not care about God or how many gods there were. I observed that he cared about the strength of his friends, but mainly in a competitive way. By the time my first month of dynastic breeding came to an end, I knew the inner workings of my husband very well. What I didn't know was what I could do about it. Retreating back into my privacy, I summoned Seline and went before the Akhus of the High Council. I was filled to overflowing with questions about my duties regarding their program. What I learned very much surprised me. They did not want me to intervene with sacred sexual teaching. Mankind was already too far removed from God and its own feelings to put the two together. It would be reserved for those who practiced the mysteries. Next I learned that I was not to interfere in any of the political or priestly affairs, no matter how much they infuriated me. Furthermore, I was not to bear children by Adam . . . ! Completely bewildered, I felt a little betrayed. I could not conceive of my purpose beyond helping the poor and enlightening the priestesses. The purpose of my entire Mission, they finally explained, was the purification of my own emotions and the clear definition of my own truth. I went into immediate reaction, clearly demonstrating to them that I hadn't learned anything yet. I was dismissed.

"I could not imagine such a complicated plan simply to test my emotional neutrality and measure my ability to stand in truth. Yet, ultimately, I did, for I am a soul that loves challenge. I accepted it all because of my soul's desire for enlightenment. I was eighteen years old, Sarah, and by twenty I had managed to clearly define my truth and temper my reactions. Adam tested me in every way. He taught me not to react by feeding off my reactions. He helped me learn the depth of my truth by offering me my untruth. When he could no longer throw me into reaction, he sent his priests to challenge me. I held my courage but not my temper. It took a full year to learn neutrality with them. I also learned the ways of the patriarchy, their lust for power and the limited perception that allowed them to dismiss the feminine aspect of God. I understood them at their core. It was blind and unforgivable.

"The more peaceful I became the less they harassed me, perhaps thinking I was coming to embrace their beliefs. I was truly bringing tranquillity into my life. However, there was one problem that was becoming a serious concern. My childlessness after three years of dynastic marriage, was impermissible. Adam had plenty of bastard children by this time to prove his virility so the blame was placed upon me. His family put him under increasing pressure to produce an heir and he reacted by breaking the law. He began forcing his way into my quarters and into my vagina, unpredictably. Becoming increasingly brutish, he was often drunk when he came. I suffered beatings and chastisement that were the final test of my endurance. It could be dangerous to take the herbs every day, for they would become ineffective and could seriously harm my body's ability to bear children in the future. I used intent alone to prevent conception, but knew that there was a danger in being caught off guard. My life, which had been tolerable, became quite the opposite. Adam had my behavior monitored when he could and began replacing my servants with his concubines. When he ordered Jerushah to leave the palace grounds and not return, I knew I needed to act. I wrote a letter to

Adam's mother explaining the breach in the law her son had made, and begged her forgiveness for my barrenness. I declared the marriage null and void for that reason, in keeping with dynastic law. We had not had the second marriage which ordinarily came after conception and the assurance of an heir. Asking nothing of her but my freedom, I gave her my honor and my love, and put the letter in a safe place until I could find a way to leave.

"Adam was to be deep in government conference three days hence, so I waited. Lovingly, I packed my power objects and crystals,p and my second purple robe. I left my entire wardrobe including my bridal dress for Adam's little sister. Adam saw no change as he entered my room to violate me and I proved no different in the level of my resistance. My life depended upon right timing, and I was more than careful. I knew which women I could trust and which I could not. On the first day of his meetings, I sent the concubine servants to select new flowers for the garden, the most coveted of duties in the spring. I asked two of the priestesses to accompany me to the traders' market to search for special cloth to drape a worn lounge. We walked to the market without being followed and I made my way to the trader's booth, the man who would know how to reach Petra. I had often dealt there to be above suspicion. When I arrived the trader was gone and a new one was in his place. I wanted to cry, to panic, to react, but did not. With my heart ready to burst, I turned to walk away. The man reached out to touch my arm and asked if he could help me. I turned to say no, and met his eyes. In a whisper he said 'I am Petra'. I wanted to hug him, to laugh and to cry from joy, but I didn't do that either. I told him I was interested in seeing something from the Red Sea. He understood. He would have something to show me tomorrow but I would have to come soon after sunrise for he was leaving for the east.

"We understood each other's unspoken intention. I had a plan. I did not see Adam that night for he had drunk himself to unconsciousness with his associates. I went back to the High Council one more time and received clearance to leave. I had passed my final tests in the market place. It would be years before I had truly achieved tranquillity, and stillness, but I had learned to harness my emotions and act from my heart and mind together. This was the seed of wisdom that this part of my life had planted within me.

"The next morning, shortly after dawn, I donned my most worn purple priestess robes and with the two priestesses, whom I trusted beyond doubt, left the palace through the back garden gates. No one in the city gave a second thought to three priestesses out early in the morning. I gave one of them the letter to deliver to Adam's mother. To the other, I gave most of the money I had saved and all of my jewels. I asked her to give them to Jerushah for my last project in Ur. I wanted every pregnant woman in Ur to receive proper midwife care with safe births. I wanted all newborn babies be received into the world like heirs to the throne. This gift from my heart helped to neutralize the energies that I had used to prevent conception with Adam. I knew he would have his heirs, but they would not be from my womb. It was, regrettably, my only farewell to Jerushah whose friendship had meant so much to me.

"I had no cherished farewells with my companions who accompanied me to the market. We moved quickly in separate directions. Petra was waiting for me and silently led me through the chaos of the early morning market to the south city gate. Here he had a boy holding three donkeys for our journey. He secured our bags to one animal and we mounted the others. Before long, we were nearer to Babylon than Ur. Our journey was well under way. If Adam came to my bed that night, I would be well out of his jurisdiction. It was an easy ride for I had been that way before and the countryside was magnificent. Petra was silent but watchful, the perfect guardian. I was turned within, searching for the larger picture of my experience. He was the one on a Mission now.

"We had spent many days in this silence when something remarkable began to emerge from my consciousness. We were approaching Haran when I saw the greater picture. The patriarchy was here to stay, at least for four thousand years. How was the feminine to survive during this time and through the unspeakable oppression that would come with it? It would only survive by harnessing the emotions, acting through hearts and by standing in the truth, whatever that cost. Like a bolt of lightening, the knowingness came to me that these were codes that I carried for the planet. If I could achieve mastery of these very important gifts in my own life, they would be released into the collective mind to support all the women who would follow me for four thousand years.

"Sarah, magic is created with realization. This was self-realization, the purpose of my soul on Earth. I was in elation. I let out a joyful shriek that aged Petra ten years. It was cathartic, releasing all of my harbored resentments toward Adam. It freed me totally and I remain free to this day. I remember hearing something like the beating of the owl's wings at my ears and knew that the High Council breathed a sigh of relief as well. Seline was flying happy circles above us. It was one of the biggest days of my life.

"After some time had passed, I would look back on my days in Ur and realize that many of my key codes were opened as well as the planetary codes that I carried. I had a real sense of gratitude towards Adam even if he didn't understand. I would be struck from their history but not from the collective consciousness of their women. The gifts I carried would be activated and released as I continued to work towards my own enlightenment. The Divine Plan was flawless. How could it be otherwise?

"To return to my story, Petra and I reached Haran where I was received by the women's temple. He found room at the house of a friend and we stayed several days. At the temple I met Eve, a young woman of striking beauty and delicacy. Her hair was raven black and her eyes deep brown. She had a lively countenance and a quick wit. She was the daughter of a Phoenician prince who spent much of his time at sea. She was unhappy in the temple, sure that something more awaited her in this life. I was touched by her sincerity and called upon Seline for more information. My vision had never been clearer. I saw her with Adam, bringing forth his heirs. I saw more than that, but did not reveal it to her. They had karma to play out and, many generations later, she would be blamed for the loss of their fertile homeland at Ur. They were soul mates willing to learn from each other. As it happened a king's messenger arrived from Ur in search of the queen. I sent Eve in my place and never heard another word from Adam.

"Petra and I took the road south along the river and into Damascus. Here we spent several nights enjoying this center of trade and philosophy. I began to long for home, whatever it looked like now, so we pushed on to the south. When we arrived in Jericho my family was shocked. I had seen my father several times in Ur but had not indicated that I was unhappy. What could he have done? My inner knowing told me that they were disappointed I was no longer married to a king. I simply informed them that my duties had been fulfilled. Now I was free to live my life as I chose. In this way I made it quite clear that there would be no more arranged marriages, if there were any at all. I had truly matured while in the north. Coming into my soul purpose gave me the strength of a warrior. I was a Warrior Queen, there was no doubt - not with the force of the body but the mind, heart, and spirit.

"I asked after Abida and found that she was contentedly raising her family in the countryside. We stayed in Jericho only one night, for I longed to be with my sisters at their new temple. Mother told me they had moved the year before. Everyone missed their wonderful energy in Jericho. I was truly anxious to be under Leah's careful guidance again after having assumed so much responsibility at such a young age. We rode south along the salty shores of the Dead Sea then west towards the Red Sea and the holy mountain of Horeb. When we could see the water in the distance I began to image Mek in my mind's eye. I had not forgotten about him, I had merely put him in a safe place away from my emotions for those years. I sent so much intent his way that he dropped what he was doing and rode out to meet us. Petra rode on ahead as Mek and I jumped to the ground and greeted each other with great hugs and lusty kisses. Mek was a man with whom I could be free, with whom I could fulfill my soul's purpose. I believed this with all my heart and soul, and so it was.

"Leah and I had a happy reunion with days of storytelling, laughter and tears. I did not tell her about my encounters with the High Council until much later in my training to become high priestess. She told me that I had passed through a certain portal of enlightenment, the first initiation, with my emotional work. She thought that my being more mentally inclined made this task easier. The emotions I felt were rage and anger at what I perceived as injustice to me or to others, resentment toward people who did not agree with my beliefs, and a certain arrogance about my role in the world. I had seen the truth about injustice, it is illusion, Sarah. It is precisely the creation of our thoughts to present us with this test of worthiness. I had learned to forgive and harbor no resentment in my life - not towards Adam, my family or anyone who would have previously disappointed me. I had courage, love and compassion and much knowledge, but Leah told me that knowledge was not wisdom. When I asked what my next task was, how I would walk through the next portal, she gave me one word, detachment. I was to detach from feelings of self-importance, from opinions of others, from knowledge and from my own personality.

"I tried not to be discouraged. Being humbled in such a way was a good beginning and harboring no resentment towards Leah was the first test. Sarah, it took me years to find that portal. It was not until I was in my late forties that I realized I did not have to be the one always teaching, that I could become a listener and let others teach me. It occurred to me that I didn't need to hold onto all the knowledge, the information, that I had gathered so I began to dispense it. I encouraged others to teach and listened to their ideas. I let other people bloom. All the work I did to release myself from attachment to knowing and to being someone important made me a far better leader for these women. It worked against the core of my personality, my warrior woman, to be sure. I began to see a different woman emerge - one who centered her power in simplicity, truth and peace. More and more I moved into the world of energy, intent and dreaming. I began to understand the essence of women as I hadn't before. Our power lies in our innate ability to intend and dream the future, Sarah.

"As I became more deeply involved in what might be considered magic, the mastery of energy, Leah suggested that I begin spending time with the magi. I was already seeing Mek in a social way, though we had not consummated our relationship. We took long walks beside the sea, shared sunsets, laughter, warm embraces and tender kisses. I did long to enter a sacred sexual relationship with him and he with me but we were happy to explore the possibilities in the beginning. The magi were free to do whatever they wished with their personal lives so long as they performed their duties for the community, honed their skills, and taught others. Mek was working with the weather, learning to bring the rain, to part the clouds and quiet the wind. He apprenticed under a wise old man who had learned the craft from one before him. This community was in direct lineage to the Brotherhood of Magi established by Aman-Ra and they held the secrets which he brought to them from Ak-An. They were the most powerful men on the Earth to my thinking, but by far the most humble and reserved. They could become invisible to others to protect their identity or their lives. From them I learned not only magic but humility. One does not need to be outwardly important to complete important missions upon the Earth, in fact the more one can cloak oneself, the better. I spent many years with the magi and eventually was able to part with my self-importance and integrate my personality.

"After I had returned to temple life I did not participate in the sacred sexual practices with the other priestesses and Leah did not require it of me. I had left before I was ready to practice what I had learned from the older women and my experience with Adam had numbed me. I recognized that I had lost something, my innocence, my enthusiasm, and my trust of men. Before Mek and I could enter a deeper relationship it was necessary for me to heal these aspects of myself. I had successfully suppressed my sexual self. Mek knew this and allowed me the time for healing. He proved

[81]

to be worthy of my love and my trust, facilitating a great healing within me. The priestesses worked with me and sparked the flame of desire within my body again so that, at twenty-five, I came into my womanness for a second time. I felt my wholeness once more, but differently, more softly than when I was younger, and with a little more wisdom. Finally, when I felt ready to be present for Mek and to honor all that was in me, I spoke with Leah about it. Mek and I would not marry. We were committed to our respective communities and I was to be the leader of mine in the future. Yet we were not going to run away from our love. Leah suggested a very special cave situated in the low cliffs above the lake. She took me there to see it and I knew it was the right place. I could see myself sitting with Mek at the mouth of the cave, the starry night above us.

"I would not reveal my plan to him. I asked him to find soft skins and I did the same. Carrying everything a fair distance to this cave, I climbed up the cliff from the shore. I brought oil lamps and incense, sacred oils and pure drinking water. Pointed quartz crystals were used to set the sacred star within the cave and I had built a little altar for other crystals and the incense. I was in readiness on the day of the highest Sun. It was a hot day and would stay hot that night. We would not need a fire and the Moon was dark as well, so the stars would be ours. I had arranged the skins layer upon layer in a soft bed, and had spread upon them the lush cloth my father had given me for my wedding to Adam. Never had I used this gift, but carried it with me to Ur and back again. I had made a pillow of goose feathers and covered that with another cloth, an exotic red and orange silk print from the far east that I had found in Ur. Our covers were soft woolen blankets woven by the priestesses from the Midianite wool.

"On that very special night, I brought a small oil burner to this room of the eternal flame in which we sit, and borrowed fire for a lantern to take with us. Carrying bread for the morning, Mek followed me on the narrow path. When I led him to the cave door he was speechless. He wept to know the care I had taken to prepare the sacred space for us. Holding me in his arms for a long time, he whispered that he loved me - that he had never loved anyone else. I had no doubt that we were soul twins about to enter the dance of union upon the Earth. We did not hurry, but sat in the cave opening just as I had visioned, gazing at the stars. Seline flew over the lake and perched herself on the cliff above the cave. When the sky was black with night I slipped within the cave lighting the oil lamps - four in all. I lit frankincense upon the altar where I'd placed the sacred oils. Mek came to me and we knelt facing each other on the skins before the altar. Fair, blonde and blue-eyed, he looked like a god. He was perhaps much like the Akhus of old for his blood was nearly pure.

"He reached out and plucked the stay from my hair, which sent it cascading down to my waist. I loosed the neck of his robe and let if fall, exposing his body to below his waist where his robe was cinched with a braided cord. I reached for the tiny jar of spikenard and, holding it over his head, crushed it in my grip and let it drip onto his crown. Laying the fragments down on the cave floor, I used both my hands to anoint his head. His eyes shone like sapphires as the light came into him. A surge of passion moved through me from the Earth to the heavens and I did not let it go. I took the jar of sensuously scented oil and began to massage his neck, his strong shoulders, his muscular back and chest. He moaned as the body's tension released and the heat of desire fired within him. Time after time I experienced the rushing of the Earth's energy within me and filled my body with it. My frequency was rising with my desire.

"Mek loosed my robe and let it fall to my waist. My breasts were ample with soft pink circles around erect nipples. Taking some oil in his hands, he caressed my neck, throwing my hair behind me. He massaged my shoulders and then, drawing me to him, my back. He pushed me away, took up more oil and began to massage my breasts in circles, moving energy as he'd been taught by the priestesses at his raising. Loosening my cord he stroked my belly, and the fire built to unbearable heights within me. He reached behind me and pulled me to him again from my buttocks and I felt the fullness of his maleness against me. Bending down, he kissed me, more deeply than he ever had. His tongue reached within me as his maleness wished to and I released myself, panting. I glanced at the soft furs and bedding and he gently laid me down upon them. Taking up more oil, he stroked my feet and legs moving deftly towards my womanness. He began bringing pleasure to me there and I rode the waves of bliss that came with every stroke. When I could take no more, he slipped off his robe and came within me, gently stroking until the world split open. We rose together in the Divine vibration and our souls escaped into the void. We floated there until a light came to us - first a ray of white light, and then a flood of crystalline light clearly alive with energy and sound. We were in ecstasy for as long as we could hold that frequency, then gradually flew back down to the Earth into our bodies. We had made love with body and soul. We had touched the heart of God and would return many times over in the years that lay ahead. We lay in each others arms coming in and out of sleep that night. We made love again and again in different ways, honoring our bodies as sacred temples, then slept soundly in each other's arms until the sun was high.

"This period with Mek was the sweetest part of my life, Sarah. It was when time stood still and we knew we were gods. I cannot explain it another way. Later, we were able to hold our passion longer and longer and Mek was able to save his seed and his energy without losing the bliss. We did not meet often but certainly more often than the constrained relations of a dynastic marriage allowed. We were free to do as we chose. I conceived our first child, Nora, on that sacred night. As you know, she is with us here delighting in the gardens of the temple. Mek and I had two daughters and a son. They were brought up in the temple and the boy, after his raising, lived in the magi community. My second daughter, Miriam, chose to marry a Midianite farmer. She dyes and weaves the most elegant woolens from their sheep. Our boy, Shem, has remained as a magus, apprenticing with the number magic in their community. He looks in on me often now that Mek has passed over and he is very close to his sisters. Quite different from my family situation where only two people raised me, these fortunate children had entire communities that love and support them.

"With the help of the midwife and Mek, I birthed our babies in the cave. When I look back at that time I realize that motherhood brought the full opening of my heart and the deepest expression of the feminine energy from my wombspace. It changed me forever, as it does every mother. My warrior days were but a memory as I held the young ones to my breasts. As they grew, they taught me everything about life that I'd been ignoring. My time in Ur seemed a dream or a past life. I believe everything changed that day outside Haran when I knew my soul's calling. From that moment on, my life has been one remarkable event after another. I have been very blessed, Sarah, very blessed.

"Leah passed over when I was fifty-two. My children were raised when she began the final stages of my training, so she drove me very hard to separate from self. I had so many blissful experiences of God in meditation and in love-making that I had no longing to be tied to the things of this Earth, especially my self. She wanted me to anchor my light fully before she left. Because I was beyond my fertile years, an opportunity was at hand. She told me I stood before the gateway to my higher self - the part of me that is God. She urged me to acknowledge my god-self and live my life from that perspective. Light was piercing into my body from above, so she knew I was very close. I immediately shifted my consciousness into trance state and connected to light. Leah, knowing exactly what had occurred, gave me a tremendous smack on the back. My whole being lost focus. I felt myself split with a part of me that was heavy and dense, and it vanished. I was in light, so much so, it was blinding. My eyes had opened wide with the impact. Leah looked at me, forcing me back into this world. She lightly kissed my cheek and thanked me for relieving her of this one worry. I was stunned.

"As I spent my days trying to integrate the God-presence that was with me, Leah spent hers preparing to leave. She was an old woman, in her nineties, an absolute pillar of integrity with respect to the codes of light. On her last night we sat together in this room as you and I are this night and she told me the story of her life. It was as much a surprise to me as I am sure mine has been to you. She knew that I would hold the codes with honor and train the next in the lineage to do the same. She passed just before dawn with a smile on her face, in grace and peace. As God works magic when angels pass over, you were born that very day. I looked at you in your mother's arms wrapped in a safe, warm blanket. I saw the disc of Annu between your brows and within your heart. I gave praise to God for such a gift, such a strong soul and a warm heart.

"When I came into my light that day, all remaining codes in my soul body opened and activated at once. That night my body shook off my bed as the light found its way into every aspect of my being. It did not hurt me, rather it made me laugh. I saw before me all the women who have carried these codes since Mir-An-Da. There are no words to express the strength, beauty and wisdom of each one of them. I released everything I was carrying and became the light. I became God. Now I am able to tell you that I carried codes for women of the future. I will be judged harshly by the patriarchy, as all carriers will be, and their stories will portray me as likened to the bad seed for both men and women. It doesn't matter, Sarah, and it cannot harm me for I have released, as part of the Akhu's program, the thought forms of equality and balance into the collective consciousness. True, I have also released lesser energetic impulses to give women strength and steadfastness in their truth, for they will need these in times to come. I have released codes of consciousness for self-realization - for knowing one's calling - and for the sacredness of sexuality and conscious child-birthing. But Sarah, listen! I have found a way to God and that is the most important energy that I leave on this planet. My work is finished. My beloved Mek has been waiting for me these past five years while you matured in your duties. I anticipate the merging of our souls as we had experienced in our first love-making.

"Sarah, you will have a wonderful life as high priestess. God has smiled on you for you will not be challenged from without. However, you will be challenged by the High Council to carry out your duties and seek your own soul growth. You must be in communion with the Akhus to fulfill your calling. Let us end this night with a journey to Ak-An where Seline and I will take you before the High Council in the Great White Lodge. I wish you the richest of lives, Sarah, and the fulfillment of your soul's purpose."

*

Lilith produced a small earthenware vial and told Sarah to drink the contents. Sarah was surprised, but not in fear. She drank the bitter substance and asked what it contained. Lilith told her that it was the venom from a certain snake mixed with other herbs. It would allow Sarah to leave her body and travel with Lilith and Seline. Sarah was not capable of doing this without the aid of the venom. It was mild and would not have aftereffects or cause her any harm. She was to use it when she needed to be with the High Council. Her intuition was to guide her and the magi would provide her with the venom. Sarah began to feel drowsy as Lilith told her that Mir-An-Da had first formulated this potion, knowing that many of the kings and queens and the priestess of Annu would lose their ability to contact the council directly.

The two women lay back in their chairs and closed their eyes. Seline closed hers as well, when Lilith began leading Sarah out to the stars. They arrived at Ak-An and were led by magnificent light beings to the Great White Lodge. The council was in session just for them, so Lilith led Sarah to the central table where the Akhus were seated. Sarah's appearance before the High Council was brief - merely an introduction. She was told to return on her own within one month to receive her Mission instructions. The council turned to Lilith whose god-presence was apparent. They thanked her for her loyalty and acknowledged the way in which she had brought herself to full light. As she was bowing to them, rather formally, the speaker sharply tapped a baton on the table to get her attention. At that point the High Council rose and bowed to Lilith. At first she was embarrassed, at a loss for words, then she burst through the illusion and began laughing as only she could. It was contagious, catching everyone off guard. When order was restored, she turned to the speaker, hands on hips, and asked if they would kindly permit her to die. Permission was granted, and she and Sarah were dismissed.

They returned to the room of the eternal flame, easing themselves back into their bodies. Lilith struggled to stand upright, waving at Sarah to stay where she was. Standing beside Sarah's chair, she held her vibrant hand to Sarah's forehead, her palm on Sarah's third eye. Holding it there until it burned, she brought through the lineage and placed it in Sarah's energy field. Burning it further, she opened Sarah's sight so that she might watch the filaments and identify the discs of Annu in her heir who was yet unborn. Sarah was still partially out of her body, yet was certain that a hole had been burned through her head, or at the very least, that there would remain a blistering wound. There was nothing visible when Lilith finished, but to Lilith's keen eye, Sarah's entire filamentous structure had shifted its geometry. She knew every soul had the potential for enlightenment on their Earthwalk, but she could see it was not part of Sarah's soul purpose in this particular life. So she gifted her the vision, opening codes within her that might otherwise have remained dormant.

Sarah walked Lilith to her room. The old woman insisted that Seline perch above her bed that night, so Sarah opened the window and the owl flew to her mistress. Sarah had pulled some bedding in to be with Lilith through the night. She fell asleep with the sound of Lilith's rhythmic snoring in her ears. The next thing she remembered was a ball of lightning flying through the room above her as the wind blew the door and windows open. She jumped up and watched the ball fly out of the window and burst into a million sparks. Then it gathered itself together again on the treetop in the garden. The owl flew past her and out of the window, her strong wings stroking the electrified air that had filled the room. Seline flew to the treetop where owl and light became one. The light shot straight up into the heavens. Sarah watched until she could see it no longer, then turned to face Lilith. The old priestess was sitting in meditation, a smile on her face, her body lifeless. She had died consciously, harnessing the elements to hasten her journey. Sweet is the magic when a great soul leaves the Earth."

Leah Speaks

No one moved in the circle of women. All were deep in their own thoughts of Lilith and how she had shaped certain aspects of their lives. They had never thought of her as being a real woman who'd actually lived. She had always been portrayed to them as a goddess, like Isis. She held major lessons for anyone seeking enlightenment. Leah held the space for them in silence as they processed what they had received, until Karen raised her head and looked at Leah. Karen was a strong woman of forty who had struggled for years to balance her growing spiritual consciousness with the corporate world. Now she administrated a holistic healing center in Milwaukee and led groups of women through their passages there.

"Leah," she said, "this woman, Lilith, is very dear to my heart. I recognize her as Pallas Athene in Greek mythology. You've spoken of her before, but now I see another side of her, a side where she let down her armor and did God's work. This is such a metaphor for my life, Leah. Thank you."

"You are more than welcome, Karen. You know, the vanguards of the feminist movement were all strong Athenas. She comes down to us from the Greeks as the intelligent woman, born from the head of her father. She is all mind. Having no mother, no feminine nature, she was welcomed into the ruling body of Athens. She is the archetypal woman who sells out to the patriarchy. As such, she could support women who want to excel in the male world. She bears archetypal patterns that allow women to ignore or hurt other women. But that is not who she really is or was, that is how she has been portrayed by the Greeks who either did not understand the power of the feminine or feared it. She was Lilith with her owl, Seline. But let's skip back in time a little to make some sense of this.

"When Lilith lived, the patriarchy was just beginning to grab for power. The priests were being given power far beyond what Aman-Ra had specified when he had created the brotherhood of ritual and ceremony. As the priests moved into politics, the women's temples and wisdom were diminished. Lilith was stricken from the historic accounts of this era in the Bible because she would not sell out to the patriarchy. Eve is remembered as the wife of Adam and suffered accordingly. But what to do with Lilith, who's legendary life had become part of temple teachings for the women? Well, you can see how the Greeks handled it. They rewrote her and the Hebrews ignored her. Indigenous people in lands the patriarchs invaded had temples honoring her as Ishtar, one of many names for the primal mother goddess. In truth, earlier legends portrayed her as an amazon woman, a defender of the feminine, and that is much closer to the truth. She had a fine mind, completely open vision. She upheld the teachings of balance and the one God from the early times."

"I am moved by her struggles with detachment," Patricia remarked. "It hasn't changed in four thousand years, has it?"

"Patricia," Leah replied, "it hasn't changed for eons. Human nature is such that illumination comes through a form of separation. It appears a paradox, since the intended outcome is union, but it is separation or detachment from that which is illusion. All that is left then is Light - God. It is a struggle, until it is not. With that final release there is freedom."

Ellia spoke very softly. "Leah, it seems that how Lilith was remembered was such a small part of her life, her headstrong youth. She was a teenager when she was in Ur. I am touched that she had such a long life and most of it was spent with Mek. I like the way they chose to live and love. It warms me in a special way."

"They really found balance, didn't they, Ellia?" Leah replied. "I enjoyed the humor that was part of Lilith's life. I am sure she set the High Council on their heels in more than one lifetime!" They laughed, and Leah continued, drawing the evening to a close. "You may have guessed that Lilith also carried the goddess codes for the Black Madonna. In the context of her life, they take on a different look than those of Mir-An-Da, but that is another illusion. The pure energetic impulse - the thought form of oneness with God - Lilith released when she came into her own enlightenment. Living it in her own life, she gifted it to the planet to reinforce the many times it had been planted in the collective consciousness. She was a Sofia, a goddess of wisdom, and is a great model for women who seek higher consciousness. Let's ask Lilith to enter our dreams tonight. We will meet at breakfast tomorrow and share her insights."

They extinguished the candles and wandered out beneath the stars. The twelve women stayed breathing the pine-scented crisp mountain air as Leah went off to her cabin alone. As she reached the steps to her cabin an owl called out from the tree above her. The women were hushed. The owl called again, and they heard Leah call back. Each of them felt a current of electricity run up their spine. After Leah's door shut, they huddled together hugging one another, laughing and crying and asked each other, "Who is she really?"

Jedidah

Leah speaks

There had been a lively discussion of the night's dreams the following day, each dream showing evidence of Lilith's presence. The group talked all morning, sitting in a casual circle on the side deck of their meeting room. Beside them a clear mountain stream tumbled over rocks on its way to meet the river, and the great snow-capped mountain rose before them. In the afternoon, they initiated circles of growth, each woman in turn presenting her work to Leah and the group for evaluation and assistance. They would continue for four days until each woman had participated. In these sessions Leah guided them on their own journeys, their own unique paths to enlightenment. In the shaman's world, tremendous care was taken to clear and balance the lower chakras, the gateways to the shadow self - the so-called dark side. Recognizing and owning these aspects of self was the first step in transformation. The path of liberation through shamanism was not one of denial. It required one to take full responsibility for one's life, to blame no one else. In this way the power to shatter the illusions that mask the reality of God was acquired. Nor was it a path of devotion for there was no hierarchy, no guru, simply different levels of consciousness. Leah was a master, she was charismatic, but she was not their guru. She would not allow it. She was their friend and counsel, their sister and teacher, and a companion on the path who had blazed a trail for them.

These sessions were the heart of the work and the women gave of themselves freely. They had come to know sisterhood in the sharing of their innermost thoughts and behaviors with trust and love. They had discovered the commonly held behaviors that were archetypal patterns in all women. As Leah brought through the story of the lineage, they acknowledged the part of self that was typified by each character. They came to know themselves as part of a collective - womankind. Leah saw this as a vital step in healing, and expanding consciousness for these women. Healing the collective required becoming the collective, and owning it - as unsavory a task as owning one's own dark nature which sprang from it. These women were engaged in high level healing for all women and they were depersonalizing their lives in the process, which brought them one step closer to God.

Leah did not try to control the stories of the women as the lineage came through her. She allowed them to speak their truth. They came from a clear and quiet place within her, like a stream flowing through bamboo, that she had created through her own process of healing bloodline and soul lineage. She was one with the lineage, having expanded her consciousness to be them. It was a more universal place of awareness and as the stories were told aloud for the first time, this great process of healing was coming to completion within Leah. To be one with your bloodline and one with your soul lineage could spontaneously heal them. To be released from the memory and the patterns they create in this life and all those to come required expanded consciousness and universal awareness. She was beginning to see limitless pos- sibilities of healing separation, for that was the only source of dis-ease. She was opening the next door for these women who would find greater union with the Divine in the process.

When they came together in sacred space that third evening, Leah was pensive. Having fallen into a deep dream-filled sleep after the group session, she had taken dinner in her cabin to hold the energy of the dream, for it was a gift of understanding about the woman she was ready to bring to life. A few more pieces of the puzzle had fallen into place for her - gifts coming through the lineage. Everyone was ready to begin as soon as she sat down.

"My beloveds, I have a very rich story to tell you tonight about a woman who lived in the most perilous of times for both the bloodline and the lineage of light. Her name was Jedidah. She was a queen and a high priestess in Jerusalem during the fall of the kingdom of Judah. Before we can move with understanding into her life, it would be best to recount the centuries between Lilith and Jedidah - particularly events pertaining to the blood- line and the lineage of light converging on Jerusalem, when we'd left them far to the north and south in our last story. Abraham, the patriarch of the Hebrews, the dynastic heir through Adam of the lineage of Aman-Ra and Mir-An-Da, left Uruk and began the wandering period. They had lost Ur to the encroaching Chaldeans and were forced from their adopted homeland. As we have come to know the story, Eve was blamed for the loss of paradise because she wanted to taste the forbidden fruit. This fruit was knowledge and truth. The apple is symbolic of the Sun, which tells us that the blame was metaphorically being placed on women who pursued enlightenment. We can imagine that the priests might have had something to do with placing this blame on Eve. Women were living the teachings Lilith had given to Jerushah and must have embraced them wholeheartedly to have engendered such a heavy dose of blame.

"So the Hebrews who left, primarily the dynastic family and those who did not wish to live amongst the Chaldeans, followed Lilith's path to Haran. There they stayed for many years before heading south. Eventually, they made their way back to Egypt where they had originated, but understand that some of them stayed in Haran and in Canaan as well as Moab. As a small tribe, Abraham's son Jacob and his family, left the famine plagued lands to the east and arrived in Egypt where one of his sons, Joseph, was then governor. We know from the bible stories that they came and went from Egypt a number of times and were generally on good terms with the pharaohs, many of the lineage holding high positions in government. Initially, the pharaohs recognized them as sons and daughters of the Akhus for their blood retained some integrity. The Egyptian dynasties were no longer of pure blood but they were aware of their pre-deluge history. Later dynastic pharaohs became hostile towards the Hebrews and, as you know, there were a number of exoduses to the east.

"When Moses, a banished pharaoh of mixed blood and the dynastic heir to Adam, led the final exodus from Egypt his band first settled in the region around Mt. Horeb (Mt. Sinai). Here they came in contact with the magi and the priestesses of the temple of Annu. They brought with them their belief in Yahweh, the patriarchal one god, but also all the pagan worship that existed in Egyptian culture at that time. The Egyptians were worshipping Aman-Ra in the form of the Sun instead of the Akhu concept of God. He and Mir-An-Da had become myths. When Moses went up the mountain he was visited by a representative of the High Council, Aman-Ra himself, who handed him a set of sapphire tablets that would help him govern his people. When he came down and found his people in idolatrous worship he shattered these tablets in rage. A second set of clay tablets, given to replace them, reflected the true frequency of the tribe. The High Council was concerned about the bloodline and the program. The Egyptians no longer held the key, but there was great potential with the Hebrew lineage because the heirs of Aman-Ra had kept the blood fairly pure. Their patriarchal god-vision, a distortion of the primordial balance found in God and all things in the universe, was the only drawback. The High Council was counting on the lineage of light to hold the balance.

"In time, the Hebrews started taking lands away from the Phoenicians and Canaanites in the north. They had a great military leader, Joshua, with whom they won the promised land. After Joshua, there was a period of poor leadership and loss of gained lands until the time of Saul, the first anointed king, who reunited the tribe. At his death, the kingdom was split. Saul's daughter had married David of Bethlehem who then became king of Judah in the south. In time, David won back Israel in the north, and became the king of all the Hebrews. It was at this time that the High Council intervened to rejuvenate the bloodline in the form of Solomon, son of David and Bathsheba. Solomon was a god incarnate who came to revitalize the Hebrews. He brought magi from the Red Sea to reestablish the brotherhoods in Jerusalem. The temple of Solomon was a brilliant composition in magic. Outwardly, Solomon believed in Yahweh, but inwardly he understood the balance of the masculine and feminine in God. The tribes were not in solidarity under Yahweh and would not be until after their period of captivity which we will discuss later. Solomon's greatest virtues were justice and tolerance and he allowed the people of his land to follow their own beliefs. He was, perhaps, the only king who did not force his beliefs on the population. Solomon brought forth the Grail code of kingly service and judicious rule to the people, which was of principle interest to the High Council. He was also brilliant and brimming with excitement.

"Solomon was directed by the High Council to establish a women's temple in Jerusalem for the priestesses of Mt. Horeb and that is how the lineage of the codes of light came to the Holy City. Solomon's dedication to reestablishing the Golden Age of Aman-Ra and Mir-An-Da was tremendous, but his life was not as long as theirs. When he died the kingdom again split into north and south and his son, Rehoboam, took the southern throne which included the tribes of David and Benjamin. The northern kingdom suffered constant harassment from its neighbors and eventually fell to the Assyrians in 722 BC. The ten tribes of the north were assimilated into the Assyrian population, lost forever to the program.

"During Rehoboam's reign in Judah and for centuries to come, paganism existed side by side with Yawism. The priestesses of Annu from Mt Horeb were not Yawists. Their high priestess was well aware of the High Council's need for them to be in Jerusalem to create some balance for the bloodline. She also knew that the only way to fulfill that Mission was in secrecy and silence. They appeared to embrace whatever the king at the time was advising without succumbing to prostitution. Solomon had allotted them great privilege which served them well in the times that were to come. Within the inner sanctum of the temple, in the place of the eternal flame, they honored the balance of the one God and kept the legacy of Annu alive.

"Right after Rehoboam took the throne of Judah there was an invasion by Egyptians who stole many treasures from Solomon's temple. Rehoboam became obsessed with the security of the borders which fortuitously began a three-hundred year interval of peace. The lineage of kings that followed Rehoboam seemed to alternate between strict Yawism, paganism and indifference. During these times the people did as they pleased, thus the strict Yawists were never really able to abolish paganism. The Hebrews tended to be Yawists and the Canaanites whose homeland they usurped worshipped Baal, the creator god and Astarte, the mother goddess, a clear representation of Isis coming through Lilith. Baal was a composite of Aman-Ra and the Sun. This cult was still using human sacrifice as a way to appease the gods. Mankind was in a true amnesia about its origins.

"It was into this climate that Jedidah was born in 663 BC during the reign of the most despised of all the kings of Judah, Manasseh. Manasseh earned this distinction historically because the Yawists were the ones recording history. The pagans would surely have seen him as a messenger of Baal. Manasseh reverted to paganism in a most decadent way. It is said, by the Yawists, that he sacrificed his first-born son to the gods. Jedidah was to live through the most perilous of times for both the bloodline and the codes of light. Her task was to bring both through intact. Here, again, the bloodline and the lineage of light were brought together to serve the future. The bloodline would suffer some important lessons as the lineage of light held the consciousness and expanded it for the next phase of the Planetary Ascension Program.

"Now, let us imagine ourselves in the Holy Land during that

time. We are welcomed into a small community of mud-brick dwellings near cliffs overlooking the Dead Sea." Leah closed her eyes and began. "The year is 577 BC. We find Jedidah, white-haired and weathered at eighty-six, preparing to pass the codes of light to her daughter-in-law, Hamutal, the next high priestess of Annu. Hamutal's hair and eyes are dark and her skin olive. She was the mistress, then second wife of Jedidah's son, Josiah. They are sitting in the temple room of the eternal flame which is hidden in a cave beneath the community dwellings. Jedidah had moved the priestesses to this location in the desert near the Dead Sea in 598 BC at the urging of the High Council, when the safety of the codes of light in Jerusalem had been in jeopardy. We find them sitting on pillowed earthen seats carved from the walls of the cave. Oil lamps on the cave walls give a yellow glow and the eternal flame burning on the altar illuminates the golden disc of Annu. Jedidah has set the sapphires in the six-pointed star grid which had become known as the Star of David during the renaissance of the mystery schools while Solomon reigned. The cave is energetically activated, bringing their frequencies into the range that will open the necessary codes in Hamutal.

"At Hamutal's feet there sits a stunning girl of twelve years. Her dark hair and olive skin contrast sharply with deep blue eyes that are reminiscent of the Akhus. She is Hamutal's granddaughter and Jedidah's great-granddaughter, Tamar Tephi. She has been born and raised in the seclusion of this temple community because she is an Akhu, a god incarnate, born from the genes planted in her mother's womb by a Siriun team of geneticists. Her mother, the wife of Hamutal's son Mattaniah (King Zedekiah), is a priestess of Annu. She had understood the necessity of protecting Tamar Tephi and had allowed grandmother and great-grandmother to spirit the baby away. As a girl child it was not expected that she stay at the palace. She was of no use to the patriarchal dynasty as an heir and Jerusalem, especially the palace, had not been safe. In time, Tamar Tephi's mother had returned to the community to spend time with her daughter as she grew into a young woman.

"Tamar Tephi and Hamutal are both crucial to the program. For the first time in the history of this seeding, the lineage will be passed to two women who will each carry it forward as directed by the High Council. Jedidah had worked with both of them preparing for this day. Jedidah's vision guided her to prepare Tamar Tephi from birth knowing that she would still be young on this day when she would receive her Mission. Jedidah found her capable in every way and was grateful that Tamar Tephi was old enough to have experienced her raising and many of the mysteries of the temple. Hamutal reaches out to touch Jedidah's hand to receive her blessing, and Tamar Tephi holds the edge of her great-grandmother's worn black robe. Jedidah's brown eyes are lustrous, filled with light, as she looks down at Tamar Tephi and then across at Hamutal. Hamutal is in her forties. Threads of grey are woven into her dark brown hair and signs of weathering have given her face character. These have been difficult times in which to survive, let alone hold consciousness for a world out of balance. Tamar Tephi has been spared that world for her Mission was not to involve the Hebrews."

Jedidah speaks

"My beloved daughters, my time of completion is at hand. I have only to relive my life for you - to pass you the power of my lessons and my knowing. You both hold the mysteries and the teachings of the lineage in your hearts. You both bring your own gifts, your own richness to the lineage of light, as you have in so many other lives. You are both in communication with the High Council at this moment of expansion for the lineage and the blood. When the Akhu blood was seeded in ancient Egypt, it brought crystalline codes of God consciousness to the planet, not for the first time but it was the first seeding in many millennia. The bloodline of Aman-Ra and Mir-An-Da is receptive to genetic manipulation and direct incarnation of the Akhus to strengthen the blood or perhaps more precisely, to refresh the memory of the blood. Throughout the colonization and intermarriage programs of Aman-Ra, the crystalline codes have been spreading into many distant lands as people carrying them migrate and marry into existing tribes. One of Aman-Ra's Missions was to plant the seeds of consciousness in many people.

"However, the colony sent into the lands of Mesopotamia was ordered not to intermarry with other tribes. They were to maintain a high percent of Akhu blood in their leaders to facilitate these incarnations and genetic manipulations. In this sense, the Hebrews were chosen people. Now the bloodline is experiencing a time of karmic repayment for having chosen the warriors' path. These ways will not end for them until they see the feminine aspect of God and bring their own lives into balance. They are stubborn patriarchs, so it will be hard for them to transform. You have come, Tamar Tephi, as a gift from the star beings to the lineage of light, but you will not enrich this bloodline. Tomorrow morning you will leave this community for the first time and for-ever. You have been aware of your Mission since before your birth. It is no surprise to you, apart from the timing. It is imperative that we move now for your opportunity awaits you.

"Hamutal, the original lineage of light will remain here in this community for many centuries. This sisterhood will be of service no matter how oppressive the political situation may become. There will be protection from the Akhus who want the lineage to be in this place for the next phase of the program. Make certain that all who carry the light in the future maintain the sanctity and the secrecy of this temple of the eternal flame. It is the heart of the lineage until a time in the future when we must carry it within our own hearts. There will be a great woman coming soon who will take it to a distant land when our work here is completed. Her energy is already touching the Earth from the morning star, though her physical form will not appear for hundreds of years. More I will not reveal to you, for speaking of the future can some-times put limitations upon its evolution and her path must be clear.

"Now, I make ready your way into the future with the giving away of my life. I was born in the village of Boscath to parents who had been childless for fifteen years of their marriage. From the moment of my birth, I was raised like a gift from God. An only child, they wanted the best for me. I do not remember making any effort to be like my mother, Sarah, though I helped her in every way I could. I recall spending a great deal of time listening as my father, Adaiah, discussed politics, religion and the situa-tion in Jerusalem (a shameful mixture of both), with his friends. Father was a regional governor, a man of some importance. King Manasseh was trying to force his pagan, idolatrous ways on the Yawists. There would have been a war in Jerusalem if he were not so feared. As it was, the devout Yawists moved into silence and many left the city, unable to tolerate the behavior of the king, his court, his priests and the people. Both feared and hated, he was a truly ruthless man with no concept of kingly service, only self service. What he gave to the people was license to behave as he did, without morals or conscience. I have learned not to judge, my daughters, and Manasseh was a great teacher for me in that respect. What I relate to you today are the feelings I experienced during those times and not the wisdom that was born of them.

"My father entertained my questions and, in time, I became politically astute for a young girl. I also loved the garden and spent hour upon hour working or just sitting there. I spoke freely with the plant people and the spirits that guided the energies of the garden. Whenever I was in nature it spoke to me and I listened. This was how I learned for I had no formal schooling. When I was nine years old, I began to dream of a golden disc of the sun. It had a very powerful face and a great radiance. The dreams persisted and I finally shared them with my mother. She had heard legends about the priestesses of Annu who had lived at Mt. Horeb for thousands of years. Mother thought, perhaps, that I was finding part of my life connected with them through my dreams, she was very intuitive and wise. I insisted upon knowing if the priestesses still existed there but she could not tell me. I begged my father to find out and he, being the obliging parent that he was, asked an acquaintance who knew a magus from that region. When word got back to father, he informed me that there was still a small group of the holy women at Mt. Horeb, but that the majority of the priestesses of that sect were in Jerusalem. I wanted to visit these women but Father and Mother insisted that I was too young. Finally, Father suggested that if I still wanted to visit them in several years, he and Mother would inquire as to the possibility of my raising with these women.

"It was at this point in my life that I began to learn patience and surrender. I let go of my desires and allowed my life to unfold without bothering my parents. My dreams continued and became more detailed. Seeing the same women in my dreams, I participated in ceremony with them. Eventually they began teaching me spiritual lessons. I would get up in the morning and repeat the lessons to the spirits in the garden so that I would not forget them. They were teachings about God and the star beings who visited the Earth. I knew I could not discuss them with my parents and felt I was living two different lives. My parents did not push to betroth me before my raising for they cherished having me with them. For this I was grateful. By that time, I had waited almost three years to meet the priestesses of Annu and wanted no distractions from that great event.

"My father had traveled to Jerusalem numerous times during that three year period. He had brought news of the turmoil and the pagan worship of Baal and Astarte by the king and the people. Father was a Yawist. He believed in one Father God named Yahweh. He no doubt expected me to believe as well for he had no knowledge of my hidden education. I would often whisper a request to the priestesses before falling asleep and was usually rewarded with answers to my questions. When I asked them to explain the difference between Baal and Astarte, Yahweh and their God, an older priestess came to me in my dream. She said her name was Lydia and that she wished for me to know the truth. She said that God was not a man, not a patriarch, as the Jews believed. She said God was not Baal and Astarte as the pagans believed. She told me that God was all things, male and female, living and dead. God was an Energy like the Sun that shone on everyone all the time. It was a vast energy, something universal, unimaginable, yet if I wanted to feel that Energy all I had to do was become tranquil inside. Anyone could feel It because we *were* It. I awoke from that dream a changed young woman.

"I had been given a truth so great I could live at peace with the concept of God from that moment on. That morning I went to the garden and sat, completely still. I could hear the spirits quieting themselves once they knew I had not come to play. My seriousness was apparent. I began to do this every day. It was not difficult for me to sit still because I had learned patience. The difficulty was in stilling my mind's activity. I would try not to think, but thoughts would enter my mind. I tried concentrating on the word God and my mind stilled somewhat. Eventually, I felt a hum inside and just gave myself over to it and it grew. I felt as if I were floating off the ground. I was very light. It was my first experience with the frequency of God. I rolled on the ground laughing and laughing. I was so excited and filled with joy from the experience.

"Finally Father brought me the news that I had been accepted for my raising at the temple of Annu in Jerusalem. We had not discussed it in three years so you can imagine my elation. He and Mother had agreed upon this initiation after hearing of the women's behavior in the other temples. The temple of Annu for some strange reason seemed to be able to exist in the chaos without becoming part of it. Their concept of God might have something to do with it, I thought. So excited was I, that my quiet time became very difficult. Thoughts were racing through my mind now. I didn't really know what to expect from my raising with these priestesses. I knew what the other young girls in Boscath experienced at our local temple. It was not what I expected of the temple of Annu, which had an ancient energy associated with it. No one could tell me about it. Once again, I practiced patience.

"We had family in Jerusalem where we were able to sleep and have our meals when my time came. Father was not allowed in the temple but saw that Mother and I arrived safely that evening. There were surprisingly few young women, only six, for the size of

Jerusalem. Later, I discovered that the priestesses were very se-
lective in their choices of young women for the teachings. A feeling of familiarity overcame me as I entered the building. We had
been guided to the altar room by young women in blue robes. I
knew we were not in the real temple, the part of the building
where only the priestesses went, but I could feel the energy of
that space in the altar room. We stood in a half circle before the
altar, our mothers right behind us. A young priestess announced
the arrival of the high priestess who floated into the room in robes
of black, accompanied by four priestesses in purple robes. I looked
at the face of the high priestess and gasped. It was Lydia from my
dream. She smiled at me in a most engaging way as I regained my
composure.

"The ceremony began with the cleansing of our energetic bodies, to wipe away the soiled energies of Jerusalem. Then Lydia
gave us the teaching of the blood mysteries, the coming into womanhood, and the power of the feminine aspect of God. I do not
know how my mother was reacting to what the Hebrews called
heresy. I suspect that in her heart she knew this about God. Deep
in her heart, every woman must know this. There came the time
of parting with my mother before entering with the priestesses to
spend the night and come into our womanness. She backed away
reluctantly as I moved with the other young women through the
doorway to the next set of rooms. Lydia was present in my room
that night. Her presence lent an energy of the Mother to the ritual.
I was a very naive child who socialized little with other girls, but
was swept away by the beauty of the ceremony and the awakened
energies of my young body. Experiencing God in new ways, glorious ways, I saw the Divine light in the eyes of the priestesses who
initiated me. Lydia broke my shield of virginity and I bled my first
blood. It was collected for me so that I could make an offering of it
to the Earth.

"That night, curled up in the arms of the priestesses, I did not
need to dream of them. Instead, I found myself dreaming of my
garden in Boscath. All the plant and nature spirits came from
their hiding places to be with me. It felt like another initiation,
but also like a farewell. When I awoke the next morning the priestesses asked me to share my dream. I told them of the garden and
the spirits, the joy and the sadness. Lydia seemed to hear me on
a deeper level than the younger priestesses and she asked me to
take a walk with her. She led me to the temple gardens and asked
me to communicate with the spirits. I sat very still and opened
my heart to them. Before long they began to come out of hiding

and tell me of life in this garden. Apparently Lydia could see them as well, but could not hear them. I interpreted for them so that they could express their wishes to her. She seemed very grateful and asked me to continue walking in the garden. Then we went back into the temple building and through a series of hallways and stairways that were very confusing. Opening the door of an interior room, she directed the two purple-robed priestesses within to wait outside. She pulled me in and I stood before the solar disc. Below it, on an altar, burned the eternal flame. Tears rolled down my cheeks and the feeling of God came into me. I trembled in recognition of my life and Lydia took me in her arms.

"When I was quieted, she eased me down on a pillow and sat across from me. She wanted to look at me. I went into the stillness, closing my eyes and saw her luminous self before me, so beautiful, so pure. She told me she had been looking for me, calling to me, and I told her that I had dreamt of her and her teachings. Laughing, she said she had tried many ways to draw me to her. She was happy the dreams had been good for me. I bore the golden disc of Annu on my third eye and within my heart, she told me. I was marked to follow in her footsteps and had very important work to begin very soon. I told her I was ready but that my parents were very attached to me. Though I was twelve years old, they had made no attempt to find me a husband. She understood, indicating that no part of my life was a mistake, that every detail was part of a plan. I had reason to believe it was not my plan, but not wanting to appear ignorant, I remained silent. She would speak to my parents. To be marked in such a way was a very high privilege. My position would bring much honor to my parents and far greater rewards would be forthcoming as my life progressed. Here again it was time to practice patience - to arrest my curiosity and allow life to unfold. I could already see a pattern of lessons emerging in my life centered around patience, stillness and allowing. These must be important for me to learn, I concluded, or the lessons would not be so difficult. After thanking Lydia, she allowed me a few moments alone in the room with the great solar disc. It was exactly as I had seen in my dream. Precisely the disc that we sit before this night, my beloved daughters. I had found my real home.

"I never returned to Boscath, but spent several days with my parents in Jerusalem before they returned me to the temple. It was a difficult parting for them, however Lydia had told them something of the future and they were able to put their personal desires aside so that I might follow my soul's path. I saw Father

every time he came to Jerusalem and sent my love home with
him to my mother. My days were divided between temple duties
in the garden and kitchen, very intense training sessions with
Lydia, meditation and devotion to God, and social activities with
my sisters. I was very comfortable at the temple and the days
passed quickly.

"One spring day in my fourteenth year, Lydia called me before
her in the temple of the eternal flame and took the simplicity
from my life forever. She told me that she had received a request
from King Manasseh. He was looking for a wife for his son, Amon,
who had just turned fifteen. He wished his son to marry one of
the fine priestesses of her temple. She looked at me in a more
serious way than usual and simply stated that the bloodline of
King David was in serious trouble. This was obvious to all who
could see. It could have been a purely political maneuver on the
part of King Manasseh but that was of no concern to Lydia who
had been waiting for this opportunity. I was told that I was to
marry Amon and eventually become queen. This was my path.
She also told me that I would bring a son into the world who
would be a strong leader for Judah. These were to be my first
important tasks. I was not to be concerned about the temple since
it was doubly protected by the Akhus and the magi. there seemed
a ring of truth in her words so I believed her. I knew from the
chatter of the priestesses that Amon was a handsome young man
with an eye for beautiful women. I was not a beauty like our Tamar
Tephi here, but had an inner light that was very attractive. I had
been trained in the sacred sexual practices but this service was
given to very few young boys at their raisings. We served only the
sons of the magi and members of the brotherhoods who were still
keeping the mysteries alive in Judah. I had had only one sexual
experience in my life in the capacity of a sexual priestess with one
of these young men. His name was Jeremiah. I recognized him as
my soul twin. Our experience was magical, but our lives were
being directed by those of greater power. Again, all my lessons
had come forward - be still, be silent, allow, and believe in the
higher power.

"My audience before the king brought up a few more issues
in my young life. Amon was not present. This was not about finding someone whom he could love and be happy with in marriage.
It was about an heir to the throne, bringing good stock into the
bloodline. Manasseh was unusually well-behaved that day owing
to the presence of Lydia who would not have allowed me to go
alone. However, we had to endure his interactions with the many

nearly unclothed women in his court. I felt shame for them and knew that was an important lesson for me. Merging myself more fully with these women, I understood what lay beneath their masks of playfulness and seduction. I felt the anger, rage, fear and repulsion in these women. Later, I was to learn that their parents had sold them to the king as slaves to his passions and cruelty. Several of them were his own daughters. My feelings of shame turned to compassion. Manasseh was a lecherous old man who was soon to be my father-in-law.

"Asked to express my political opinions, I bit back my truth to appear neutral. Lydia made it clear to the king that I would remain a priestess under her tutelage until I was fully trained. He agreed, knowing that this marriage was no more than a breeding formality. I would be quartered in a separate part of the palace with its own access to the streets. Manasseh dismissed us, telling Lydia that she would be notified about the date of my wedding. He asked one of his daughters to show us my future quarters on our way out. They had been lavishly decorated in preparation for this moment. I was without words. Lydia was not. She ordered the young woman to have the furnishings in one small room removed to give me a quiet space for my meditations and work with the priestesses. She inspected every room, its contents, entrances and exits, while I stood like a statue in the middle of the sitting area. I could see the bedroom, the bed covered with soft cloth, pillows, and weavings in pale colors. Through a doorway to the right I could also see the gardens which were for my private use. I was sure I had landed in paradise until the thought of being here alone entered my consciousness. Lydia was checking to see that I would be safe, but I was concerned about being lonely now that I had so many sisters in my community.

"When we were back on the street, she told me that she would have the magi cast a protective energy over all the doors and windows. Nothing would harm me. I voiced my concern about being alone and she smiled. She understood that I was really voicing the fear of being harmed by Manasseh or Amon. How could I be alone with a garden full of spirits? How could I be alone when I was to see her almost daily? She assured me again of full protection and doubted that I would have much interaction with Amon except during the month of dynastic intercourse. It was somehow important that I interact in this way with the bloodline. It was my calling though I knew not its nature at the time. I thought of the love I had felt for Jeremiah and a sadness swept over me. That was not what this lifetime was about for me."

*

Jedidah found herself back in the sadness of that time and suggested they walk up on the cliffs to watch the sun set. It took some time for them to climb from their subterranean cave to the cliffs that surrounded their community. The fiery disc of Annu hung low on the desert horizon. As always, there was a blessed stillness to the scene, the cliffs dotted with robed priestesses in evening ritual. They drank of the Sun, feeding their energetic bodies as the ancients had. That was the beauty of this ritual for all of the priestesses. It linked them with their origins and everyone who had come before or would come after them. When they were engaged in this ritual with Annu, there was no time. All was present, contained in the universal life force coursing through their bodies. They felt blessed. Jedidah prayed for the future of the codes of light. She saw part of it in Tamar Tephi's sunlit eyes. She saw the other half in Hamutal's wise countenance. The Divine Plan was a wonder beyond comprehension. As the last golden rays of Annu danced in her ancient eyes, she thought about Jeremiah, what they had lived through since that time when they were so young, and the freedom that awaited them at the end of this Mission. She thanked God for the privilege of serving.

The priestesses lingered in the afterglow of the sun as violet and pink rays reached across the sky to them. The colors deepened, then began to fade as the chill of the desert night moved in upon them. They slowly returned to their community moving single file along the clifftop path - sacred silhouettes against the evening sky. Hamutal and Tamar Tephi moved to Jedidah's side as they descended to the dwellings and then helped her down into the cave of the temple where she resumed her story.

*

"Ah, my little sisters, we had come to my wedding, my marriage to the next king of Judah. It was a grand excuse for Manasseh to have a decadent celebration. I had lived in our simple community and before that with conservative parents, so I had never seen such extravagance. It was so overpowering I could not even react. You could say that my senses became dull or numb. It was my first opportunity to come face to face with Amon who treated me with respect and with reserve. I repeated empty vows to this handsome young man, and he to me. Manasseh, already drunk on wine, cheered loudly, beating his fists on a skin drum. I was embarrassed for him and for Amon, but need not have wasted my time. As soon as the vows were spoken, the celebration began in earnest and Amon proved to be his father's son. There were musicians, exotic dancers, many jugs of wine and more food than I had ever seen. Fortunately my parents and Lydia were also there. When I could take no more, we stole away to my quarters where I had a wonderful visit with my parents.

"I was served meals in my quarters while life in the palace continued as before the wedding ceremony. Preferring not to interact with the family unless formally requested, I excused myself to my priestess duties when, in fact, I was just trying to maintain my frequency in surroundings that kept pulling it down. This was my first major test. As my vibration increased, could I hold it when everyone around me behaved in complete unconscious density? In the beginning I could not, so I retreated to my quarters. Eventually I could hold it in the face of anything, including death, for death would surround me. Lydia and the High Council had really put me to the test. The secret of my success was to be without judgment. As soon as I truly let go of my opinions and expectations of Manasseh and his court, my frequency stabilized and began to rise.

"Visiting Lydia almost every day, I continued my training and paid little heed to what transpired in the king's court. Working hard to learn about the stars and the energetic composition of the universe, it seemed as though I was part of that universe when I could feel God in meditation, and I longed for more understanding of this. Lydia taught me the history of the order and helped me profit from the lessons of all those who had held the codes of light before me. We are not individuals, my daughters, but one long incarnation of a soul group. As a group, we have called great lessons to us and also great service. When Lydia told me the history as I have given it to you, I could not separate myself from any of those women. I felt I had lived all of their lives. In this way, she helped me adopt a more universal concept of the soul.

"It was not long before the month of dynastic intercourse arrived. The Sun was at the summer solstice three months after our marriage, which took place on the feast of equinox. Amon had much more experience with women than I had with men, yet he had never made love to a priestess, and had not been given the secrets of sacred sexuality at his raising. Temple prostitutes had taught him at his father's urging. He was open to my suggestions, being young and somewhat intrigued by me, and seemed grateful for my suggestions. The month became an enjoyable time for both of us. Although I had no sense of love for Amon, I performed my priestess duties with sincerity. I was blessed with conception which sanctified the marriage and, if I were to birth a male heir, would release me from dynastic intercourse for six years. My son, Josiah, was born the next spring, a male conceived at the highest position of the sun. He was destined to be a great leader with natural, high male energy. For this reason, I began working with him as an infant to soften him and sensitize him to his feelings. Manasseh and Amon paid no attention to my nurturing. They were happy to see Josiah occasionally, happy to know he existed and they didn't have to be responsible for him. I began taking Josiah to the temple when he was a baby. I continually surrounded him with feminine energy. He responded very well and delighted the priestesses but was never to enter the room of the eternal flame. A sweet and tender little boy, he and I played in the garden while he was still open to Spirit. I was amazed at how much he could absorb for one so tiny.

"When Josiah was six years old and the month of the dynastic marriage was due, Manasseh became ill and died suddenly. He was an old man and had ruled for over fifty years living the kind of life that would have killed others prematurely. The palace went into mourning and I was spared the month of dynastic intercourse. Instead, I was to prepare to take the throne with Amon as his queen. I could not see the kingdom changing at all. Amon was made in the image of his father. The cheers of the Yawists at Manasseh's death were short-lived. I watched Manasseh's courtiers release themselves from their long-held fear of the king, for any one of them could have lost his head in an instant. Many felt he was insane and perhaps his insanity had come with the disease that killed him. Their relief was short-lived, for Amon, though just twenty-three, walked right into his father's shoes.

"Our coronation was another grand celebration, but this time I exercised my rights as queen and made it a celebration for the people and not a court orgy. Amon did not mind, thinking this a good political move. He was young, handsome and charismatic. Arousing the crowd with his fervor, he then drank himself into a stupor. I left the celebration after a short time and took my crown and son to my quarters with my parents who had come to Jerusalem for the event. We played with Josiah that day in the garden, watching him build palaces of little stones and I wondered what would happen next.

"Shortly after the coronation, while returning from the temple one day with Josiah, I chanced to meet Jeremiah on the street. He was in his mid-twenties by that time, but I recognized him easily. Our eyes met and he smiled. Excusing himself to his friend, he asked if he might walk with us to the palace. He called me his queen. I laughed and in a voice too low for my royal guards to hear, I remarked that it would surprise me if Amon stayed in power for long. Jeremiah agreed. I asked what he had been doing since the time of his raising. Blushing at the memory, he told me he had entered the priestly brotherhood. He was developing his abilities as a seer, but was quite involved in the political situation in Judah as well. News traveled through the brotherhood quickly and accurately via a network of brothers spread over much of the civilized world. His eyes were a sparkling blue, his hair light, long and in curls. With a rather intense countenance and prominent nose and chin, he looked more a rabble rouser than a priest - and I told him so. His answer delighted me, for he was a priest who was not allowed in the temple! Well, naturally not, I supposed, if he were with the brotherhood. He would have supported neither the pagan's view nor the Yawist's. To my surprise he told me he did support the Yawist's for the simple reason that they might restore order to the kingdom. The brotherhood was sworn out of politics because political involvement risked their integrity, yet they saw some potential within the Yawist movement for the equitable rule of Judah.

"By the time we had reached the palace gates I had dismissed the guards. I regretted the brevity of the walk hoping to have more conversation for I had not been so stimulated since the days in my father's house. Turning to Jeremiah, I asked if he would visit me to talk again. He felt it best to avoid the court of Amon. I understood completely and indicated to him that I lived in separate quarters. If he would oblige, I told him I would be delighted to receive him at my private entrance two days hence at noon. No one would have the slightest idea of his presence and Josiah and I could both benefit from his acquaintance. He agreed and we parted in the manner of old friends who chanced to meet every now and then.

"I received Jeremiah regularly at the street entrance to my quarters. My quarters were well removed from the court since they had originally been designed to house the widowed queens who were respected but given no power. The gardens were completely private and brimming with flowers and trees. Josiah, an energetic six-year old, wanted to play continually with Jeremiah, who was happy to entertain him. In the years to come, they would form a strong bond of friendship and Jeremiah would be a great influence on certain aspects of Josiah's life. He and I spoke to Josiah often of kingly service to the people, of fairness and justice, and brotherhood. Josiah understood that this was a part of our lives he did not discuss with his father on those rare occasions when he saw him.

"From Jeremiah, I learned of the hatred for Amon within his own court. Of course this was the inherited court of his father Manasseh and Amon was too indulgent of his desires to pay close attention to those around him. Since I seldom saw him, I said nothing of this to Amon. I knew that I was not in the palace to be a visible force as queen. My work was to be with the invisible, with the preservation of the bloodline, now represented in Josiah, and the codes of light. Jeremiah saw this very clearly. The world might shatter and fall around me, but I would be as a pillar of truth and integrity. I would be the light for those who could see.

"Just two years after taking the throne Amon was assassinated by men in his own court. I could see it coming, but did nothing about it, although I was not an accomplice. Neither was Jeremiah but he foresaw it clearly. He felt that radical Yawists, who had suffered through Manasseh to await the future, were probably responsible. Fifty years of Amon was not what they had envisioned. We never really knew who it was that killed him. He was found, his throat slashed, in his private quarters. The kingdom was in turmoil - the Yawists and Baalists at each other's throats to gain power. The court convened and the majority of them deemed it wise to support the continuation of the House of David for there would, at least, be some continuity. Josiah, at the age of eight, assumed the throne. He would not officially be sovereign king until eighteen but, nonetheless, he already represented the Divine authority. At the suggestion of Jeremiah and myself, he appointed Shapran, a moderate Yawist and trusted friend of my father, as his royal secretary and adjunct-general. The rest of the court he dismissed. You can imagine the uproar. My dear Josiah simply held up his hands and reminded them that there existed in this court a cold-blooded murderer. It was impossible to know their motive, thus, in all fairness, they would all go. There was no argument. He dismissed the entire household staff, including relatives of Manasseh and Amon, as well as the priests who were associated with the court.

"The palace was staffed again with those we could trust. Our needs were not lavish so they were few in number. Josiah did not

create a court around him for some time. Shapran, acting as re-
gent, brought intelligent advisors to speak with us. I say us because in those first ten years of his reign, both Jeremiah and I
were quite active in shaping Josiah's political career. This was
not known to the kingdom. They began to see fair and equitable
decisions coming from the palace. The heated animosity between
Yawists and Baalists cooled. Josiah did not take sides with them.
He allowed religion to follow its own course separate from the
government. The poor began to feel some hope and the wealthy
sat in needless readiness to defend what they had hoarded. Even
when he came into his own power, adopting his own beliefs and
priorities, he remained, in general, a fair and just ruler until his
death.

"Though I was a widow, Jeremiah and I remained as friends.
Our love could not have been greater but we both recognized that
earthly union would jeopardize the Mission. It was during this
time that I realized Jeremiah was a true star being. I would learn,
much later, that he had been taught to communicate with the
Siriun High Council through his training with the brothers, who
recognized him as an Akhu. He was to become a visible force for
the Mission while I remained an invisible protector of the codes of
light. We were working together, twin souls united in our souls'
callings. There was a beauty in the way we could love each other
and remain detached. Sometimes, I think he longed for marriage
and a normal life. I would not have been offended if he had taken
a wife, but he never did.

"Josiah grew in many ways during those ten years before coming of age. He experienced his raising at the temple of Annu. He
was strong and handsome yet gentle in manner. I have heard he
was a wonderful lover. Dear Hamutal, after all these years there
is no need to blush. Josiah did not wish to marry before he came
of age, which gave me ample time to find an appropriate wife for
him. The only way to enrich the bloodline without intervention
from the Akhus was conjoining the line itself. I found a young
woman who was related to Josiah through his great-grandfather
Hezekiah. Her name was Zebudah. She was well mannered and
very pleasing to the eye. Josiah was agreeable so I sent her off to
the priestesses of Annu for the sexual training she had not received at her raising. She was very appreciative and remained
with the priestesses until her marriage. I had some concern about
enriching the more unsavory aspects of the bloodline but was
encouraged by both Lydia and Jeremiah in my choice of Zebudah.
She and Josiah were married shortly after his coronation - both

glorious celebrations for the people of Jerusalem. He appeared a wise and just king in every way.

"I was thirty-three years old then, sure that I could relax for a time and resume my priestess's life. It was then that the book was discovered. Soon after Josiah's coronation he ordered the renovation of a temple for the Yawist priest Hilkiah. During the restoration, a book was found by Hilkiah. It was apparently an old text of Yawist teachings. Hilkiah gave the book to Shapran who passed it on to Josiah. Josiah was no scholar and had never learned to read Hebrew, so Shapran read the book to him. Then he called Jeremiah and myself into his quarters and Jeremiah read it to him again. Jeremiah and I felt strongly that it had been planted in the temple by the Yawist priests who felt discontent at Josiah's support of freedom in religious worship. It was a book of Yawist laws, very strict and patriarchal. Nothing of that nature was openly practiced in Jerusalem though the strict Yawist priest undoubtedly held to the concepts. Jeremiah and I advised Josiah to treat it as a historic document and incorporate what he wished into his own beliefs.

"I saw something snap in my son. It may have been the opening of some bloodline code that he carried. Perhaps it was the code of fanaticism! He changed overnight and became a religious zealot - sure that Yahweh had appointed him the savior of Judah. Jeremiah and I were dumbfounded. Josiah made the discovery and content of the book public and launched the most energetic and extensive reformation period of our history. The pagan temples were destroyed. The worshipers were deported and all references to Baal and Astarte were stricken from the kingdom. Of course, the pagans simply went into hiding as they had many times before but there was no visible paganism in Judah. I had alerted Lydia who summoned the magi to protect the temple of Annu. Josiah had been initiated there and knew that we embraced the dualistic nature of God. The magi's power was supreme. Josiah did not harm the temple and seemed to have forgotten its existence. It had become invisible to him.

"One of the biggest lessons of my life became clear at that point. I realize now that Josiah and the bloodline had activated ascension codes within my energetic body. My task was to detach from my only son, the boy of my heart, and let him follow his own calling, to allow him to hold his own beliefs, and avoid judging him because they did not agree with mine. I also had to refrain from judging Jeremiah, who reacted publically to Josiah's transformation based on his well-known distaste for religious law. He carried the codes of service to the people with freedom and equality. I also had to be there for both of them as friend and counsel. It was a blessed time for me, and a true release from judgment. I saw all that transpired and was able to find a quiet place of truth within me. None of it mattered. It was all illusion. What did matter was the Spirit moving through me and all things. I began to communicate with the High Council in my meditations to provide some outside support.

"This reformation continued for three years. At the end of that period Josiah invited the entire kingdom to a great feast on the spring equinox. He even invited our Assyrian neighbors who had run ten of the tribes of Abraham from the north three hundred years ago. Whether he knew it our not, he appeased the pagans by holding this feast when they would have held their spring festival. It worked well to unite the people and it became, once again, a traditional passover feast.

"Zebudah had produced a male heir during the first year of her marriage to Josiah. Dynastic rules prohibited further relations between them for six more years. Their son, Jechonias, was seven when his brother, Jehoahaz, was born. Josiah felt secure with two male children and the reformation an apparent success. It was at this time that the Assyrians began losing power to Babylon. Josiah turned his attention to the military. He trained himself as a soldier and a leader in battle. His charisma and reputation for fairness assisted in reorganizing the army into a fine fighting force. With the people and the army supporting him fully, he began to take territory back from neighboring tribes along the Red Sea and in Philistia. These tribes had moved into Palestine during the various reigns of Solomon's successors. Succeeding at all that he endeavored, he endeared himself to the people. He began taking territory from the weakened Assyrians in the north with the dream of reuniting Israel and Judah for the first time since the days of Solomon.

"During this time period, when Josiah was in his thirties, Jeremiah came into the fullness of prophecy. He spoke in the name of Yahweh - obviously a politically astute choice. He was not speaking in public yet, but did confer with me about the days to come. It was disheartening to know that all that Josiah strove towards would crumble at his death. The official court prophetess, whose name was Huldah, also warned Josiah that Judah would fall, but not in his lifetime.

"I conferred with the High Council who assured me that the bloodline would continue but that a crucial person was yet unborn. That is all they would reveal to me. I spoke with Lydia who was, by then, in her seventies. She felt it had nothing to do with the blood, but rather the codes of light. She had someone she wanted me to meet and she brought you forth, Hamutal. I could see the golden sun upon your brow and within your heart, dear one. I knew you were to be my successor. Remember? You were already twenty, a dedicated priestess of Annu who had just come, at Lydia's bidding, from our temple at Mt. Horeb to Jerusalem. You were beautiful in every way. Your light was very bright and clear. It was then that I saw a soul hovering around you that looked like the sun itself. It was our dear Tamar Tephi, of course. There were four of the lineage in the temple room of the eternal flame that day. That, I am sure, was unprecedented.

"I suggested to Lydia that Josiah take you as a second dynastic wife since Zebudah had been childless for twelve years. She agreed and you did not question the workings of the Divine Plan. You were moved into the palace adjacent to my quarters and I saw that Josiah was in Jerusalem for the month of dynastic intercourse. The marriage took place after your conception of Mattaniah. It was a quiet marriage, unknown to most of the people, but sanctioned by the priests and the court. The birth of a boy was a shock to both of us since we expected Tamar Tephi. Her golden soul of the Sun came again just after the birth and hovered about Mattaniah. I then realized that she would be his child and that he needed the protection of the priestesses. Josiah, who was completely preoccupied in the north, gave us no argument when you and Mattaniah moved back to the temple. You were the lioness protecting your cub as the political climate on our borders began to warm. I remained at the palace with Zebudah and my grandsons.

"Josiah was in the north moving his army towards the sea through the mountain pass at Meggido when he met the army of Neko. The Egyptians, allies of the Assyrians, were disturbed by Josiah's aggressiveness. They sent their army by sea to meet and defeat Josiah. In truth they had more to fear from the Babylonian Empire which, allied with the Medes, was defeating the Assyrians soundly in their northern borders. Josiah was severely wounded in a surprise attack. He was brought back to Jerusalem in his chariot and, within days, died from wounds to his internal organs. Zebudah and I spent his last days with him, dressing his wounds and softening the blows of his defeat. Sadly, he revealed to me that in the midst of the battle he had had a vision of a far greater defeat. He felt the deepest regret that he had failed his country, that he had lost the key, the key of kingly service, to a quest for territory and power. We recounted all he had done for the people, reinforced the great love they had for him, but he died in a despondent frame of mind knowing that the freedom he strove to protect was lost to his people.

"I mourned the death of my son as did all of Judah. He had been a great light in this land that had suffered much from poor leadership. I had not always agreed with him but admired and respected him for following his passion and his own truth. The Egyptians, though proclaiming themselves victors over Judah, kept their distance during this period of mourning, waiting to see how the court would move to replace Josiah. The court would naturally have chosen Jechonias who was twenty years of age at that time and who already had a son of four years. Instead, fearful of Egyptian reprisal against their decision to name a king, they put his fourteen-year-old brother on the throne. Jehoahaz had not been trained to lead and would have been a weak king whatever the circumstances. He had no drive for power. The court used him, like a sacrificial lamb, to force Neko's next move. Within months of his reluctant coronation the Egyptians were in Jerusalem. They forced their way into the palace, held the court at the points of their swords and took my grandson from their midst. The court was told to await the decree of Neko with respect to their next king. They were to make no independent decisions. Their actions left no doubt that Judah belonged to Egypt.

"We had no word from Jehoahaz after he was exiled to Egypt. Jeremiah's contacts assured me that he had been treated well. I grieved then not only for my son but my grandson. However, I did so from a place of serenity and surrender. Neko appointed Jechonias to the throne as a puppet king. His name was changed to Jehoiakim, another show of power from Neko. The military was shattered. Judah's defenses against the Babylonians were in the hands of the Egyptians who cared nothing for us. Jechonias/ King Jehoiakim's reign became one of rebuilding from the ruins of war and time. Being an aggressive young man, the rebuilding programs kept him centered on something positive. Soon he built a second palace at Ramat Rahel where the remaining military had a stronghold and he moved his family there for safe keeping. Never did he step beyond the bounds set by Neko, so there was peace in this borrowed kingdom for a time.

"Shortly after Jehoahaz's capture, Lydia summoned me to the temple. By then, I had completed my passage into the circle of the elders with the cessation of my bleeding. Fifty-four years old, I was a widow who had lost her son and one of her grandsons. Through it all, I felt more and more the presence of God within me. Lydia surprised me that day. She sat with me as I sit with you to pass the codes of light to me. Telling me of her life of a true dedication to the sisterhood, I heard of her sorrows, her joys, her losses and her triumphs, and I heard of the Mission as it has come down through the ages. Profoundly moved, I was deeply sorrowed that she had chosen this time to leave the Earth. She laughed softly and said that she was not leaving the Earth, but setting a precedent. These were times of precedent, she declared. She was retiring to the community on the Red Sea for she felt her strength waning and knew the coming years were mine. On that day, she wanted to pass me the robes of high priestess so that I might truly come into my calling.

"In speaking of my purpose, she mentioned only that I would be guardian of the order as it made a great transition. About a decade hence, we would once again separate ourselves from the bloodline to protect the codes of light. That was always to be the highest priority. I would receive my instructions from the High Council and we both knew that you, Hamutal, were to replace me when I had finished my Mission. As she finished with me, she fully opened my third eye and connected me to the lineage of light. My light body, which I had been struggling to anchor fully, came firmly into me. I have had the sight ever since and have worn the black robes of high priestess. It was then that I left the palace and moved back to the temple of my maidenhood. It was wonderful to be home again after so many years away. Zebudah, her grandson, Jechoniah, and her daughter-in-law Nehushta [wife of King Jehoiakim(Jechonias) and Jechoniah's mother], were at Ramat Rahel so the palace was left to the patriarchs.

"Jeremiah and I still had regular discussions about the fate of Judah. He came fully and openly into his powers as a Divine channel during the reign of Jehoiakim. People were reverting to paganism and Jehoiakim was ignoring it. The Yawists appealed to the king. All that Josiah had created was crumbling. What really happened was that the illusion fell away and people began worshipping publicly again. Jeremiah still argued against the book of laws, hoping the homeland could come to peaceful agreements that benefited the people rather than the priests. He was adamant that a curse would befall the kingdom in the future should temples continue to be used as places of prostitution. It hurt him deeply to see the abuse of women, and their participation in this corruption, because he had been raised by the brotherhood to

[114]

respect their sacredness. A small circle of disciples followed him and occasionally acted to defend his life for his outspoken prophecy. What good was a prophet in silence I ask you?

"Jehoiakim had been the appointed king just four years when the Egyptians were defeated by the Babylonians under crown prince Nebuchadnezzar. My grandson was twenty-four years old and for the second time in my life, I witnessed the mysterious codes within the bloodline open and activate. An aggressive young man to begin with, he had had the good sense to limit his energies to sport and building, but he began to speak of war against the Babylonians. It was absurd, insane. I began to think that these spontaneous bursts of aggression were a kind of defect within the blood of the House of David that denied the very codes of kingly service for which the lineage stood. We had had children on the throne since the death of Amon and now they were not even anointed kings. I could not imagine how this fit into the program of the High Council. Using the techniques now familiar to me I journeyed to the council to consult with them.They told me that the blood would remain powerless so long as the line denied the feminine aspect of God. I was told that the bloodline would serve the program more consciously if it were removed from the world of politics and war, and concentrated more on spiritual matters. Of course, they were right. Judah was a shambles.

"Jeremiah had a scribe by the name of Baruch who wrote down the specific prophecies concerning the future of the kingdom. Jeremiah ordered Baruch to go to the palace and read them before Jehoiakim, which he did. The prophecies foretold the loss of Judah and the destruction of Jerusalem at the hands of invaders. Yahweh laid the blame on the pagan practices and weakness of the throne. The king tore the scroll to shreds and ordered that Jeremiah be arrested. His disciples fled with him to the brotherhood community on the Dead Sea. I could see very clearly that Jerusalem would eventually fall. While Jeremiah was at the Dead Sea he secured for me the cooperation of the brotherhood to begin the restoration of an old village inland and near their community for our sisters. That village, inland from the Dead Sea, is the same village in which we are now sitting.

"When Mattaniah was twelve, he experienced his raising at the temple and was then sent to live at the palace with his half-brother. The next year Jehoiakim challenged the Babylonians now led by Nebuchadnezzar who sent his northern vassals into Judah to defeat him. He was taken captive to Babylon. His son, twenty-five year old Jechoniah, returned from Ramat Rahel and assumed the throne. Nebuchadnezzer himself stormed Jerusalem and took King Jechoniah captive as well as his family, the entire court, and a goodly number of intellectual and wealthy citizens. They sacked the palace and the temples, and then appointed thirteen year-old Mattaniah as king, renaming him Zedekiah. Hamutal, you were brave indeed to move into the palace with your son during those perilous times. The temple of Annu survived unscathed due to the protection cast by the magi years before, but I knew it was time for all of us to move out to this community in the desert. Our brothers assisted us and again cast protection around our dwellings. We were once again brothers and sisters together just as we had been beneath Mt. Horeb and in Egypt during the Golden Age. I sent our priestess, Neiah, to you to bear King Zedekiah's children. Hamutal, you did well with their marriage. When Zedekiah was fifteen, they married and five children came one after another, breaking all the rules of dynastic wedlock. I truly believe, as much as I loved him, that Zedekiah's blood was not complete. It is no fault of yours, Hamutal, nor Neiah's. What could she do? I am convinced it was more the composition his soul requested, a karma of some sort. He was not very intelligent. However, my dearest Tamar Tephi, you came into the world as the third child and the only girl of this weak grandson and king. As soon as you were able to leave your mother with a wet nurse, Hamutal brought you to the desert.

"Jehoiakim's threat on Jeremiah's life was no longer viable since the former king was in captivity. So the prophet priest returned to Jerusalem and again stirred up all those who would listen to him - and the numbers were growing. People began to believe in his prophecies. At the same time they began to doubt Yahweh's original proclamation that they were the chosen people. Chosen for what? For punishment? Jerusalem was a hotbed of religious turmoil. I give credit to the Babylonians for staying out of the religious arguments and for giving the exiled Hebrews complete freedom of religion and scholarly pursuit. It is certainly more than our kings would have done for them.

"When Zedekiah turned twenty-two, I once again saw the codes activate in the blood to produce an unstable aggressive leader. Zedekiah allied himself with the pharaoh Hophra who openly encouraged him to launch a campaign against the Babylonians. Hophra knew it was suicide for Judah and he never intended to support it wholeheartedly. Nebuchadnezzer swept through Palestine destroying town after town. Jeremiah stormed the court and delivered the terrifying words of Yahweh to Zedekiah. Jerusalem would fall, he would be killed, his family would fall to the Babylonians. If he did not care for his homeland, what of himself? Jeremiah walked the streets of Jerusalem in tears, an oxen's yoke around his neck, advocating submission to the Babylonians. Jeremiah had been to Babylon and knew that the Hebrews in captivity there were not unhappy. Jerusalem and the Hebrews could survive that way. The Fatherland could survive. Zedekiah had him arrested and imprisoned for desertion as he attempted to leave the city for Anathoth, his family home. He was first thrown into a muddy pit within the guardhouse courtyard. Afterwards he was moved to the palace prison and remained there until Jerusalem was lost.

"My heart went out to your mother, Tamar Tephi, but I could not risk having the boys anywhere near the communities here. Neiah was brave to stay in Jerusalem during the siege of the Babylonians. For two years they battered against the city walls until the city fell. In those two years the people starved and suffered from many diseases. Zedekiah remained stubborn. When, at last, the Babylonian army broke through the gates of the city, he fled like a coward leaving his family behind. King Nebuchadnezzer seized the boys and your mother. While locking them in the palace prison, Jeremiah was found and released. He begged for Neiah's life and won it, then he implored her to leave the city with him for the situation was hopeless. She wept for her sons, but knew she had no choice. Jeremiah convinced her that they had no political use for her and would probably force her into prostitution to humiliate the throne. After tearfully kissing your terrified brothers farewell for the last time, she allowed him to remove her to safety.

"Your father, King Zedekiah, was captured trying to make his way to Ramat Rahel. He had not travelled very far. They brought him and your brothers to Babylon and tied him to a post in the square outside the palace gates. Encouraging the citizens to gather around the spectacle of their fallen king, the Babylonian general under the order of his king brought your brothers to the square to face your father. One by one, their heads were cut off as your father watched in horror and shame. I am sorry Tamar Tephi, do not cry. You must know this. It is necessary for the awakening of codes within you in the future.

"When they had finished executing your brothers, they gouged your father's eyes from his head that he would see no more. There," she gasped, her eyes moist, "I have said the worst of it. He was dragged off to prison where he died within a few short months.

Jeremiah saw that your mother was returned to us in secrecy. That was six years ago. We nursed her back to emotional wholeness, but it was not easy. You were the light that allowed her to heal, Tamar Tephi. Jeremiah stayed in Jerusalem for some time helping the poor and ailing who were not taken into Babylon. The Babylonians took the higher classes, the intellectuals and high priests into Babylon and left the poor and the needy behind. Much respected in Babylon, Jeremiah was offered a position in the court of Nebuchadnezzer, but refused it. In time, he returned to the Dead Sea where Baruch recorded all that had transpired in his life."

*

Jedidah took the tearful Tamar Tephi in her arms and soothed her. She had known nothing of the siege nor the fate of her brothers and father. The knowledge had been hidden from her but she would have heard of it in her travels. Jedidah did not want her to find out in that way. She wiped the girls eyes with the end of her sleeve and produced from her pocket a second set of six perfect sapphires, each wrapped in a soft black cloth. These she placed in Tamar Tephi's hands and around her neck she placed a golden disc of the Sun, a perfect replica of Annu hanging behind the altar. Tamar Tephi thanked her great-grandmother and looked at her grandmother's approving eyes. She sat back upon her pillow, more centered and more grounded than she had ever been.

*

"I am almost finished, my daughters. I want to speak now of the future, for it holds more hope than our past. We will stay here with the brothers for a long time. Eventually the Hebrews will come out of exile and take back Jerusalem, but we will not return there. The House of David will not regain the throne but the bloodline will have undergone a cleansing, the removal of that lust for power, the flaw in the genes. The descendants of Jechoniah will return from exile and come to live with the brothers and sisters as our communities combine. We have always worked in secrecy, holding power in the realms of the energetic, and will continue in that way. Hamutal, the Babylonians will not even see these communities, and neither will the Arabs. We will be visible only to those with eyes to see. In time, a great woman will come into the sisterhood, holding the lineage of light. She will be ac-

[118]

companied by a great man who will come into the brotherhood and into the lineage of David. Again, the lineages will cross and the world will change forever for these two will be Akhus incarnate. These are the only prophecies you will receive from an old lady like myself.

"Tamar Tephi, I have given you the sapphires of the high priestess. I have given you the disc of Annu to keep close to your heart at all times. It will connect you with the sisterhood here. Tomorrow morning you will leave us, my darling. I will miss you more than you will know, but it is part of my path to detach and allow you to bloom as a rose. You will leave with the purple robes of a vowed priestess for you will give me your vows before we end this night. In time and with maturity you will know when the black robes are to be yours and these I send with you also. You will leave also with fire from the eternal flame. Jeremiah will accompany you to Egypt along with two of the brothers and two priestesses of Annu. One brother is a magus, a master of energy, and the other a priest, a master of devotion. In Egypt, you will all secure passage on a ship bound for Iberia. From Iberia you will journey further to the Isle of Gael in the northern ocean. You and your companions will establish temples and a mystery school in this very holy land. You will find great stone monuments left by the Hyperboreans - a very old seeding program of Ak-An. Respect these monuments for they are messages to you from the gods who walked the Earth. They will remind you of balance, of the four elemental powers and of our mother, the Earth. They will give you a map of the stars in their ancient skies. In Egypt, Jeremiah will take you all to the ancient city of Annu, called On by the Egyptians, the pyramid temples, and the great lion monument. He will explain that part of your past to you. In your new land you will notice that the monuments are similar but really quite different. Seeing these sacred temples of the past will open wide the codes within you that you might live your Akhu heritage.

"The other important thing awaiting you is your destiny. On the Isle of Gael, Tamar Tephi, there lives a young king named Eochaid. He is the twin to your soul, my darling one, and you are his queen. Your love will be pure, your life will be long, and your children will be many. He will hold you in his heart and give you a good life. You will seed the Akhu codes onto this Isle of Gael as well as the codes of light. You will bring the truths of Mir-An-Da and Aman-Ra and they will spread. In the future, that which we hold here will join with lineages you begin there. You are planting the seeds of a golden age, Tamar Tephi. Do not let the flame go out. Let no impurity enter your being. Yours is the path of absolute integrity and light. I know you will not fail. I am very happy for you, my little one.

"When Jeremiah sends me word that you have all arrived at your destination, I will gladly leave this world. He will do the same and you will honor him in his death. We are old and have seen far too much of the illusion on this planet. However, until you have arrived safely in the arms of your beloved, our Missions are not complete. Even so, Hamutal, I wish to turn my duties over to you this night that I might spend my last days holding sacred space for our little group of travelers. Now, Tamar Tephi, resplendent Queen of the Gaels, I would like to hear your vows."

*

Tamar Tephi was brilliant, like a newly formed star. She knew her destiny and was happy to begin her time of service. She expected Jedidah to be watching over her from spirit world for years to come if not her whole life. She gave her vows to her great-grandmother, kissed her grandmother, folded her new robes over her arm and went off to sleep with her treasures. Hamutal and Jedidah sat for a long time holding hands and gazing upon the disc of Annu.

In the morning, Tamar Tephi accompanied Jedidah back into the temple of the eternal flame. Jedidah gave her a small oil lantern and together they used a wand of woven grass to light it from the eternal flame. She had oil enough to keep this tiny flame burning until she arrived at her destination where it would be kept alive until the temple was built to hold it. They went to meet her traveling companions, with Tamar Tephi wearing the purple robes of the vowed priestess. Jeremiah was waiting with the four other travelers who added the warmth of their excitement to the cool pre-dawn. The young ones went about loading the donkeys as Jeremiah and Jedidah slipped away into a nearby garden. They embraced and kissed each other for the first time since they had made sacred love at his raising, nearly seventy years earlier. They cried and spoke their passion and love to each other as if it would make up for a lifetime apart. She reminded him that it was only human love, that union in God awaited them. He reminded her that this life had seemed an eternity. She agreed. They had lived through the most treacherous of times and had held their truth through it all, he in the thunder of the prophet's words and she in

[120]

the silence of the priestess's heart.

Jeremiah took from his pack an object wrapped in red cloth. He carefully removed the cloth to reveal a black stone, smoothly polished with years of reverent care. He told her that the brother-hood was asking him to carry this stone to the Isle of Gael and to entrust it to the lineage of Tamar Tephi and Eochaid. It was said to be the stone upon which Jacob rested his head when he saw the ladder to heaven, and was symbolic of the bloodline's com-mitment to kingly service, for which Jeremiah had been the ma-jor advocate. Tamar Tephi's seed would use this as a reminder of kingly service because the lineage of the House of David would no longer be serving the Hebrews as earthly kings. The stone would not survive the future if it stayed in Palestine. Jedidah under-stood. He asked her to hold the stone to her heart, bless it and charge it with feminine energy. When she gave it back to him, he wrapped it carefully, replaced it in his pack and embraced her again. They walked back to the group of travelers with measured steps, each one a reminder of the transparency of their Earthwalks. The stone held an energy beyond the limitations of time. It was past, present and future at once. They both knew the Mission would not fail.

In Egypt, Jeremiah took the young people to the ancient temples across the Nile from ancient Annu. Tamar Tephi awak-ened to deep remembrance of her origins and the others too felt the past merge with their energetic bodies. Jeremiah, himself, felt his heart reach out to the star that called him home. While they waited for passage on the ship, he thought to inquire about Jehoahaz. With little investigation he was able to locate him in Annu in one of the great libraries. He had been fully supported by the dynasty to pursue whatever activity he liked. The only stipu-lation had been that he was not to return to Judah nor have offspring. He was led to the study of the ancient times and the history of his bloodline in Egypt. Having heard the news of the fall of Judah, he felt that an ancient karma was being played out. Jeremiah agreed for no one had listened to reason or to Yahweh. Jehoahaz looked happy and stronger than he had ever been in Judah. Jeremiah told him that his mother had died shortly after Jerusalem fell but that his grandmother Jedidah was still alive. Jehoahaz had smiled and told him that she would probably not die but melt into the landscape. Jeremiah agreed.

After their safe arrival on the Isle of Gael, Jeremiah sent a message back to Egypt by return ship to be delivered to one of the brothers in the port. The message was brought to the Dead Sea and given to Jedidah. It was from Tamar Tephi and stated that King Eochaid was much more wonderful than Jedidah had said he would be, that the sacred flame was burning brightly on the Isle of Gael, and that she had felt her great-grandmother's presence every day of her journey. She thanked her and sent love and deep commitment to the Mission. Jeremiah also sent news of Jehoahaz to Jedidah knowing that she had loved him well. Lastly he sent word that he was leaving this world and begged her to join him whenever she felt the call of Ak-An.

Jedidah received the news of Tamar Tephi with complete delight and little surprise. She was so connected to the child she felt her every emotion. The Mission in Gael was underway. She was cheered by the news of Jehoahaz, and sent blessings to him for a happy life. Her Mission completed, she arose early the next day and said farewell to Hamutal, Neiah and her other beloved sisters. Jedidah, more serene than ever, walked out into the desert towards the Dead Sea and the rising Sun. No trace of her was ever found.

Leah speaks

Leah opened her eyes, then shut them again to assess the energetic state of the group. Many of the women had had deep emotional reactions to the tragic losses which Jedidah had experienced in her life. The group energy was a little fragile so she asked everyone to sit up straight and begin taking deep breaths down to the abdomen. She asked that they release the emotion on the exhale, making it loud and strong. As the emotional charge began to neutralize, she quieted them and pulled the energy together.

"I had a dream this afternoon, my beloveds. In the dream Jedidah was delivering white doves to the communities of the sisterhood and brotherhood in the desert. She was serenity itself and the birds, representing peace, protection and freedom, were her gifts to those she'd left behind. It was so touching, so meaningful to me, that I dared not break the energy of her gift until she'd told her story. These birds represent the Holy Spirit, that feminine aspect of God, which Jedidah truly embodied. The doves were also harbingers of one who would come after her, one who knew the name of God, and who bore the goddess codes of union. On her Earthwalk, Jedidah opened codes of consciousness for universal truth, hopefulness, and peace. Codes of right action were activated and released through her experiences with the flaw in the bloodline. The energies released allowed the blood to correct itself over time. She mastered tolerance, humility, non-judgment and invisibility or non-ego. For her soul, it was another incarnation, another opportunity for enlightenment and mastery. To me, she represents the highest expression of the guardian of the codes of light.

"Jeremiah reactivated the Grail Codes of kingly service seeded by Aman-Ra. Of course, they were not realized in his lifetime, but that is usually the case. His was a life of sacrifice and service and it was not in vain. It is a pity that he is represented as such a Yawist in historical texts because his heart and soul understood the one God in its fullness. The brotherhood to which he belonged has been the active component of the current Siriun Mission since the times of Aman-Ra. Like the lineage of light, this soul group has been dedicated to healing separation from God for eons on the Earth. Many of these brothers have moved into the realms of the Ascended Masters, but they are still fully dedicated to the Mission. We will meet them again and again as our story continues, but to tell their story would take another week."

"Perhaps next year?" Sonia interjected cheerfully.

"Quite possibly," Leah laughed. "There is also the whole story of Tamar Tephi and how her life and legacy evolved. We will meet part of her lineage in a few nights in another rich story. Needless to say, when the Celts made it to the British Isles, there was already a strong temple tradition in place as well as the Brotherhood of the Magi.

"I see Jedidah as a central pillar, a pivotal point in the program. She held the ground and let the chaos sweep by her. When it was over, all that was left was peace. She did not succumb to the illusion. The bloodline of David continued and modified in Babylonian captivity. For the first time, the Hebrews wrote their history, producing the books of the Old Testament. Also, they wrote the Torah, their book of laws, and came to know themselves as the Jews. The roots of the more esoteric practices of Judaism and their ancient connection with the Egyptian mysteries were presented through the brotherhood. These have been held in secrecy for thousands of years, coming and going from this reality relative to the availability of acceptable recipients. When The Word, The Logos, cannot be heard in purity, it will not be spoken, but it does not go away. IT IS."

Mary

Leah speaks

Everyone came to the evening session refreshed after a late afternoon trip to the hot springs. Leah had a way of leading them
through any activity with higher purpose and intention and so it
was with the hot springs. Their energy was so high it was difficult
to eat dinner. This was precisely what Leah wanted. Her aim was
for the energy of tonight's story, the energy of this woman's life, to
become an inseparable part of them. For this to happen, they had
to be in very high frequency and receptivity, as they now were.
Leah focused on her own presence because the energy of Mary
began moving through her during meditation at the springs and
she wanted to provide some background information before she
took her finger from the dike and gave way to the flow. All was in
readiness as she entered the room. She wore a long blue-black
silk top that was delicately splattered with stars. To the women,
it looked as they imagined the temple ceilings of Annu must have
appeared to the priestesses of old. Leah returned the loving gaze
of her apprentices, and then connected with the eyes of Sananda
from the high place on the altar.

Slipping a deep blue velvet bag from the pocket of her black
silk pants, and planting her bare feet firmly on the floor, Leah
invoked the one God, the Divine Mother, the Akhus overseeing
her work, the lineage of the codes of light - her sisters through
time, the great White Brotherhood, the elements of the Earth, all
Earth's creatures, and Mother Earth herself. The women felt these
energies fill the room and sweep them into an uplifting vortex.
Lowering herself to one knee, she opened the bag and poured
into her hand six perfect sapphire wands. The women gasped.

Leah smiled and blew on the stones. Then she rose and set the six sapphires in a Star of David around the outside of the circle. She connected them with her intent after she had stepped inside the star. The configuration of the sapphires set the circle of women in the hexagon within the star, the center of the honeycomb. Energy was moving and everyone could feel it. Then she modified her original grid in the center of the group to make a five-pointed star.

"Did you know that, over time, Venus traces her path through the sky as a five-pointed star, my beloveds?" she asked.

"I remember reading that somewhere," a slight blonde woman replied.

Leah smiled. "I did too, Emily. I never forgot reading it either and found that it was in all the deeper layers of the feminine mysteries. The five-pointed star is the feminine star. Its energy connects us to Venus. The six-pointed star is more closely associated with the brotherhood, Sirius, and the star beings there. It represents the masculine and feminine energies as well as heaven and Earth coming together in unison. The five-pointed star relates Earth to Venus, our sister planet, you see? I have found it useful to grid the five-pointed star for specific work with women or my own feminine nature. Tonight, we are using it to anchor energy from Venus for that is the residence of the next pivotal member of the lineage of light in our story. She no longer works upon the Earth but guides consciousness from our sister planet. This Venusian ascended master brought the last coded impulse of God-consciousness to Earth. She released the goddess codes of the Black Madonna at the close of her life as Mary Magdalen, which she will recount with us this night. Until the release of the next impulse, part of her consciousness will remain on Venus as guardian of that which she carried." Leah centered Mary's picture in the grid with Jesus alongside her. "She will have much to say about Jeshua as well, but first I am to provide you with some background material to fill in the gap between Jedidah who died in 577 BC and Mary who was born in 3 AD. The accuracy of what I share is doubtful, but what the history books provided me."

Leah lowered herself into the cross-legged position she always favored and began. "We left the upper class Hebrews, including the king and his family, in Babylon. Jeremiah had told them to make the best of it and they did. They were in Nippur to the southeast of Babylon – a select group of exiles who held the intellectual and priestly reins of Judah. If the brotherhood had not operated in secrecy, the leadership might easily have been disputed, for the sons and daughters of Annu were a powerful force working quietly at the north end of the Dead Sea. Within forty years, Persia defeated Babylon and many of the Hebrews returned to Judah, which was then under Persian rule. They were given religious freedom, their temples were returned to them, and they were encouraged to intermarry with the invaders. There was a general decrease of the already weak Akhu blood as this occurred, but not within the high lineages of the king and priests. The Zadok, the anointed high priest whose lineage could be traced to King David's time, was the new 'king' of the community who ruled with a council of elders, the priests and Levites. The kingly lineage of the House of David was prevented from assuming the throne. The Hebrews had returned from exile with the Torah and the solidarity of religious purpose known as Judaism. From this point on, they became known as the Jews. Control of Judah, now Judaea, changed hands with each new world power down through the centuries.

"In the middle of the first century BC, Judaea was a province of the Greeks, part of the Hellenistic kingdoms. Antiochus IV, in direct contradiction to his treatment of other cultures assimilated into his kingdom, violently opposed Judaism and did all he could to abolish the temples and prohibit practicing the religion. Yahweh was equated with Baal while Zeus reigned as king of the heavens. You can imagine the kind of reaction this provoked. Perhaps Antiochus would have benefited from a course in Hebrew history. A revolt began in Lydda which lay between the Mediterranean Sea and Jerusalem. A man by the name of Mattathias Maccabaeus of the priestly clan of Joarib refused to offer a pagan sacrifice in his temple. What is more, he struck down a Jew who was willing to offer sacrifice. He and his five sons, the famous Maccabees, fled to the mountains and rallied a group of guerrilla fighting men. The pious Hasidim, the conservative sect of Judaism, were among their supporters. After Mattathias's death in 166 BC his son Judas became the next leader of the group and eventually his brothers regained Jerusalem. The temple was restored in 164 BC, an event that is still commemorated as Hanukkah. The Maccabees were also called Hasmonaeans, another name for the priestly clan of Joarib.

"Around this time, there were two pivotal occurrences relevant to our story. With the Hasmonaean rule, during which the kingdom was free for eighty years on the strength of treaties with Rome, Jonathan Maccabee declared himself to be high priest, a title previously exclusive to the Zadok lineage, not the Joarib lineage. The other pivotal event was the eventual installation of the Hasmonaean lineage as the kings of Judaea and their seduction by the material world. With these two deviations from tradition they lost the support of the Hasidim who considered them usurpers of both the priestly and kingly lineages. Nonetheless, the last of the Maccabee brothers succeeded in ousting their conquerors and established peace. It was at this time, around 140 BC, that the Hasidim, proclaiming themselves to be the faithful remnant, marched *en masse* out of Jerusalem to the Dead Sea where they joined the brotherhood and the lineage of light. Leading the group were Zerubbabel, heir to the Davidic lineage, and the Zadok. What developed was the first Essene community at Khirbet Qumran. Jerusalem became a more cosmopolitan city, a melting pot of invaders, and the whole face of Judaea began to change. This influx of the Hasidim from Jerusalem increased by hundreds the number of people in the combined communities on the Dead Sea.

In 63 BC, Rome moved in from Carthage to seize Jerusalem and Judaea. Julius Caesar installed the Idumaean, Antipater as Procurator of Judaea and his son, Herod, as Governor of Galilee. The Idumaeans were Arabs from the south who had recently converted to a form of Judaism. They were not from the lineage of David or the Hasmonaeans although, when you understand the way in which the near east was populated, there is no disputing the fact that Arab and Jew came from the same lineage of Abraham. Looking back beyond that, there were few people anyone encountered there who did not have some of the blood of Aman-Ra and Mir-An-Da in their veins. Antipater was soon killed and Herod became king of Judaea after incorporating Sumaria into his jurisdiction as well as Galilee. The eighty years of independence gained by the Maccabean revolt was over - not to be regained for over two thousand years. Also of consequence to our story, Judaea sustained an earthquake of some magnitude in 31 BC, which destroyed many of the dwellings at Qumran. It was in the rebuilding of their communities that the brotherhood, the sisters of the lineage of light and the Hasidim merged into the common Essene community at Qumran.

"It was into this environment in Judaea, that Mary Magdalen was born in 3 AD. Herod had died after a final burst of brutality born of his own paranoia, and was succeeded by three district governors; one ethnarch and two tetrarchs, the sons of Augustus. Government was stabilized in Galilee where Mary was born but the central district, which included Jerusalem and Qumran, the old Judah, was plagued by bad leadership resulting in a series of petty governors. Within the Jewish society, there existed several distinct sects, not unlike the Hasidim who were considered the pious ones. The Sadducees, supposedly related to the priestly line of Zadok, were rich, influential landowners. They were pacifist laymen connected to the temples. The Pharisees were also laymen of the middle class who called themselves the Haberim, the equals. This sect arose when the Hasidim marched out of Jerusalem to join the communities at Qumran. The Pharisees were a progressive group of men, more related to the synagogue than the temple, who supported social causes. Their agents, or lawyers, were the Scribes who had become the intellectual elite, the interpreters of the laws of conduct. The Scribes were part of a religious legislative body called the Sanhedrin which was also connected to the council of elders.

"The Essenes were the remaining sect - the pious Hasidim combined with our beloved sisters and the brothers. They had been influenced by Hellenistic thought through connections to the brotherhood from Egypt. Teachings of the immortality of the soul and the battle of light and dark forces were major contributions from Greece. However, we can see that these were part of the cosmology of Zep Tepi, *the First Times,* for Greece was one of the colonies of Aman-Ra, and the Greeks were very attentive to the ancient Egyptian teachings. Within the Essene community were the Zadok and the heir to the House of David. The Essenes felt these were the only true priests and the only true kings. In their doctrines, we can find the old teachings of Annu, the ancient heritage of the star beings, because the Hasidim came to learn of their true origins from the brothers and sisters. I should also mention the Egyptian Therapeutae which was part of the Qumran community. This group was part of the brotherhood in the times of Jedidah at the Dead Sea and a branch of an order of brothers from Egypt - the brothers through whom Jeremiah delivered his last message to Jedidah. These brothers regularly traveled back and forth between Heliopolis and the Dead Sea. They were magi and skilled healers, masters of plant medicine, and healing with stones. Though the Therapeutae was thought to have been invented by Pharaoh Tuthmosis III, heir of Thoth, and great-grandfather of Moses, the pharoah simply revitalized the teachings of Aman-Ra, forming a new mystery school. The Therapeutae had a large contingency at Qumran and maintained a small community in Egypt.

"That completes the background information needed to help

understand the events and circumstances of Mary's life. Jeshua was already nine years of age when her soul incarnated on the Earth. Her birth was not heralded by prophecies because the lineage of light has always worked in secrecy. Her life, as history reported it, was fabricated by the fearful patriarchs because she carried more power than all of them combined. Her grateful acceptance of that anonymity allowed her to complete her mission without harm to her life or the lineage. It has taken two thousand years for the consciousness of the western world to begin accepting her relationship with Jeshua. As we let go of the beliefs that have held us in darkness for all of this time, the energies that she released on the planet can be of some value to us.

"Now my dear ones, would you mind if we took a small break at this point to watch the setting Sun in silence? I would value the time to disperse the mental focus of this introduction and allow Mary's feelings and perceptions to move through me."

Everyone nodded in agreement and, stepping carefully outside the energetic field of the sapphires, they wandered out to the lawn to watch the sunset. They re-entered the room in the magical light of the hour of power, stepped back within the star, and seated themselves. As Mary's energy began moving through Leah, they felt a radiant warmth enter the circle and some could see light emanating from her, especially around her head.

She began almost at once. "I see Mary sitting in her favorite spot, atop a bench padded with sheep skins in her cave of solitude in the white mountains of Sainte Baume of southern France in the district now known as Provence. Little beeswax candles flicker around the perimeter of the cave and a tiny oil burner sits upon an altar near the cave wall. A Star of David with six sapphire wands has been cast on the floor of the cave. All is in readiness for the passage of the codes of light. Mary is sixty years old, fair-skinned, with long golden-red hair falling in a neat braid to her waist. Her dark eyes are huge, liquid pools of light so much like those of the ascended masters. She wears the black robes of the high priestess or Magda-elder of the lay Nazarites, the organization through which the priestesses of Annu ministered. Her delicate hands reach out to the young girl opposite her who looks like an adolescent version of Mary. Her name is Gabriella. She is Mary's granddaughter, the child of her daughter, Tamar. Gabriella, at fourteen, is dressed in the blue robes of a novice of the priestesses of Annu. She puts her hands upon her grandmother's for a few minutes connecting energy and sharing love."

Leah had closed her eyes to remain detached from her role in the circle and soon the words of Mary began to come through her.

Mary speaks

"Gabriella, my dear one, I am being called to continue the work I have begun here from other dimensions. Do you understand? I must shed this earthly body and live only in my body of light. I know you understand. I have prepared your way in this world and it will be easy for you, Gabriella. I know it has not been easy thus far. Our little community here will nurture you and, in time, you will become a great teacher and healer. You have a natural ability to understand the word and the works of God, my child. You also have the mark of the high priestess, the disc of the sun, upon your brow and within your heart. That is a position you will assume with time, as well. Until you are ready, Sister Anna will fulfill those duties. However, on this night I pass the lineage to you, a task that must occur face to face, high priestess to high priestess. As I gift to you the story of my life, there will be parts of it you will not understand, the politics of men and their struggle for power, but it will reach you on some level. I am obliged to leave out nothing of importance.

"So, Gabriella, we begin. I was born in the city of Capernaum which sits along the Sea of Galilee. That was sixty years ago. My father, whose name was Syrus, was the chief priest of the synagogue in Capernaum. He was born to the Jairite priestly clan which serviced many of the synagogues in our region. My mother, Eucharia, was of the royal house of the Hasmonaeans who had ruled Judaea before I was born and who were defeated by the Romans. Her father, Menahem, founded the Samaritan Magi, a branch of the brotherhood in our region. These magi came to honor my beloved, Jeshua, at his birth and during my time with Jeshua, were led by our dear friend, Simon Zebedee. My mother was considered the most beautiful woman in Capernaum and she looked, to me, like a queen. I had good blood by Jewish standards. This was necessary for the completion of my mission. I had some consciousness about my soul and the other realms as a small child. I have always held a memory of God and became something of a channel for wisdom that my higher self carried.

"So, as you might imagine, I was a strange child and truly strange things started coming from my mouth from the age of three onward. I told my parents of the great beings who oversee the evolution of consciousness on Earth and told them many things about my future. They did not laugh at me, but listened intently. They knew, I am sure, that I had the gift of prophecy, but it was never my intention to be a prophetess. I was just open to my gifts at a very early age. Probably this was the result of many lifetimes struggling to achieve enlightenment. After many such lives, it is possible to have a spontaneous remembrance revealing something of one's light. I think this is what was happening to me as a child.

"My family was wealthy so there was no need for me to labor in our home. I spent every minute I could in nature, at the sea, by the rivers, on the hillsides, and in the meadows. I was nature's child. Mother Earth helped me to hold my light and increase it. Oh, Gabriella, I have so loved the Earth. It is for that reason that I had agreed to come to serve here and that I will continue to watch over her when I leave. She is going to become a brilliant star someday, my child. She will come into her light. too.

"My most vivid memory from childhood was the visit of Jeshua and his mother. She was the Magda-elder, the high priestess at Qumran, and was called Mary. She was your great-grandmother, Gabriella. Jeshua had completed his childhood studies and had been through his raising the year before, which would have made him about thirteen years old. I would have been four years old, a small child, at the time. It was the first time I had met either of them for they lived with the Essenes at Qumran. Mary had left her younger sons, James and Joses, at Qumran, and had traveled with Jeshua and Simon Zebedee north, along the Jordan, to see my mother. She and my mother had been good friends before Mary was called to join the order and moved to Qumran. When they arrived, I rushed right into the arms of Jeshua who hugged me and twirled me in the air above him. He was already strong of body, but not like Simon who was built like a bull - even then. There is a special grace that descends when twin souls first meet again on the Earth plane. I can only speak for myself and the feeling of great peace that filled my heart as I looked into Jeshua's soft blue eyes. It elevated my consciousness to incorporate him into my vision of this Earth Mission for he was so integral to much of it. We three children knew our importance to each other immediately and took the first opportunity to steal away to the water, leaving mother and Mary deep in conversation.

"I showed Jeshua and Simon my love of simply being and did not think of the serious tasks that lay ahead of us. We skipped stones instead. Laughing, we ran about, and sometimes I was on Simon's shoulders. That night my parents allowed me to go with the boys to the hillside and sit beneath the stars. Jeshua spoke

[131]

of our star, pointing it out and he also showed us a very bright star that was about to set, saying we had a deep commitment to that planet, Venus, as well as Earth and would feel equally at home there. I made him tell me stories, all that he could remember, of our life on the star. He told me of great wars in the middle of Orion, energetic gateways or portals to deep space, and the Heart of God. I was enthralled, all the while sitting on his lap. I never wanted to be outside his heart space, Gabriella. He was open and loving like no one I had met, and not from his training - at least not at that point. It was the degree to which he naturally held light and love within his being. Even at thirteen he was teaching me to be fully open and to love. Those were cherished moments because they were carefree and conscious at the same time. I was blissful, as though I was being held in the arms of God.

"At the time of his visit, he had just finished his studies at Qumran and was about to embark on the next part of his mission. He told me he was being sent to Egypt to live and study at the Therapeutae. I must have looked alarmed for he told me not to worry, that he would return to me, of that I could be sure. He lovingly teased me a bit about being only four years old and that brought a smile to my face. Simon was taking all of this in with his usual ease. He would be a life long friend to both of us. He was studying at Qumran to become the next head of the magi. We turned our conversations to magic and I had the best time listening to Simon's stories. I remember Jeshua's gentle laughter, the softness of his voice, and the reddish-golden curls of his long hair. Simon wore his black hair loose and wild, down to his shoulders. His eyes were intense, brown and not nearly as large as Jeshua's. Perhaps it was the softness of Jeshua's eyes that made them look so deep and large. I remember them as being very kind.

"Our guests stayed for four days, affording me many opportunities to speak with Jeshua and his mother. She was a woman of serenity and delicate, almost childlike, beauty, and unfathomable depth. I was to find out much later that my mother had called her to Capernaum to look at me, the strange little girl who spoke of the stars. Mary returned to Qumran knowing that she had located the next in the lineage of the codes of light in the daughter of her friend, Eucharia. She saw the golden disc upon my brow and in my heart even as I ran past her into the arms of Jeshua that first day. Her vision was as clear as my own would be for she too was an Akhu, but from the star Arcturus. Her soul was called to collaborate with our program to bring forth the energy of the Divine Mother upon the Earth. This energy will nurture humanity during the troubled times ahead and help the Earth prepare for her ascension. You will hear much more about your great-grandmother as I continue for we became very dear friends. When she, Jeshua and Simon left that day I did not know that she would call for me at my raising. My four-year old vision was oddly focused on the greater Mission rather than the details of my life. I did not know that I would go to live as a sister at Qumran, and I did not know that I would not see Jeshua again for over twelve years. I did know that I loved him from the depths of my soul. I held those days in the very center of my heart, dear one. I knew that my destiny was intertwined with Jeshua's.

"He and his mother gifted me with a sense of peace and trust which saw me through the remainder of my childhood, allowing me to enjoy my youth. I knew that everything would be as it should be. When I was five my parents brought a very good teacher into our home to tutor me. I was taught to write and speak Latin and Greek in addition to my own Aramaic and Hebrew languages. I was taught the history of the known world, basic mathematics, the legends and myths of all people, and, at my urging, some astronomy and astrology. For the latter, my parents searched all the way to Jerusalem for a tutor. I loved learning and had a quick mind. When younger brothers and sisters came into my life I swept them up and introduced them to the glories of the Earth. It was a wonderful time as I recollect it. I loved my parents very much. They gave me every opportunity in life which was most unusual for a girl child. Mother also taught me the womanly arts, but sewing, cooking, weaving and the like were not strong interests for me. I did like the garden, the growing of food, and the mixing of medicinal herbs. Now I know that these were strong within the lineage of light.

"Father let me try catching fish and taught me about money, fairness in business, and how to bargain - though Mother was much better at this than my father. I wanted to help him at the synagogue, but was forbidden entrance except in the women's section on the Sabbath. I wanted to know why. He was firm about the rules but handled me delicately for a chief priest. By then, I was eight years old, and better educated than any boy my age - perhaps any boy of any age in Capernaum. I can recall the conversations very clearly, Gabriella. Listening intently to all he had to say, I allowed it to enter my heart, then I would feel something move within me, as though the wind had blown open a golden doorway. Words came to me. They were my words but they felt like someone else's. I looked him squarely in the eyes and said, "Beloved Father, I know God, and God does not see me as separate. God sees me as God. Please excuse me from the Sabbath for my heart must align with its truth. I know that your religion honors the role of women, but the role is not in equality." He was at a loss for words. Any other father would have punished me severely, especially one who was chief priest. But I was not impudent or angry, simply stating the truth as it came from my Essence. I really believe that he heard me, and I understand now that I came into my truth, aligned fully with my higher self, that day. It was that higher part of me speaking from my wisdom. He had activated that code within me. I had had no use for it, even though it was within me previous to that day - truly, from birth. Sometimes the challenges in life are the greatest gifts, my child. We cannot predict how or when the codes will open or be activated within us. Oftentimes it is with conflict.

"Jeshua and I had both made soul commitments to heal our bloodlines. I was faced with the priestly clan of Jairus and the Hasmonaean dynasty with their warlord guerrillas, the Macabees. Jeshua would heal the blood of the House of David so that all those following him in the lineage would be free of the karma, beliefs, and patterns that had evolved over the millennia. His mother's blood was pure, healed by the Divine Love of her own incarnation. For both of us, there were hierarchical and patriarchal institutions and patterns of exclusivity, greed, violence, discrimination and self-righteousness all blinding the blood from the truth. We could look back on our common ancient heritage and see a warring, near barbaric tribe of people who conquered and deprived others of their homelands. There was an ancestral ego in need of healing as well, for all the transgressions done in the name of Yahweh and their desire to be the chosen ones. I began that process with my father as I stayed in my truth meeting his conditioned beliefs face to face. Something dissolved in him, perhaps a melting of these beliefs, at least to some degree. Jeshua and I healed these useless energies in our blood so that you and all those who sprang forth from us could be released from them as well. Now we are pursued by those who embody them, including our own people who do not understand our mission. It will continue until they awaken from their slumber.

"Jeshua and I went further, Gabriella. We healed our soul lineages, freeing all those souls in the lineage of light and the brotherhood from the grip of separation, opening the door for resurrection, ascension, and complete enlightenment, whenever

Mary

those souls would incarnate. This was a gift for the future for many of those souls would come to Earth to assist in her ascension. Jeshua demonstrated complete soul healing - taking his own healing to the level of the collective. It will be a long time before this is fully understood because it moves in the energetic planes and is not visible in this reality. One day, many people will remember who they truly are and, in an instant, will release all the pain and misery they have carried in their blood and soul memory. It will be replaced with love in the heart and crystals of light will open in their blood. This is what Jeshua and I have released into the energetic field of the Earth. We have seeded a Golden Age for the future and we will guide humanity toward it, from other dimensions, as its time approaches.

"I have run ahead in my story for I was yet a small girl when I became impassioned about my father, but no matter. My father was powerless to change the rules of the synagogue and never confronted me about my absence on the Sabbath. I spent my time with the Earth. In fact, I was sitting on the Earth one Sabbath in a grassy meadow near the sea when I first had my menstrual bleeding. I was not quite fourteen, the year in which girls experienced their raising ceremony, but Mother had shared some of the mysteries with me. I felt the warm liquid. The Earth pulled it from me. I lifted my skirt and sat upon the Earth allowing her to be nourished by my feminine power, giving her back what she had given me. Staying there until the Sun was low in the sky, I then slowly walked home leaving little drops of blood along the way. Mother was very excited. She had had everything prepared for that day and supplied me with pieces of sheepskin sewn to ties that held them in place. I was content to sit on the Earth but did as Mother expected since my natural plan would not always be convenient, especially when sleeping.

"The next day she asked me to sit with her in the morning Sun. It was her way of welcoming me to the women's world. I did so, and she began to talk. She began to reveal the plan that she and Mary, Jeshua's mother, had made for me. I would be fourteen in several months. Ordinarily a young girl would be betrothed after her raising but we had never spoken of husbands. She told me that I was being invited to join Mary's Order of Dan, the lay Nazarite sisters, at Qumran. She made no mention of the lineage of the codes of light because Mary had not told her who I really was. Also, she said nothing of the solar discs. Simply, she said that I was to join the sisters. It was the greatest honor imaginable. I had asked about Jeshua, but there was no news of his

[135]

return. Often, I felt him in my heart space, and I would be at Qumran when he returned. I was ecstatic. Of course I would miss my parents but usually a girl did not stay at home past fifteen. My parents task was completed with me. I was to be received at Qumran at the time of my raising as a highly educated young woman who knew her truth, but had had little chance to exercise it.

"When that time came, Mother and Father both accompanied me to Qumran. We followed the Jordan south from the Sea of Galilee, and found the community just inland from the Judaean hills which overlooked the sea. My need to be nourished by water was to be well satisfied. It did not seem to matter that it was "dead" water. Mary was told of our approach and went to the edge of the village to greet us. There are quite a strange array of mud brick buildings, housing tents, and open air workshops. I came with nothing, as instructed. My father, I believe, may have given the community my dowry, a custom I became aware of when I rose to a position of authority, but I cannot say for certain. My parents were housed in guest quarters and I was taken to a tiny room that I would share with another young novice. Suddenly my life was simplified in a way I had not thought possible. I felt very free. My parents were given tours of the public parts of the community and talked freely with the scribes and younger priests. I know that Father had some lively philosophical discussions and was quite happy being there. Mother and Mary were with each other much of the day and evening, watching their children play, mending robes and just chatting.

"I was called to my raising two days after we arrived. Mother had brought a white linen robe for the occasion. She would take it back to Capernaum with her for my sister's raising years hence. I would be given the dark blue robes of the novice. Mary wore the black robes of the Magda-elder, the Miriam, the high priestess of the Order of Dan. That is how she acquired the name Mary. She was in her mid-forties at that time. I did not acquire the title until she retired to Alexandria after your mother was born, Gabriella. I was named Miriam, more commonly Mary, at my birth, but in the community I was officially known as sister until I assumed her position. It made things very simple. Most of us were just called sister.

"At the raising ceremony there were four young women all of whom were joining the order. Our mothers stood behind us. The ceremony was held in a temple room dedicated to Isis the great Mother Goddess. That seemed strange to me at the time since the

Jews were quite adamant about the one male God. I learned later that it was a compromise the council had made with the priestesses who were there long before. My learning would go far beyond that, my child, but let me continue without further digression. Mary was announced and came quietly into the room to stand before us. One of her most remarkable gifts was the ability to move without creating the slightest stir. Even her feet touching the floor could not be heard. I would one day learn to be as graceful but at that time I felt more like an ox.

"Mary spoke the words of the blood mysteries to us in a soft, lilting voice. I am quite certain that I became entranced for I have little recollection of her words. The moment was beautiful for all of us. We were given red flowers to symbolize the blood and were each handed the blue robes of the novice. A celebration dinner was held that evening for anyone wishing to attend. I was happy that my father was able to participate in this way with Mother. After dinner we four novices were taken to separate places for our intiatory rites with the priestesses. My mother and Mary took me with a group of six priestesses to one of the caves overlooking the sea. In the cave there were oil lamps and soft skins, flowers and a small copper face of the Sun. While the women finished preparing the space, Mary took me atop the hill to watch the setting Sun. She taught me the ritual of bringing the Sun's energy into my eyes to feed my energetic body. It awoke something within me, a deep remembrance of having done this many times before.

"She told me of the life of Mir-An-Da, the one we call Isis now, and something more opened within me. She told me of the star, Sirius, which was called the Sun behind the Sun, for in the times of Mir-An-Da, each Sothic new year began when the Sun and Sirius rose together at dawn in the eastern sky. As she told me these things, she watched me carefully, measuring my responses on all levels of being. I could feel a power stir within me, the arousal of my Essence. She held the palm of her delicate hand between my brows telling me of the solar disc there. Her hand began to burn me but really it was melting away the illusions of this world, Gabriella. Inside my head, I saw images of setting suns, of water, of oil lamps and dark caves. I saw a beautiful young woman, golden-haired and blue-eyed. As I watched, I saw her move through her life, her marriage to a god-like man, her children, her gardens, her temple, the six-pointed star of sapphires and a shimmering golden disc of the Sun. I no longer felt the heat of Mary's hand but rather the cool breezes on the water as a barge, like a ghost, moved across the lake. Then I saw the temple baths, the great lion, the rising Sun and union with the light. I was faint with ecstasy and remembrance for part of my soul experienced Mir-An-Da's life. Removing her hand, Mary held me upright, gently grasping my shoulders. She looked into my eyes dropping to one knee and asked, "Sister, do you know who you are? Do you know the power of the lineage that you carry?" Tears filled my eyes as I came into her arms whispering "yes".

"She soothed me, stroking my dampened cheek. When I was calm again, she placed in my hand six tiny sapphires, asking me to begin using my memory to work with energy. She told me that I would be a master of energy again and use it to further the Mission. Mary explained why she had opened me to my wisdom and inner sight that night. My life and my work would be such that I needed to know who I was at that moment. There were to be no illusions from that point on. I think more than the ritual that followed, Mary brought me into adulthood in those remarkable moments we spent together at sunset. She handed me a small purse for the crystals which I slipped into the pocket of my new robes. I was led to the cave where the women awaited us. Using the ceremony that Mir-An-Da had given to the first priestesses of Annu, they brought my body into the full awareness of its womanness. Mary slipped the sacred crystal within me and broke the seal of my virginity. I rode the waves of bliss as my sisters' sensuous hands massaged and caressed my body with their perfumed oils. I was so happy that my mother could experience this with me since she was really giving me away at that moment.

"I was fully instructed in the pleasures of love-making with both men and women. Ordinarily the young priestesses would enter into sacred union with young men at their raisings to instruct them in the ways of pleasing women, but I was forbidden from this practice. There were a number of women's orders at Qumran. The heads of these orders, the Miriams and the Marthas, represented the women of the entire community. In addition, there were many women who were the wives of the scribes and other officials, and artisans, the working people of the community avowed to no order. During my youth, I lived with the celibate sisters of the Order of Dan and studied *The Way*, the teachings of the community. In addition, I had daily meetings with Mary who shared with me the truth of this community. I knew from my history that the Hasidim came to Qumran when the Hasmonaeans, my worldly ancestors, had turned the people away from the disciplines of the Torah. That was when the Davidic lineage and the

Zadok lineage came to Qumran as well. What I hadn't been taught was that a community already existed at Qumran and had existed through the whole of the exile in Babylon. Mary told me of the brotherhood and the lineage of light coming together at Qumran and the cooperation and eventual merging of their communities. They lived simply, the women holding the vibrations for the evolution of consciousness, and the men keeping the teachings and crafts of Aman-Ra alive through right action. Both did so in complete secrecy. There were many distortions of the crafts of the brotherhood arising out of Egypt. The true teachings and powers had not been in the hands of the Egyptian kings since before the deluge. The brotherhood alone held the true power of Aman-Ra's teachings. I remembered Simon Zebedee and his stories of the magi. Of course, he told me children's stories of magic and wonder, but I now realized that he was truly studying to be a wizard.

"One day, after I had been at Qumran over a year, I asked Mary why I had not seen Simon and she told me that he had gone to Egypt with Jeshua. That allowed me to ask about Jeshua who was never spoken of at Qumran, but who was on my mind a great deal. Mary told me that he and Simon had studied for six years at Heliopolis, receiving the full initiations into the brotherhood. They could have been initiated at Qumran but they deliberately chose to study elsewhere. Then they had moved to Alexandria where they acquainted themselves with the thinking of the Greeks. Now, she thought Jeshua and Simon were far away on the Isle of Britain involved in a mysterious mission. Her second son, James, had followed them to the Therapeutae and they had all gone off to Britain together. She told me they would return soon and would be very surprised at how I had matured. I laughed, remembering myself at four years of age. Mary longed for his safe return as well, for in his absence, he had been qualified as the Davidic heir, next in line to her husband Joseph who was fast approaching seventy years of age. That day is still clear in my memory for it was then that she told me of the laws of marriage for the kings. These laws were very old. They represented a mixture of ancient teachings and an attempt at deliberate spacing of kingly reigns. They were also born of the loveless marriages that were the product of political maneuvering. When the Jews came out of Babylon, those who had stayed behind in Judaea were surprised to see that the law had been altered in a significant way to favor a more balanced energy in the kings.

"The structure of the dynastic marriage was rigid. The king

and future queen were betrothed in June when the Sun was at its peak. A first marriage would take place in September, the month of atonement, but the couple was only permitted to have intercourse in December, through the time of the new moon. If a child was conceived it would be safe by March to have a second, consecrated marriage for an heir was imminent and would be born during the month of atonement. I was astounded. I had never heard of such a thing. She assured me that it was true for it was her experience with Joseph. Conception in December brought more feminine energy into the child for the Sun was low in the sky. In the old days it was quite the other way around with the month of intercourse being June which brought the fullness of masculine energy to the king. I supposed that the elders' experience in exile gave them time to ponder the wisdom of this arrangement since it was the warrior nature of the kings that put them there.

"I asked why Jeshua should be questioned as rightful heir since he was her first-born son. It was then that she revealed to me that he was born in March, precisely as it would have been in the ancient days. I asked if she and Joseph were punished for their behavior. She smiled and told me there was nothing that could be punished. Joseph was forty years old, a master of the craft, high in the brotherhood. She was eighteen years old, a celibate priestess of the lineage coming into a prearranged marriage. He left immediately after the betrothal for Heliopolis and she had felt her womb quicken without intercourse. She revealed to me that she had used the same technique to enter her mother's womb. There were patterns of the stars in the heavens, she explained, that matched the destiny of Jeshua and so he was born, at Qumran on the first day of March. On some level I understood her, for if a magi could appear and then disappear leaving seemingly empty space, and if Aman-Ra could manifest himself from nothingness, the implanting of life in a womb was not a great challenge for the Akhus. She asked me to go deep inside myself and see what my truth said about it. I had the full recollection of having participated in many such events as both child and mother. She and Jeshua were trying to purify the blood of the Davidic lineage or at the very least arrive in this world untainted themselves. I had chosen otherwise in this life for I was primarily responsible for the codes of light. I would not need their level of purification for my mission was quite different although it interconnected completely with theirs.

"So our beloved Jeshua was a son of the Sun, Gabriella. The

council of Qumran, of which Joseph was a member, spent many years debating Jeshua's legitimacy. Finally, in the face of Joseph's failing health, they voted in favor of Jeshua, the elder son, rather than James, his younger brother who had been born within the lawful structure of the dynastic marriage. I was at a loss to understand the importance of it all since there was no kingdom to rule. Anyone attempting to claim a throne would be crucified in an instant by the Romans. She quite agreed with me and explained further that the Davidic heir represented the common father of the land while the Zadok headed the spiritual hierarchy and had much of the authority within the community. The position of the father of the community was one of loving service. She used an old word, *ma-at*, to describe this and it struck a chord in my heart. It was kingly service, love without condition, without class structure, without a reason. I could see then that there existed in the community a very rigid hierarchy of men, whose principle concern was debating and interpreting the laws of Yahweh and giving those interpretations to the many scribes of Qumran who wrote them down. This had been going on for over a hundred years. Within the writings was an incorporation of some of the old teachings from the brotherhood.

"When I asked Mary how the women fit into the community she told me that when the Hasidim came to Qumran they brought their laws and scriptures with them. They had spent all their years in exile inventing new laws to uphold purity and they wrote down the history of their people as well as they knew it. The patriarchy was supported in all their endeavors. They arrived at Qumran, with the king and the Zadok, declaring that women were unclean. Men participating in intercourse went through elaborate ritual bathing to cleanse themselves before coming back to the priestly life. Can you imagine, Gabriella? Menstruating women were considered untouchable - evil. It was a complete rejection of the feminine, of the Mother, the Earth. The women of the lineage of light refused to have anything to do with them and continued to interact with the brotherhood, but these strong-willed patriarchs prevailed and managed to enforce their laws onto the brothers and sisters. There were conflicts over hierarchy amongst the women of the community too, but there was such a solidarity within the sisterhood of Annu about these issues of discrimination that we seldom argued with each other.

"At Qumran, all foods were alive when eaten, including fruits, grains and grasses. There were restrictions about where and when one could walk, when it was appropriate to speak and, as I have already described, about sexuality and marriage. The way the Hasidim came to control Qumran was no different than the many times our ancestors had forced a people into submission. All the knowledge about food, fasting and the purification of the body as a temple had already been practiced by the brothers and sisters. Many of the laws were benificial, upholding virtuous behavior and good health, but many were foolish restrictions created by the patriarchal group of law-givers. When combined with the ritual practices of the early people of Qumran they appeared as an attempt at purity which penetrated only the physical layer of their being. In the deeper layers they were self-righteous and judgmental, hierarchical, rigid and very elite. I saw none of this in Mary, Jeshua, his brothers and sisters, nor the community brothers and sisters, even though some of them were appointed to high positions. The community was beginning to manifest the division that had been infiltrating it since the arrival of the law-givers. The brothers and sisters went into secrecy again as they had in the past, becoming the inner core of the Essene community. The truth would not die. It could not.

"After learning of the politics of Qumran, I became very attentive to everything said and done by the men in the community. Understanding their politics and motivations, I was trying to imagine how Jeshua might act as the common father among them one day. Well, it was impossible to imagine unless he had been transformed into a patriarch while in Egypt. It wasn't long before Mary received word of his return from Egypt.

The three travelers had stopped in Egypt for a short respite before returning to Qumran. Just before her son's homecoming, Mary allowed me to spend much of my time in the hills overlooking the sea. These were wonderfully meditative times for me when I connected fully with the Earth, her elements, and the heavens. Each day, I filled myself with the energy and asked that any impurities be cast away to be absorbed by the Earth. I became more centered and more vibrant. One day, I was in a particularly clear place when I saw Jeshua climbing up the hill to find me. Mary had sent him shortly after he had arrived at Qumran. He had taken the time to bathe and shave his face before coming after me. I arose and ran to his arms which enveloped me. He held me close to his heart and I felt it open to receive me. He called me 'his Mary'.

"He noticed that I was no longer a child. I had filled out considerably by sixteen and the sexual energy stirred within both of us. He kissed me firmly on the lips and held me for a very long time. I remember wishing that it would never end, that we could just merge into each other and become one. But we were both celibates at the time and knew better than to allow desire to rule us and risk ruining the greater Mission. Day after day, we spent in the hills, sometimes with Simon and James but usually on our own. Jeshua told me everything that had happened on his journeys.

"The first six years they stayed in Egypt. He and Simon were taken into the Therapeutae as first degree initiates within three months. During that time they were observed and questioned. The initiation took place in a temple building in front of the whole Therapeutae. He did not reveal the details of the initiation but said that it was one in which they stated their intention to join the brotherhood. Because they had both been raised as part of the community of brothers, it was assumed that this initiation would be given.

"They were then sent off to study with the brothers - to survey all of the crafts. Simon's interest in the magi was well known but he learned something of the other crafts as well. Jeshua was more drawn to healing, especially the use of energy in healing. I guessed that if he combined that with the magnitude of his heart love he would be a revolutionary healer. There were few men I knew with his compassion and openness of heart. At the same time, he had excelled at the geometry of high magic and numbers. At the end of their first year, they were given the second degree initiation and began studying the ancient teachings, which they had begun in a small way at Qumran with the brothers there. They both did well in their studies and received the third degree initiation at the end of the third year. For this, they were taken across the Nile to a temple building that stands before the Sphinx. The Sphinx, Gabriella, is an enormous carved lion with a human face that sits like a mountain facing the rising Sun. Jeshua said it had been built by Aman-Ra long before the deluge. It was ancient. They were bathed in sacred waters and initiated between the paws of the beast at sunrise. It was an ancient custom to align one with the Sun and the stars. When the Sun hit his body, Jeshua had the feeling of coming apart, of little pieces of him starting to fly on their own. The master who initiated them used a secret word to pull Jeshua, for he saw him begin to disappear. From that time on, the brothers paid particular attention to him. Simon was completely engrossed in the study of alchemy and James, who had arrived about that time, began his initial studies, so neither of them seemed to notice that Jeshua was meeting with the high masters.

"In the same way that Mary had seen me as a part of Mir-An-Da, the masters saw Jeshua as the complete incarnate soul of Aman-Ra. They used all their magic to open him to the mysteries that he knew so well. He was taken to secret chambers in the pyramids and beneath the Sphinx where mysterious ceremonies were conducted. He passed through three additional levels of initiation without anyone knowing aside from his teachers. Near the end of his time there, he began bringing teachings through from his higher being that were crystal clear, simple and profound. He was encouraged to record them and was assigned a scribe to assist him. Allowing me to read what he had written, I wept, recognizing the teachings from the stars and Venus. These would not be accepted by the Hasidim at Qumran, but seemed not to be written for them; rather, they were written for the simple folk in the villages and the gentiles - those who still believed there was a feminine aspect of God. When he left Heliopolis, Jeshua was a master healer but, secretly, he was a grand master of the brotherhood as well. He was recognized as a direct link to the stars.

"During his sixth and last initiation, he had undergone a symbolic death ceremony in which he was given a potion to drink. It was bitter, vile, but put him into a deep trance sleep immediately. He was led by a strange looking being of light out to the star Sirius, where he met the Siriun High Council. At their approval, he was taken to the Great White Lodge of the brotherhood and the initiation was completed with the ascended masters. His participation in their Planetary Ascension Program was revealed to him and he was told to come to them whenever assistance was needed. He saw past death and had no fear of it.

"By that time James had finished his third initiation. He and Simon accompanied Jeshua to Alexandria. There they were in the center of new thought, primarily Hellenistic, which they discussed and debated every day. It was a time of mental exercise and the formulation of a new philosophy based on the wisdom moving through Jeshua that he would one day teach to all people. They spent a great deal of time in the libraries of Alexandria which contained most of the known information in the world. There Jeshua began to have visions which reached far into the future. He saw the geometry of the Earth grids - the lines of energy on the Earth - and the geometry of the celestial grid of ascension consciousness that he would put into place with his work. I was told that I held the codes of this consciousness and he was to act on them. He spoke with Simon and James of important places on the Earth where the two grids were to be connected, where important future events would occur. From their conversations and what became a highly motivated study of the world, they developed a plan.

"It was this plan that took them to Britain and Caledonia. Britain was to be the land to which James would bring the new teachings in the future. There was a place there, in the west country, where he was to establish a following. It would be important in the distant future for it served as a connection between the Earth and celestial grids. It could act as a doorway to other dimensions for this reason. The three initiated brothers sailed to Britain from Alexandria, stopping for a brief time on the coast of Iberia. They spent several years in Britain working with the land and teaching the people. The land was prepared to receive the grid connection. It was called Glastonbury by the Britons. The people were also very receptive to the teachings for they lacked the rigidity that existed in Judaea. They moved north into Caledonia and its northern isles and activated grids within the Earth that would hold the future of the bloodline of David and the secret teachings of the brotherhood. After finishing their work in Britain they sailed to Gaul and crossed to the Mediterranean by land. Near the sea, just inland from Massilia, they located another sacred part of the land, not for grid connection so much as the germination of the philosophy. They worked with the land there to connect the brotherhood and secure the region for the lineage of light. This geometry was set in a way that connected this land to Venus. Gabriella, you were born on that land and we sit upon it at this moment. It will not be protected forever, but long enough to allow the seed to germinate and not be lost. From Gaul, they journeyed back to Alexandria and then to Qumran.

"It took weeks for Jeshua to tell me the details. I am giving you the important points only. His sixth initiation was the ancient king-making ritual from Aman-Ra, though in Aman-Ra's time it was for both kings and queens. He had passed through the doorway of death and had survived. The grand master had not received this initiation though he held the power to administer it. No one had received it since the time of Thoth who bestowed it on the Divine lineage of ancient Egypt. Thoth was Aman-Ra incarnate and came to reestablish the mysteries that the kings and brothers were losing as they slipped into human consciousness. Since the time of Thoth, the brotherhood had been holding the king-making ritual in secrecy for the one who was to uplift human consciousness once more. Jeshua was nineteen years old

[145]

at the time. His mother and I were the only two people who knew the entire story of Jeshua's time away because she and I were the pillars of the new temple. She held the energy of the Divine Mother, and I the Earth Mother. We were white and black, the representations of the duality as well.

"I knew my calling, but all this was quite overwhelming for me. You can imagine my shock when Jeshua announced that he was leaving again. We were sitting in our favorite spot overlooking the sea. He'd been reading his notes about compassion to me and I was deeply moved. Then he turned to me and said he would be going away again for a little time. Tears welled up in my eyes and he took me in his arms. He promised that he would return as soon as he had finished what awaited him. I asked where he was going and he did not hesitate to tell me. He would journey to the high mountains of Tibet and India. I knew that his would never be a normal life and, with some difficulty, let go of my attachment to him. I felt as if I were in the center of a whirlwind. All that I could do was sit still. This was good, for it was exactly what he asked of me. Jeshua asked me to anchor the grid right where I was sitting. I would always be connected to him in that way and we would be doing what we had come to do. My task was to tap into the Earth and send him the energy. Later in our lives we would see this reverse - he would send me the lightening and I would ground it into the Earth. It was how we worked together. He asked me to practice *ma-at*, goodness freely given, at every opportunity, to prepare me for the future.

"Several more months passed before he left but the energy of his withdrawal was apparent. He would never stay long at Qumran for he did not agree with the council or Hasidim. Not one to argue, he sought out those who understood him. Simon stayed behind and became quite active with the Zealots, a group of political terrorists who wanted to end Roman rule in Judaea. He also practiced high magic and was my greatest ally amongst the brothers. Simon was the lover of Salome, a priestess in the Order of Asher. She was a very powerful young woman, a master of plant medicines, and was also very close to Mary. In time, we three women would be the dearest of friends. Jeshua asked James to stay at Qumran to represent the lineage of David should anything happen to their father, Joseph, who had grown increasingly frail. James would assume great responsibility at Qumran because Jeshua would refuse it. He could not live outside his truth. It would be an imprisonment for him. Needless to say he was not well liked by the Hasidim, the priests, or the council. They were

[146]

afraid of his new ideas. He confided to me that it would be easier to unite the pagans of Briton with these new concepts than the pious ones within his own community.

"Before he took his leave of me, we walked to our favorite spot together for the last time. Our feelings were too strong for many words. We spent a long time just sitting together, our hands joined. As the Sun began to sink behind the mountains to the west he turned to me and asked if I would make a promise to him. Of course I said I would, and he asked me to wait for him. He asked me to remain celibate, as he was, for one day he wished to make me his wife. It would not be soon and we would, necessarily, have a dynastic marriage. The time and space for it would be provided by the plan. He held me to his heart as I wept again. I had strong emotions with Jeshua as he seemed to open my heart and expose my every feeling. In truth, I told him I would gladly wait for him, for there was truly no other in my life. He knew that the celibate priestesses kept the spark within alive by loving each other and he had no objection. This was absolutely sacred to us - a ritualistic practice of pleasuring much like our raising ceremonies. Jeshua told me that he would bring the sacred spikenard ointment from the high Himalayas for our wedding. It would be the finest, the most fragrant in all Judaea. I asked him if he had told his parents of his plans. He had told Mary but not Joseph. She had felt his choice was a good one. He said that Joseph would not be alive when he returned. He had spent a great deal of time with his father while visiting Qumran for he knew he would not see him again in this life. We parted again, as he rode off with his uncle's caravan to the far east.

"Mary arranged for my entrance into the Therapeutae at that time, to learn the healing skills of the brotherhood. Studying with the energy masters and the masters of sacred geometry, I wanted to understand the spatial relationships in the grids that Jeshua described to me. They were fascinating - indeed captivating. I worked very hard to learn how to hold and move energy within the filamentous structure of the universe. Then, I was taught to bring that energy through me and into the human body to assist in eliminating disease and emotional distress. While maturing and discovering my calling, I frequently repeated some of Jeshua's writings to myself and his ideas began making a great deal of sense. He would be the common father of the people but not in the way they expected and not just the father of the Hasidim, the Sadducees and Pharisees. I saw him reaching out to touch the Gentiles and the Samaritans, the troubled, and the simple-minded.

[147]

He would be as father to all.

"Unbeknownst to himself but hardly unexpectedly, he came into that role just over three years after his leaving when his father, Joseph, died. James stepped in to play the role of the dynastic heir in Jeshua's absence without irritating anyone on the council. James really enjoyed the political life at Qumran and played the role very well. He would, eventually, lead Qumran while his brother set about his mission.

"It was shortly after her husband's death that Mary invited me to take the vows of the dedicated priestess. I saw no reason not to take them, since I had already fully engaged the Mission. The next step in commitment to the lineage, taking the vows, did not exclude marriage or sexual relations. In taking the vows, I found there were only ten priestesses of Annu at Qumran, which surprised me, for there were many sisters. Mary took me into a hidden temple, which was in a cave beneath her dwelling space. No one knew of this temple except the priestesses of Annu who were all gathered there in the darkness. A single flame burned in a large oil lamp, the eternal flame of Isis, which stood on an altar in front of a huge golden face of the Sun. It was my first time in this temple room and it took my breath away completely. The priestesses were gathered in a half-circle around the altar, in front of which Mary stood facing me as I knelt before her. Much like the first initiation that Jeshua went through in Egypt, I was asked to state my intent and repeat the vows of the order after Mary. These were promises to uphold in the living of my life - the teachings that had been handed down through the lineage from Mir-An-Da. I also agreed to speak to no one about the secrets of the order or about the temple room that I was in, for the brotherhood did not even know of it. Ours was an order where personal possessions and ownership were not permitted, so I was required to take a vow of poverty and detachment from the material world. I also agreed to love God and to find God in all those around me, to honor our mother the Earth, and to work in harmony with her elements.

"When my vows were finished, the priestesses came to embrace me as one of their own. They then left, climbing back up to Mary's quarters and the outside world. Mary and I were left in the temple together. It felt very uplifting to be in her radiance as well as that of the flame and the Sun. She asked me to sit upon some soft pillows which she laid before the altar. Mary explained that the high priestess would ordinarily spend some time with the vowed priestess discussing the women's calling within the order and the world. Since I was fully aware of my calling and she and I had spent many hours together already, she had decided to begin my training and assume her position at once. Questioning me about my meditations, the guides that came to me in dreams and meditations to counsel me, and any voices I might have heard within my head, she asked if I had ever been approached in meditation by a council of elders, the Akhus, to whom I had made my soul commitment. Nothing of this sort had ever happened to me. Mary was satisfied and explained that it needed to occur - that I needed to open myself to other realities.

"As soon as I assented, she walked over to a small chest standing in a wall niche and withdrew a tiny glazed earthenware vial. Bringing it to me, she bent to one knee, removed its stopper and told me to drink the contents. She said it would be bitter. I remembered the story that Jeshua had told me of his initiation in Egypt, and his experience of dying and I must have looked worried. Reading my thoughts, Mary assured me that this was a gentle potion used by the priestesses and the brothers to transport them into other dimensions. I would sink into a deep trance and she would lead me on a journey to the Siriun High Council with whom I needed to be in close contact for the years ahead. She felt this would open me to spontaneous journeys in the future so that I could speak to my superiors without needing the bitter potion. If, for any reason, I needed further assistance or wished to travel to other dimensional realities, including my own shadow reality, she would be happy to procure more of the potion from the magi who held the secrets of its formulation.

"I had to trust her decision and her sincerity, feeling that my life was in her hands. It would not be true to say that I was without doubts at that moment or during my life with Jeshua. Part of this life's work was to eliminate doubt. Betrayal and the loss of trust that accompanies it were past-life experiences for me that I wished to heal on a soul level. I would see the many faces of betrayal in my life and learn to trust in the Divine Plan without question. So I drank the bitter gall and forced myself not to gag. I had tasted bitter root medicines and some bitter vegetables but nothing can compare to snake venom for bitterness, Gabriella. Fortunately it was but a few minutes before I was slipping into an altered state of consciousness as your great-grandmother eased me down onto the pillows. As I began separating from the many layers of this reality, Mary, in a commanding voice, led me through the dark and sinister places into the light. She steered me in the direction of Sirius and to the Great White Lodge of Light where I found the High Council. They were waiting for me. Indeed, they are always waiting for us, Gabriella. They convene to serve us. Do not ask me what they are doing otherwise or simultaneously. I could not even guess. Maybe they exist only because we call them into existence.

"The chamber room was simple and the Akhus were direct with me. My job was to assist Jeshua with his Mission and correct his course when needed, for he would be pushed and pulled by those who had agendas different from his own. I was to act as a tower of strength until the moment when the tower shattered and the illusion would be revealed. The codes of consciousness I was holding would be opened by Jeshua and activated as the Divine Plan unfolded. Many of the codes involved resurrection and ascension but there were also codes of the feminine and the deep connection to the Earth that are necessary for spiritual enlightenment. They asked me not to weaken in the face of confrontation with others who feared me or were jealous. I had agreed to a life that would not be easy. My soul longed for mastery in union with God and so I had designed a life wherein I would experience separation in every conceivable way until I found the oneness within. What I learned of the codes of light was invaluable, Gabriella, and it is important that you understand this also. If you are carrying codes of consciousness one of your most important duties is the complete healing of all layers of self and its release. When enlightenment is attained, codes are activated that elevate planetary frequency. It helps no one for a woman of the lineage to turn away from her personal healing, or allow herself to be stuck like a mule in the mud.

"The High Council showed me what my higher self had designed for this life. I saw many visions of the future dance before me after they withdrew. Those visions have all come to pass, my child. I was horrified at the time. It all seemed utterly senseless. However, as the future unfolded, I could see the workings of the Divine within it. I have been back before the council many times since and have relied on their wisdom, especially when I arrived in Gaul. For a long time now I have not been before them for it seems that once one is willing to be received into the light, the wisdom is easily found within.

"Returning from my experience, I found Mary in her own deep trance, with my hand in hers. Gently squeezing her hand, I saw her astral self slip back into her body. She opened her eyes, smiled at me, and helped me to a sitting position. I felt a heaviness in my head but was otherwise alert and excited about my experience.

We sat and talked of the future together and held each other for a long time. We both possessed a great love for Jeshua.

As the years passed, my work became more focused. I learned the ways of the high priestess from Mary while opening myself to the sisters of the other orders and the lay women. My gift to them was a deep connection to the spirit of the Earth, and an understanding of her elements and playful spirits. Their gifts to me were many. I came to understand women and the deep archetypal patterns they carry in their blood and culture, seeing how they played out in myself and in the others. A suggestion that we begin meeting to speak of them in sisterhood evolved into a healing circle where a great wisdom that had been lost to most re-emerged from the unconscious. Our numbers grew and we gained a kind of power that the men never could understand. It was a knowingness of who we were, who we had been, and who we could be. If women do not connect to the Earth and learn to bring her energies through themselves, they are not able to tap into their innate powers. It was our purpose to learn to use that power to clear away old patterns of behavior. I could see the light increasing in all of us.

"My connection with the magi continued and I began working in our shelters for the sick, which dotted the landscape of Judaea. It was particularly important to remain healthy and clear when working with the sick. Without holding a high frequency you could not help anyone. By bringing a great light into the shelter, the sick would immediately begin to recover. This training was part of my apprenticeship with the Therapeutae who maintained a collaborative relationship with the core of Qumran, the council and scribes. They were brotherhood working as teachers and healers in loving service. It was work beyond the interpretation of scripture but many opinions were held by the Hasidim about intermingling with the wretched and sick. The brotherhood believed that all men and women were one, united in the energy of creation. I really enjoyed my time out in the world serving the sick. It was an opportunity to practice energy mastery and to apply the knowledge I had gained in my studies. I educated them about better ways to eat, cleanliness and honoring their bodies. Helping people and listening to the stories of those who were seldom heard were things I loved doing, and I found a place of peace in this service to the needy. All people are wise beings, Gabriella, even the most destitute."

*

Mary had sat in perfect stillness while allowing the story of her life to flow forth unabated. Gabriella sat patiently, and heard the coded messages that would awaken aspects of her mission within her. However, she had begun to squirm about so Mary stopped to allow her to run out where she could find a place to empty her bladder. On her return, Mary kissed her cheek and they both took long drinks of pure spring water before Mary continued her story.

*

"Jeshua returned from the east when I was twenty-four years of age. I hardly recognized him, Gabriella. It had been eight years but it was not age that had changed him. His hair was still golden-red and longer than it had been, but his face was bearded and he looked very thin, as if he had eaten little. He bore a radiance that was unmistakable. There was the presence of God within him. I was not at Qumran when he arrived so I did not see him before he had cleansed himself, rested and eaten of the food of life. On my return from our shelter near Bethany, I found him deep in conversation with the elders. He was telling them of the holy men and women he had encountered in the far east and the philosophical differences and similarities between the many religions he had now come to know. When I appeared in the courtyard, he was describing the thread of truth than ran through them all, and the foundation teachings of the Akhus, though he did not use that term with the law-givers who believed that Yahweh gave the law to Moses.

"When he saw me in the dusty purple robes of a traveling priestess he arose immediately. He was radiant, in the pure white linen of the Essenes, and I dropped my bundles to run into his arms. Gathering me up, he kissed me long upon the mouth, showing no shame for our love in the presence of his elders. I had forgotten that he was now the king, the common father of these people, and had grown into a mature man himself. Though feeling the leanness of his body as I embraced him, I did not concern myself with his health for he had become a temple of the Divine. His eyes had deepened, like bottomless pools, and were even softer than they had been. Also, his speech had softened. A gentle master, he had a strong conviction that reformation was in order for this community and for the Jews.

"I cleansed myself and changed into clean robes before we walked to our hillside spot overlooking the water. He would tell me nothing of his travels until he had heard every detail of my experience over those eight years. I had felt strongly connected to him many times and he knew of those times for he had felt my nurturing energy. Jeshua was delighted that I had developed my skills and was enjoying my service work at the shelters. He was also pleased that Mary and I spent so much time together and that I was learning the ways of the high priestess. Mary had seemed more vital than ever to him but his younger brothers and sister, who were all in their twenties, barely remembered him. He and James had been talking at length, and he showed some concern over James' love for leadership and his willingness to compromise with the Qumran elders. At the same time Jeshua was thankful James could do that, for he did not want to. Not only had the lineage of David passed to the next generation in Jeshua, the lineage of the Zadok, the high priest of Qumran, had passed from Zacharias to John, Jeshua's second cousin. Mary was of the Zadok blood lineage as well but inheritance patterns were long established to follow male descent. It was Jeshua and John, then, who upheld the two pillars of the community. Jeshua was the common father who carried the lineage of kingly service, and John was the high priest, the one anointed to lead the community spiritually. These were titles brought to Qumran by the Hasidim who depended on hierarchy to know who they were. Jeshua had no time for such conventions, for he saw all people as one with God and he let them know this.

"Neither did he support the recording of the interpretations of scriptures, let alone the continual discussion of their meaning which was the very core of the Hasidim. He let them know they were wasting their time and energy in these mental pursuits. God was to be found in all that contained life, in all that was of the Earth Mother, and not in the words of heavy books. In the far east. he had truly tapped into the universal matrix of God consciousness and his philosophy had become even more radical than before. Since he celebrated God in all life, he saw God in the members of the council, and he did not become angry at their blindness, but withdrew after stating his beliefs rather than causing further separation. The friends he gathered around him were of the brotherhood, his family, and the Hellenistic thinkers who were scattered about Judaea. He would not be long at Qumran as I had guessed, so we spent intensely sweet days together just after his return from the east.

"He spoke to me of holy men in India who sat in silence for years, high in the mountains. First, he studied in the Buddhist temples of the cities, but was later drawn further and further into the wilderness seeking those who were at one with God. Entering an ancient monastery in Tibet, where he had similar experiences with initiation to those in Egypt, Jeshua could see that all paths to enlightenment climbed the same mountain and eventually merged upon the peak in oneness. He did not allow dogma to enter his energetic field since it brought rigidity and lessened the light, and he had learned to filter out everything that was not pure. In that way, he elevated his consciousness with what remained - universal truth. After many years, the monks led him into the mountains to sit with the holy men. These androgynous beings were holding a consciousness for the planet that provided a doorway to those who sought enlightenment. It was an immense task for a planet plagued by wars and hatred, but there are many all over the Earth who have lived only to accomplish this purpose. The holy men taught him telepathically as he sat with them. He spent months fasting and learning to live upon the light.

"He told me of the last teacher with whom he sat. He was in a cave high in the mountains of eastern India. This man recognized the Buddha in Jeshua and after many months of meditation with this holy man, he had motioned Jeshua to kneel before him. He had placed his palm between Jeshua's brows over the place of the inner sight. A light energy had entered Jeshua, much like a bolt of lightening, and the holy man kept sending this light until even the deepest and most remote regions of his body vibrated with it in ecstasy. He had gifted him his enlightenment for he was ready to behold it. Jeshua lived in this light, Gabriella, in the light of pure ecstatic God-realization, for the rest of his life. He saw through every illusion of this twisted reality and remained ever conscious of his origins. There was nothing more for him to learn in the east so he came down from the mountains and traveled with the caravans back to Qumran, a journey which took nearly a year.

"He promised me that we would never be so far apart again but revealed his plans to leave Qumran once more. He had come to receive the ritual of kingship, a requirement of the bloodline of David. He had come to assess the political and religious energies of Qumran and Judaea. However, he was choosing to reside at the brothers' monastery at Mird which everyone called The Wilderness. There he could meditate and bring forth his future teachings. It was not yet time for him to come forward to the public, or for our union, although we experienced oneness in all dimensions beyond the physical. Part of his Mission to heal the bloodline entailed the fulfillment of prophecies regarding kingship and the messiah. He knew that John the Zadok was already working to shift the energies of his lineage, and prayed that he might succeed. They had spent many hours together in intense conversation at Qumran and though they did not always agree, they understood each other. John would also go to The Wilderness to prepare for his work teaching and initiating people in *The Way.*

"Mary arranged my work so that I would make frequent visits to the shelter near Mird where Jeshua and I could communicate in the physical. She knew that we would await the dynastic marriage for our consummation. Being with Jeshua had expanded my awareness one hundred fold. He had opened many codes of light within me, and my healing work, coupled with the simple teachings which he was bringing forth, became a passion for me. At the same time, I was helping people remember who they were and why they had come to the Earth, I was tending to their wounds of body, spirit, mind and soul. I have continued this work to this day, always expanding it as I grew in the light.

"At Mird, Jeshua brought through the teachings which would become associated with him and the peaceful, yet progressive, movement he would lead. These teachings were recorded by his personal scribe and put away for safe keeping. He did not need the records of them for he lived them every day. You have been brought up in these teachings, Gabriella, and know their power and simplicity. To see God in all things and to treat all things accordingly was the core of his message. One needed to practice the latter in order to realize the former. This is the path to enlightenment, Gabriella. To be one with the wind, the water, the fire and the Earth brings you into Oneness with God. You see how simple it is, but it requires that we not waste time or energy trying to be one with negative emotions - ours or others, nor with needless mental pursuits, for the mind knows oneness with God only through silence. We cannot hurt one living thing for that action will hurt all things, and all are equal and share equally in the grace of God. These were monumental concepts for our people, Gabriella, for they thought themselves as chosen by God. In fact they were chosen, chosen to receive this profound wisdom, but few of them really heard.

"After several years, John, the Zadok, left Mird to wander over Judaea baptizing people into *The Way.* This, to John, was a mixture of the traditional Essene teachings and those of Jeshua which guided his life. He did not seek the life of the esteemed high priest at Qumran but chose, instead, to reach the simple people of the countryside, preparing them for the coming of Jeshua who would not begin his public life for another year. Jeshua started to gather his core group of disciples around him while living at Mird. There would be twelve, the magic number of the brotherhoods and the bloodline. James and John were ministers of the brotherhood at Mird and our dear Simon was, at that time, head of the magi in the region of Qumran and a very active Zealot. Judas was chief of the scribes. Jeshua drew the leaders from the Therapeutae, the Zealots, gentile orders, and the royal families of Judaea. Peter and Andrew were the only common villagers among the twelve and they were loyal Essenes. As John went out to prepare the way, Jeshua discreetly gathered small groups of the twelve together at Mird to impart the teachings and purify their spirits, for there were those among them who looked down upon the gentiles. Also, there were several men with warrior blood and a group with scholarly mentalities. He tried to bring illumination to this unlikely group of brothers and, of course, he saw them all as one with God. So his preliminary teachings were to the disciples and, privately, to me. We met often at Mird, where I was welcomed as one of the sisters, and spent countless hours in the monastery gardens discussing *The Way* and the unfolding of our work. I would never be far from his side during the public work for I held the codes of consciousness upon which he was acting and I grounded the energies of the stars which he was bringing through his multi-dimensional self.

"In June of that next year, when I was twenty-seven and Jeshua was thirty-seven, we were betrothed. It was a quiet celebration held at Qumran in the presence of his mother, Simon, Salome, his brothers and sister and my parents. Our betrothal was officiated by the council since it was in accordance with dynastic law, but we preferred to celebrate with those who had been more a part of our lives. A few days prior to the official betrothal we had a more open betrothal feast at the house of a friend in Cana. Here, a larger group of people had gathered, including the disciples and their families. It was there that Jeshua first acted publicly when he offered a communion of wine to the gentiles who were considered unclean by the Jews. This created quite a stir as did his proclamation that all men were created equal in the eyes of God and that Yahweh, the Hebrew personification of God, was not exclusive to the Jews. Yahweh was as present in the birds of the air as in ourselves. The difference between the two was that the birds were at one with Yahweh and we denied or failed to honor that at-one-ment. This was how he set the tone of his Mission, Gabriella. That September, Jeshua inflamed the elders even further by appearing at the atonement services in the robes of a priest rather than king. He was declaring himself both priest and king in fulfillment of the very prophecies they labored to interpret.

"Shortly thereafter, we celebrated our first marriage in the home of Simon at Bethany. Jeshua had given me the sacred spikenard ointment when he had returned with it from India. I had put it away with my sacred items, oils and essences, and brought forth half of it for our first marriage. The rest I saved for the second marriage which did not take place until I had carried your mother in my womb for three months. That was over three years later. There were many friends present that day at Bethany, including Jeshua's circle of twelve disciples, his large family, many of the sisters and brothers of Qumran and Mird, and my own family. It was the marriage of the king and queen that had been passed down through the ages from Aman-Ra and Mir-An-Da. We spoke our vows in the gardens at Bethany before John the Zadok, and Mary the high priestess of Dan. We made it a celebration of the Earth and Jeshua spoke beautiful words about our relationship to the Sun, the moon, the stars, Mother Earth and all her creatures. We were all touched by his passionate prayer.

"Prior to the feasting, Jeshua was seated as king at the head of the table and I knelt before him with the spikenard and anointed and massaged his feet. This was the first marriage tradition, an act performed only by the new queen, and it symbolized the recognition of Jeshua as the common father of the land, the rightful king of the Davidic lineage. Because I was in the high priestess lineage, I was permitted to merge my essence with his by using my flowing long hair to wipe the spikenard from his feet and take the rich and royal ointment into my own being. We were as one, the marriage sealed. Simon, the perfect host, saw to every need of his guests and we honored him in every way. His affiliation with the Zealots had, in no way, diminished Jeshua's love for him. As chief of the Samaritan Magi, he was the most highly regarded of all the disciples. Judas, as chief of the scribes, was the other high ranking official. However, the difference between them was apparent since Simon possessed the depth of the secret teachings of the brotherhood and Judas had been trained in the transmission of scripture. They were both devoted to Jeshua but I felt, even then, that Judas had jealousies toward the other disciples and lacked discernment in his political affiliations. Jeshua saw the God-presence of all beings and, for the most part, overlooked the petty behaviors of this reality. What did concern him was the established hierarchy, their prejudices, and their preoccupation with mental activities.

"We began the ministry shortly after the wedding. It was in this way that Jeshua and I had intimacy, in the at-one-ment of the Mission, for the rules of dynastic marriage did not permit physical intimacy except for the two weeks prior to and including the new moon in December. He held me close to him often and kissed me deeply upon the mouth. It was not our choice to be trapped within the law of the bloodline, but we did comply with the dynastic law. It did not stop me from accompanying him everywhere. I sat at his feet to receive the teachings of my own enlightenment whenever I could. This riled some of the disciples, especially Peter who had no time for women. I was aware of his jealousies and was constantly on the alert during the remainder of my time in Judaea. Being the favored disciple, I lived the teachings with the master. What is more, I was literate in Greek, Aramaic, Hebrew and Latin and kept careful accounts of Jeshua's work. Years later, when I fled Judaea, Simon took my writings into the security of the brotherhood. They will be found one day, Gabriella, when the world is ready to receive the truth.

"When our time of coupling arrived that first year, we left the desert and journeyed into the northern hills together to a retreat of the brotherhood where we could be alone. We bathed in waterfalls, ran in green fields of wild flowers, and held each other in passionate embrace through each precious night. We learned to take our combined energetic presence into the higher realms while making love. I admit to allowing Jeshua to lead me into these higher frequencies for my baser self would surely have prevailed. Naturally, I was filled with the woman's urge to bring forth children and his desire was union with God. That first year, his energies were prevalent and I remained childless, unable to ground them into my physical body. It was not that we failed to bring the lovemaking to its conclusion. The seed could not implant because I could not hold the frequency with which it was delivered and he could not find my resonance to harmonize with it. The law would be demanding an heir to the throne but Jeshua's kingdom was truly not of this world. He advised me not to be disappointed for we had only been together intimately for two weeks.

"I spent that next year embracing the teachings at an even deeper level. We lived at Mird but traveled extensively as he actively reached out to the common people of every village in Judaea to show them *The Way*. Jeshua had presented himself to John the Zadok for baptism in the Jordan river and advocated that all people cleanse themselves of impurity in this way and embrace the true teachings of God. Denying the teaching to no one, he and I brought light into the lives of the destitute and abused. We taught *ma-at*, love freely given, and that is how we walked our lives upon the Earth. Since the days of Aman-Ra no one had been born into the bloodline who understood the codes of kingly service as Jeshua did. It greatly concerned the Sanhedrin, the legislative body of the Jews. They feared that the totality of our teachings pulled the people from the law and led them into pagan beliefs about nature and the feminine. The brotherhood, on the other hand, saw Jeshua as the messiah, the one who could lead the people back to their true God nature. The separation occurring between the lawmakers and the followers of *The Way* became more apparent with each passing year. It occurred in a small way within Qumran, where James was caught between his loyalties to the brotherhood and the council, but the separation was much greater with the politics in Jerusalem.

"Jeshua wished to awaken all people from their collective slumber. To accomplish this purpose, he used metaphor, parable, illusion, and some theatrics when necessary. This was the Mission, after all, and anything done with impeccable intent which did not harm others was permissible. Together we laid hands upon the sick and lame and moved the energy of their infirmities from them. It was not magic or miracle, simply mastery of energy applied to healing. We taught the people that right eating, cleanliness, and the correct relationship to nature and the Earth, was far more important than the spontaneous healings being attributed to us. I should say, Gabriella, that they were attributed to Jeshua, although I had equal experience and success with healing energetically. This was my work, child - to stay within my center of power while the patriarchal establishment debased my life. Many were jealous of my relationship with Jeshua and he would not hide his love for me from anyone. He loved me openly and asked his disciples to set aside their rigid beliefs and superior feelings in order to accept me fully, and tested them constantly with the openness of his feelings toward me. Teaching alongside Jeshua, I gathered the women around me and spoke to them of collective issues like betrayal, helping them reclaim their power within nature and with God. The priestesses of Annu had always taken on this responsibility and you will also, Gabriella. It is not our way to hide the light, but it has become our way to hide and protect the teachings. They will endure in secrecy until there are enough of a frequency to accept them.

"I failed to conceive at our second coupling that next year. Mary called me forward in March to speak with me of my infertility. Jeshua and I were certain that my cycles had come out of synchronization with the moon because I had spent most of my time with his group of disciples. We agreed that it would be best for me to gather a group of women around me, my own circle of twelve, to reinforce the feminine energies. If I had been at Qumran with the priestesses it would not have been a problem, for we were always in cycle. Soon after I formed this group of women, my cycles returned to normal. Salome, Mary Jacob and the Martha of our order were included amongst the women. Our sisterhood and love for each other grew stronger. We traveled with Jeshua and the disciples but slept and ate in our own group, and I used several herbs to increase my fertility.

"During this second year of our marriage, Jeshua's work intensified and his following grew. He was known all over Judaea and as far away as Damascus and Alexandria for his simple teachings and profound healings. The council of elders resigned themselves to his presence but the Sanhedrin, of which they were members, was openly hostile to Jeshua. His teachings did not support wealth, position or power, all of which were dear to the hearts of the legislative body. To the people of Jerusalem, he was an unknown, for he avoided the city completely, saying his time there had not yet come. John the Zadok had been arrested for his outspoken criticism of Herod-Antipas who married outside the rules of kinship. After a year in prison, he had been beheaded as an example to all who opposed the rule. Qumran was in shock at the loss of their high priest, but Jeshua had already declared himself both high priest and king. There was much talk of Jeshua as the messiah, the one who would free the Jews from the dominion of others. Jeshua knew this to be true but not in the worldly sense. He was trying to free them of the mental constraints that kept them from living in their God presence. The council had no ears to hear this and the younger men did not care to hear it for they longed to regain control of their country and to run the Romans into the sea.

"Simon, the chief of the magi and Jeshua's closest friend, had been arrested several times for activities with the Zealots. He had been excommunicated by the council at one time but Jeshua intervened to reinstate him at Qumran. Tempers were heated and the Zealots were avid for rebellion. Jeshua continued to walk through Galilee delivering his message of love and brotherhood while the world around him was seduced by intrigue and treachery. That third year of our marriage I conceived your mother, Gabriella. I felt Tamar quicken within my womb in February and arrangements for our second marriage were made for that March. Our love that December had been intense and she was born of the sparks of the Divine Fire that burned within us. It concerned me that she was, through my emotional body, experiencing the turmoil that rose up around us. There were times when I thought I might lose her, but the Divine Will prevailed and she remained firm within my womb.

"On Jeshua's thirty-ninth birthday, the first day of March, we gathered again at the home of Simon Zebedee, the Zealot and magus, for our second marriage. All who were present at our first marriage returned for the second and I invited my circle of women. Jeshua's disciples were politically split and at odds with each other, but kept peace during our ceremony. His disciple, Jonathan Annus had replaced Simon as the community father when Simon was arrested for Zealot activities. Jonathan opposed the baptism of uncircumcised gentiles which Jeshua and Simon advocated. Jeshua could see no uncleanness in the gentiles and Simon felt that Jonathan's attitude reflected the elitist beliefs among the Jews that would lead to their eventual persecution. As a brother, Simon believed that all actions come around to balance themselves and that only action based on Divine Truth was acceptable. Judas, who had been a Zealot until he was dismissed from their group, played the insipid game of aligning with the victor, but, in his heart, he favored Jonathan's opinions.

"It was in this atmosphere that we came together in the gardens at Bethany to complete the marriage ritual. I brought the remainder of the spikenard ointment within a thin-walled jar of red-veined alabaster. Mary represented the priestesses once again while Jonathan represented the council. Jeshua seated himself at the head of the table. He looked tired, but seemed pleased that he was to be a father at last. Telling the gathering of his deep love for me, he asked that peace prevail within the group and within our country so that our child, heir to the kingly codes of service, might be born free of the energies of turmoil. It was not to be, of course, but we proceeded with the ceremony as if it was. I had set a grid of crystals in the garden to anchor the star energy of our union and our destiny. Instead of speaking my devotion to Jeshua, I enacted it, washing his feet in a basin of heated water with scented oils and setting them upon a rich cloth to dry. Crushing the alabaster jar with my hand, I allowed the rich oil to drop upon his head. Now he was truly the anointed king for he had produced an heir. Massaging the spikenard into his scalp, I drew it out to the ends of his burnished hair. The aroma, though pungent, sent everyone into ecstasy for it was from the gods. Dropping to my knees, I lovingly rubbed the spikenard into his feet - the priestess-queen and the priest-king were one.

"We feasted. All took turns toasting our unborn child and we forgot, for the moment, that the wheels of destiny were turning. Those wheels moved very quickly, Gabriella. All that night and the next day, Jeshua, Simon and James met in secrecy. At the end of the meeting, I was asked to join them and my part in the events of the next several weeks was gently presented to me. Jeshua did not want to risk the life of our unborn child with undue trauma to my emotional body but he needed my help and guidance. They had information about the brewing of a political plot, a conspiracy to put an end to Jeshua and his ministry. The only way they could conceive of his survival was to strategically play into the conspirators' plan. It was somewhat risky but there seemed no other way. They asked me to take the priestesses' journey to the Siriun High Council to verify the orders received by Jeshua. This was their way of allowing me full participation and knowledge of the plan to lessen the trauma of the coming events. I consulted with Simon as to the efficacy of using the venom to take the journey since I doubted my ability to achieve deep trance under the circumstances. He masterfully adapted the formula to protect my child though I have always believed that your mother's fragility was due, in part, to that journey.

"However, it was imperative that I go to the High Council. With Jeshua holding my hand and Simon administering the dose of venom, I quickly slipped out of this reality and found my way to the Great White Lodge of the brotherhood on Sirius. The council made it clear to me that the only way to shift the pressure building up in Judaea was to enact the exact expectations of those carrying the dark energies. There was some risk because Jeshua was required to die to this life, travel to the higher realms to receive further initiation and embodiment of Divine Presence, then travel back into the body which Simon, with the help of James, would revive. Out of necessity, Simon and James would be locked into this reality as magician and healer. I was to travel into the other realms with Jeshua and make certain that he would return to the body, for his mission was not complete. There were really no choices since we had all made them prior to incarnation, but there was some risk of failure. The High Council reminded me of the importance of this energetic shift. The future evolution of consciousness depended on breaking a cycle of negative energy that was very resilient. This negativity had been woven into the fabric of the bloodline of the Akhus when they had fallen into the illusion of the material world. Like a deep amnesia, it kept them from knowing who they really were. They could not see themselves as one with all men let alone as one with God.

"Jeshua's mission was to be an expression of a metaphor for eternal life as well as a proof of the multi-dimensional nature of the universe. From his journey beyond death, Jeshua was to bring back, and embody, a higher aspect of himself that was capable of opening the codes I carried for the Christ Consciousness grid that was to be set in place around the Earth. There were so many layers to this one aspect of the greater Mission that it was difficult to comprehend it in its totality. The energy shifted immediately but thousands of years will pass before the amnesia lifts, allowing the Christ grid to lock into the telluric grid of the Earth, activating her ascension. The council instructed me as to the specifics of how my journey with Jeshua was to be undertaken. I would be in the temple of Annu with Mary as my guardian. Jeshua would be in the family tomb at Qumran with Simon, and yet we would both be lost to this world for the duration of the journey.

"When I returned to this reality and relayed the details of my appearance before the council, the three men showed visible relief, and summoned Mary to complete the activation of the plan. After that day my life moved so quickly it seems a blur to recall. Jeshua, in fulfillment of the twice-stated prophecies of John the Zadok, appeared in Jerusalem riding a donkey, the symbolic way for the lineage of David to assume the throne. He was not expecting to be heralded as king outside his circle of disciples. In fact, he was not even thinking of earthly kingdoms. What he did was essential to moving the plan forward and bringing the dissonant energies of Judaea into confrontation. To activate this process in the temple he reprimanded the shopkeepers and moneylenders, who had stalls in the temple, for bringing commerce and materialism into the house of Yahweh. Outwardly, it seemed an uneventful day, but the vortex of energy set in motion began calling forth all that defiled the purity of the unfolding Divine Plan. This was directed towards Jeshua and his followers, of course, and particularly the Zealots, Simon, Judas, and Thaddaeus, who were, at that time, wanted men for staging a political uprising. Jeshua was suspected by association though he took no part in militaristic maneuvers. To the Romans and the Sanhedrin, it looked as if

The Priestesses of Annu

Jeshua was the force behind the Zealot rebellion. They could not have been further from the truth. Jeshua embodied non-violence. He neither advocateed revolt, nor tried to dissuade his Zealot followers. He allowed as God allows.

"On Thursday following his entry into Jerusalem, I celebrated Passover with Jeshua and his circle of twelve in an upper room at Qumran, one place where Simon and his friends were fairly safe. It was the Essene communion feast on the vernal equinox and the sacrificial lamb was to be my dearest Jeshua. Judas, interested in saving his own life, betrayed Jeshua, Simon, and Thaddaeus by plotting with Jonathan Annus and the Romans. They were taken to Caiaphas, the high priest and father-in-law of Jonathan, who turned them over to Pontius Pilate, the Roman governor. Jeshua was brought before Pilate, who had ridden out to Qumran with his guards at the urging of Caiaphas. He found no fault in Jeshua's actions. How could he? He was completely innocent. Yet Jeshua knew that he would not escape this plot and surrendered himself like the sacrificial lamb. I cannot tell you what turmoil this brought into my life. Knowing the outcome of the messiah plan and my part in it did not lessen the anguish that I experienced through this separation from my beloved. I felt his torture, the driving force of the nails through his hands and feet, and the piercing thorns upon his head. Through every part of it, he was serene, Gabriella. In complete acceptance and bliss, he was in the light of God. My heart was on the ground and sadly the little one, your mother within my womb, shared my pain from the sudden separation. It happened so quickly when my beloved was taken from me.

"When Pilate, at the urging of Herod-Antipas, attempted to free Jeshua, the Sanhedrin called for the release of Thaddaeus instead. The Sanhedrin was interested in silencing Jeshua since he opposed the scriptures and the Torah and favored the inclusion of all people in the faith. There was no possibility of his release for the Sanhedrin had played with the fear and ego of Judas to legitimatize the crucifixion of Jeshua. However, the circle of betrayal came around to its place of origin in an attempt to balance the energies. Judas was arrested before the dawn. By late afternoon, the three men were made to carry the crosses of their fate to a cemetery garden outside the main part of Qumran. It was adjacent to the royal tombs of the House of David where James had arranged that Jeshua be entombed in the royal sepulcher. On the way to the garden, a man named Simon the Cyrene stepped in to carry the cross of Jeshua. He was an Essene brother and friend of Simon who was carrying his own cross, as was Judas. Gabriella, you must understand that the Romans had crucified thousands in Judaea who opposed them. It was their preferred means of execution. It was a slow and barbaric form of torture and death. I walked a distance behind with your great-grandmother Mary, Salome and Mary Cleophas, another of our sisters. In the confusion of soldiers, prisoners, and those who would erect the crosses in the garden, Simon, the master magician, slipped away and Simon the Cyrene performed the great service of taking his place upon the cross.

"As soon as Jeshua was upon the upright cross, my anguish lifted and I moved into my own serenity and acceptance. My higher self took over, for the task that lay before me required that I not be in emotion. I knew that all would be accomplished in a short time for no Jew could hang upon a cross on the Sabbath. James and Simon knew this as well and moved into the plan accordingly. Normally it would take days to die upon the cross but the Sabbath was within hours. The crucifixions of Simon the Cyrene and Judas were hastened by breaking their legs, but James kept this mutilation from happening to Jeshua by suggesting the administration of poison. Simon the magus, his dearest friend, came in disguise to administer the venom on a sponge soaked in vinegar to induce the death coma in Jeshua. When he began to slip from this reality, Mary and I sped away to her quarters and down into the temple of Annu. I quickly consumed the same venom and journeyed out between the worlds in search of my beloved. In this reality, James, who was referred to as Joseph of Arimathea by the community, was granted permission to take him from the cross to the family tomb where his body was laid out, then wrapped, in white linens. James and the family's friend, Nicodemus, dressed his wounds and left plentiful amounts of frankincense, myrrh and aloe in the tomb before seeking assistance in rolling a great stone before the entrance.

"Simon, the magus, came through another entrance and, in the dark hours before the dawn of Sabbath, worked on the physical plane to revive Jeshua's body as I rode out through the galaxy to support his journey back to Earth. Simon also went to the common tomb of Simon the Cyrene and Judas as well, and mended the bones of brother Simon who was carried to a healing room of the brotherhood for revival. Judas was left to die a slow and agonizing death for he had betrayed the Zealots as well as his master. After the Sabbath had passed, the Zealots took what was left of Judas's earthly presence and threw it, with his body, off a high cliff to the desert below - a feast for the vultures.

"I journeyed out and found Jeshua in a healing chamber of light within a crystal temple on the planet Venus. His etheric body was being cleared of all energetic disturbances from the ordeal. He was being guided by two Venusian healers who acknowledged my participation in his journey. I knew these women well from many lives upon Venus. The soul group of the sisterhood of Annu had a temple on the etheric planes of Venus where the lineage prepared for incarnation on Earth. When Jeshua's healing was complete, he was lifted from the light chamber and brought to me. Our communication was telepathic during this journey. He conveyed his deepest love but we were not to touch or merge in any way for he was undergoing a transfiguration to bring his monadic or oversoul consciousness into the revived body. His consciousness was expanding beyond his own higher self and his soul consciousness moving to merge with his Essence or God-Presence. Its form could be thought of as an overlord. I know that some of this is beyond your experience, dear Gabriella, but you will not forget what I am saying and one day you will merge with it in understanding. Do not forget that I carried your mother in my womb through this journey of expanded consciousness. From that point in the journey, we traveled together. My purpose was to hold the space for him to complete this transfiguration and to guide him back when the frequencies he integrated would ordinarily have been too high to be held in human form.

"We journeyed next to the star Sirius where we were received in the lodge of the Great White Brotherhood. For the brothers, this was their closest lodge to the Earth and the gathering place of their great soul group dedicated to planetary ascension. They worked intimately with the Siriun High Council who guided all genetic seedings on the Earth. We were taken to a healing room in a temple of shining platinum metal. There, Jeshua was placed upon a soft healing table and a team of brothers who were trained in energetic healing began to work upon his emotional body. I watched as these masters of energy cleared the emotional impact of the betrayal, torture, and crucifixion from his field. Along with this clearing went every emotional blockage from all lifetimes of the monadic consciousness. I could see them working through all time and all dimensions.

"When the healing was complete, we were taken to the Siriun High Council who spoke with us about the remainder of our Mission on the Earth. We were to have some time together - time to bear children who would carry the bloodline of the Akhus into distant lands where it would flourish and open the next gateway for the Greater Mission. We would then be parted to allow our individual missions to unfold within the brotherhood and sister-hood. Though apart physically, we would work together on the energetic planes to manifest the Christ Consciousness grid around the Earth. This journey opened planetary codes within me, which allowed Jeshua to return to Earth as the Christed One, to set the grid in place. Our work in the energetic planes has been to move energies within the grid, and make enlightenment and the Christed Self more accessible to those who intend it.

"When the High Council finished their discourse with us, we were taken on board a Siriun ship and transported to the star An in the belt of Orion. There we were greeted by a group of light beings who guided us to their healing temple. The temple was made of the purest gold in the shape of a beehive. We were led up the steps and into a healing chamber, at the interior of the hive. The walls were golden hexagons and the ceiling a Star of David with its hexagonal center. I was conscious of the codes opening at the sight of it and again when bees began to emerge from the walls. They swarmed around Jeshua's prone form pulling at the mental layers of his energetic body. They cleared it of thought forms and images that did not support the Christed Self. The bees came down through the layers of his being and elevated him from the table. I sensed that they were raising his frequency to a new level with their own vibration. When they had finished, they laid him gently down upon the table and flew back into the walls. He was vibrant - at a level of energy necessary to pass through the Stargate of An on his quest for transfiguration.

"The Siriun ship located the stargate. It was a huge ring struc-ture of gold with symbols engraved within it that were unknown to me, yet code-opening in their significance. When we approached, the gate rotated, locked into place, and the ship passed through it moving deep into space toward the star Vega. Jeshua was known and expected at all of these stars for the beings there were work-ing in collaboration with the brotherhood. The brothers had origi-nated in many star systems, for they were an intergalactic orga-nization, and Jeshua was following his own star path back to the light. On Vega, his spirit body was healed of all illusion and any experience of separation from God. He was infused with a green light and the seed of God remembrance was planted within his heart. It was very touching. I can tell you now, since I have taken this journey on my own in preparation for my passage, that this part of the healing is deeply moving and very expansive, for the

[167]

green light is love.

"We were guided back to the Siriun ship which took us swiftly to Lyra, our star of origin in the galaxy. That is to say the place where we entered this galaxy from the Heart of God. Our journey took us through a magical landscape of the higher spirit world. It was filled with symbols and reminded me of a paradise on Earth, perhaps the landscape in which Mir-An-Da lived. We climbed a pristine white marble staircase that wound up a hillside past orchards of flowering trees, gardens of perfection, pools of water with swimming swans, and fields of green with grazing unicorns. As we walked through this magical world I saw the bloodline and our mission unfold into the future to merge with the Christ Consciousness grid. It was as if the grid were being woven as we absorbed that world of higher consciousness. We arrived at the top of the stairs and faced another stargate. This one entered the void which contained the Heart of God. I could not enter the void with Jeshua for this was his personal journey to God. I held the space for him from the top of the stairs as he entered the void. I have recently completed this journey myself and know, from my experience, that there is a sublime peace in the void, an immersion in the darkness that expands the self to universal proportions. When the light of God pierces through the void it is like lightening striking through the dark sky. Every aspect of the being is elevated to God-consciousness and infused with the gifts of love, forgiveness, grace, and compassion. This experience heals separation completely for it is Divine Union. I sensed when it was time to call Jeshua back to me. He emerged from the void as resplendent light, the transfiguration complete. Returning to this reality, we followed the stairs to the Siriun ship which awaited us. We moved swiftly through the galaxy and the stargate of An to Sirius. There, in the lodge of the Great White Brotherhood, the brothers gathered from all dimensions to kneel before one who held the light of God. From that point on, Jeshua has been an ascended master of the brotherhood. He returned to Earth as the embodiment of love and compassion to complete other aspects of his mission.

"I awoke in the arms of Mary, his mother, before the great disc of the Sun in the temple of Annu. He awoke in the sepulcher of his royal lineage to a smiling and very relieved Simon - the true master magus. Jeshua was resplendent, and Simon dared not touch him. Simon, who had kept a vigil within the tomb, saw that Jeshua's wounds had vanished. Jeshua infused him with the deep love of God and Simon was so profoundly moved that he was healed of his aggressive tendencies in an instant. They were melted in the warmth of Jeshua's love. Jeshua was well beyond enlightenment. He was transfigured into the Universal Christ. Simon, with uncommon strength, pushed the great stone from the tomb opening, and they emerged. It was Sunday, just before dawn. After I was stabilized with food and drink, I left Mary and ran to the garden tomb. I found the stone rolled away and James within, folding the linens. He told me that Jeshua was gone. I turned to run looking for him and he appeared before me, his light so intense it blinded me. He warned me not to touch him for he was still integrating the energies of transfiguration. I fell to my knees for his blessing and he poured forth his love upon me. I wept with joy for the love of God and the success of that very difficult mission.

"Jeshua went off with Simon and James to meditate in one of the caves near Qumran. I spent long days in meditation myself, recalling the journey and trying to balance the energies of the child in my womb. Jeshua would appear periodically to the disciples, his mother and myself, but it was a long time before I could touch my beloved husband. I brought your mother, Tamar, into the world that September. She was a fragile child from the start so we stayed within Qumran to strengthen her. I could see within Tamar the wounds of separation, for she had taken on so much of my emotion during the crucifixion. Also, I could see the effects of the celestial journey for she was so transparent she had difficulty staying in form. She grew up among the priestesses and made two very special friends of the young women who tended the medicinal gardens. Her time at Qumran became a study in healing and she was exceptionally gifted in that regard.

"Following the dynastic marriage laws, Jeshua and I waited three years and three months after the birth of your mother to come together again in physical union. It was a sublime experience for both of us as our souls came closer to merging. Your uncle, Jeshua, was born of this union. He would be the next king in the lineage of David for he was the firstborn male. The bloodline required that two sons be produced, but restricted sexual union after the first son for six years. During this time, the children and I stayed at Qumran since Tamar was thriving under the tutelage of the sisters. Jeshua and Simon spent most of their time at Mird but appeared often at Bethany where a growing number of followers came for instructions from both of them. During that time period, Mary felt the call to live out the completion of her time on Earth in Alexandria. She called me into the temple of

The Priestesses of Annu

Annu beneath her chambers and passed the codes of light to me, as I am passing them to you, Gabriella. It was then that I learned about her Earth Mission which would continue for thousands of years on the inner planes. She brought forth the Divine Mother energies which nourished the souls of Earth. It was quite different from my own mission but within the sisterhood of Annu our assignments were identical - to continue the lineage in the silence and wisdom - the gift of the feminine spirit.

"Before she left, there was a great gathering of all the sisters and she passed the black robes of high priestess to me publicly. I assumed the roles of the Magda-elder in the community and high priestess among the Nazarite Order of Dan. Mary took three of our priestesses with her to Alexandria. There would be sweeping changes in the sisterhood, the brotherhood, and the Essene community during my time of leadership. The waves of change were already beginning to rock Qumran as well as all Judaea on the stormy waters of Roman domination. As your uncle grew into a child, I began to teach the gospel, the good news of *The Way* again. I had had deeper experiences with Jeshua than any others who were teaching but I never revealed them. Living *The Way* totally, I taught from my heart. The disciples began to separate into groups, each evolving their own style of teaching and their own interpretation of *The Way*. Jeshua allowed this to unfold for he knew, with few exceptions, it would be several thousand years before the human energies could be purified and elevated enough to genuinely practice *The Way*. Until that time there would be power struggles and issues of domination that would seek to destroy *The Way*. That is why he spent much time in writing, as did I, to preserve the teachings for that time.

"When our son, Jeshua, was four years old, his father traveled to Damascus to attend a meeting of all Jews concerned about Roman domination, for the yolk was ever tightening. On the road to Damascus, he met a man named Saul who was an administrator for the house of Herod in Jerusalem. He actively opposed the Essenes and particularly the Nazarene sect to which Jeshua belonged. Jeshua knew who he was and challenged him with the force of Divine Love to stop his persecution of the community. In Damascus, Saul was momentarily blinded by the light put forth by Jeshua and afterwards became a convert to *The Way*, and renamed himself Paul. He began a movement, centered in Antioch, to establish a new religion based upon the teachings of Jeshua. However, these teachings were fanatical - founded largely on fantasy, for what did he know of Jeshua's life? Again, Jeshua al-

lowed this as part of the unfolding path of purification for mankind. He told me that truth would eventually be born from the
fires which would one day rage as a result of Paul's efforts. Paul
was leading people into the greatest power struggle since this
starseeding began. Peter was swept up in it immediately as he
grasped the power he'd always longed to possess. Integral to their
teaching was the debasement of women, and I was a particularly
popular target for them. They complained often to Jeshua that I
had too much power. I can hear his gentle laughter as he told
them that what I really had was too much wisdom, understanding, and love.

"James became the leader of the Nazarenes and started a
church of *The Way* in Jerusalem. James had always dealt fairly
with all and never abused power, so it pleased Jeshua that his
brother would hold the light in a city where he, personally, had
never been comfortable. Simon, whose past as a Zealot compro-
mised his safety in Judaea, sailed to Cypress with Salome, some
of the sisters of Ashar, and many of the magi. There they began
the Gnostic sect, a group of brothers and sisters who dedicated
themselves to preserving the truth of *The Way* and the teachings
of Jeshua. Simon returned to Judaea many times but moved
quickly and silently through the land under the protection of the
brotherhood. The brotherhood of the magi grew in Cypress under
his guidance.

"When the six years of dynastic separation following the birth
of our son was completed, Jeshua and I came together in union
for the last time. I was forty years of age and would not be able to
bear children again after another dynastic separation. We took
special care with each other to honor every aspect of our being.
We also gave each other the freedom to move into the next phase
of our mission upon the Earth. I conceived our second son, your
uncle Josephes, in the dwelling of the high priestess at Qumran,
directly above the temple of Annu. Josephes did not see his father for many years for I was forced to leave Judaea with him in
my womb. As political turmoil raged and the factions of new religion continually assaulted me, Jeshua became very concerned
about the survival of his family whose blood held the codes of
kingly service for the future. We journeyed together to the Siriun
High Council and learned that it was time to move, both physically and energetically, because an era was ending in Judaea. I
was to take the lineage of light to Gaul where the next phase of
our mission would unfold. How this was to be accomplished was
our immediate task.

The Priestesses of Annu

"My Hasmonaean bloodline connected me well with Herod-Antipas who was also half-brother of Jeshua's disciple Thomas. Herod was exiled in Gaul where he had been given lands by the Romans. Through his son in Jerusalem, I secured my safe passage and refuge. At that time, James and his Nazarenes were openly hostile to the Romans who were persecuting and killing followers of *The Way* in the Jerusalem church. Months later, we heard that Thaddaeus had been captured and executed. Jeshua asked Simon and Salome to accompany me, the children, and the remaining handful of the priestesses of Annu to Gaul. He was leaving for Galatia in the east on a teaching mission. Our family and my community were dispersing and I held responsibility for the temple, including the great disc of the Sun that had been with the priestesses since the time of Mir-An-Da. There was no way I could transport it to Gaul. If it fell into the wrong hands, its gold would be melted down without a thought to its meaning. I journeyed again to the Siriun High Council who were, as always, prepared to help me. They told me to seal the temple entrance in my dwelling, making it invisible to anyone violating the peace of Qumran. Some years would pass before Qumran was destroyed so there was no need to involve the rest of the community in the dispersion of our order. The brotherhood was establishing a center of operations on the etheric planes in the Arabian desert. The Sun disc would be moved into that dimensional reality for safe-keeping until the world could hold its vibration again.

"I was relieved to leave the Sun disc in the hands of the ascended masters and made the necessary alterations to the trap door in order to seal it. The priestesses of Annu and I laid a new floor over it to mask it completely. I gathered together all the sacred items I could transport along with a few belongings of our family and was ready to leave within one month. Jeshua had already taken his leave of me. We had spent our last day together in our spot upon the hill. Knowing my courage, he did not fear for our safety. Simon would be my guardian for the rest of my life while James would, in time, assume considerable responsibility for the boys. I did not question the greater Mission for if we had stayed together in Judaea the lineage of light might not have survived. Jeshua was not ready to live in Gaul for he was seeding the teachings to the east and subsequently would move toward the west. It was the end of our marriage and he gave me full freedom to wed again as I chose. I would not hear of it, of course, for the typical life with a man was not for me. He was then over fifty years old, though he appeared half that age. I knew I would not see him again for a long time, if at all, and imprinted his image upon my third eye where it still remains. We parted in deepest love and spiritual partnership to serve the greater Mission in yet another phase of our lives.

"A month later our party arrived at Ratis on the shores of Gaul. We made our way inland to Acquae Sextiae, an old community that had become a refuge for the Jews. I was, to my surprise, honored as high priestess, queen and spiritual messenger of *The Way*. I saw immediately that this community was a fertile field in which to plant the seeds of truth. Josephes was born in September of that year. His birth heralded the new beginnings for the bloodline, the lineage of light, and the brotherhood that formed the core of the settlement in Gaul. Tamar had suffered greatly the loss of her friends at Qumran but was strong in spirit and understood the need to emigrate. She was already an educated healer and herbalist who was able to find those in need of her services as well as others ready to continue her education with the healing herbs of Gaul. It did not take her long to adapt to the lush surroundings filled with medicinal plants. She had brought many seeds with her from Qumran.

"After living over forty years in the deserts of Judaea, I found myself merging with the spirits of the water from the voyage onward. Acquae Sextiae was home to natural hot springs where I restored myself after the birth of Josephes. I visited them frequently over the years and used the water therapeutically in healing others. My time in Gaul was my soul's gift to this body after the austerity of life at Qumran. Sometimes I was hunted by the followers of Paul and Peter who felt Salome and I were witches preaching heresy, but it was quite easy to become invisible when necessary. Simon called their's the faith of fools for they created a false dogma to legitimatize their authority. The priestesses helped me establish a temple of Annu and some years later a healing mission which Tamar supervised. We were not harassed by the Romans for we were under Herod-Antipas' protection, but I cannot say that the bloodline will be so secure in the future, Gabriella.

"When your uncle Jeshua was of school age, he was sent east to Caesarea to be educated. He was looked after by the brotherhood, Simon, and his uncle James, who were committed to him as heir to the House of David. At twelve, the year of his raising, he returned with James, our Joseph of Arimathea. He then spent a number of years in Britain with his uncle who had been preaching the gospel there since fleeing Jerusalem after Jeshua's crucifixion. James had been arrested when the Romans learned that

The Priestesses of Annu

Jeshua lived on, but escaped prison and fled to Gaul, then Britain. The disciple Philip was in Gaul where he had come to teach *The Way*. He commissioned James to go to England with twelve disciples to open the Britons to the teaching. Of course he had been there with Jeshua and Simon as a young man to prepare the Earth to bring forth protection for the bloodline. James traveled back to Jerusalem often for he had interests in metal trading throughout the western lands. The children were always protected when they journeyed to Britain to work with their uncle.

"Young Jeshua was crowned prince of the House of David at sixteen in the synagogue at Corinth. He was then official heir to the throne, after replacing his uncle in that capacity. Also, he became the chief Nazarite, the head priest of Isis, the Mother Goddess. It was only the priestesses and priests of the Nazarite orders who held, in secrecy, the truth of Mir-An-Da, whom the world had come to know as Isis. We were devoted to the Mother Goddess. I thought it was quite extraordinary that we were able to stay in that truth throughout the days at Qumran when the Hasidim was so powerful. It shows the strength of the sisterhood and the brotherhood and gives me hope that the greater Mission will succeed. Now, your uncle is twenty-six and one day he will marry and produce an heir, Gabriella. The bloodline will continue. As you know, Josephes has stayed close to me. I believe he does well at the Druid mystery school for he shows great enthusiasm and intelligence. He has Simon's flair for magic as well, which will be further developed with the Druids. Simon and Josephes are together when Simon is in Gaul and it was he who arranged for this schooling. He is such a handsome young man I am sure he will marry well and seed many children. Now that Simon is Bishop of Massilia he has been in our lives more than in the past. He has been the most faithful guardian and the dearest friend a person could want. Keep him always in your heart, dear Gabriella, for your grandfather and I have loved him well.

"That brings me to your mother, Tamar, my beloved daughter. She was an angel, Gabriella. I have shared her story with you endlessly. Dedicating her life to healing, she was selfless and often neglected her own health in her commitment to others. She held the codes of light and they came through her to you, my granddaughter. I could do nothing to stop her work with the lepers except to take you from her when she became ill with leprosy herself, for I could not risk the lineage to her dedication. She was such a frail young woman, such an etheric being, that she really had no chance. I know it hurt you to be parted from her at a time

[174]

when you were becoming a young woman, but you understand the necessity now, I am sure. Tamar became quite ill and hid herself away in shame. This caused me to remember the separation she experienced in my womb when Jeshua was crucified, and I knew there was a need for her soul to act that out in this life. Becoming an untouchable, she ran off into the mountains to die alone, and took the potent herbs of death when she could stand life no longer. I am so grateful that you sprang from her womb, Gabriella, for you carry the codes as well as the blood. Your mother never revealed the name of your father, my love, but I see within you the blood of Simon the magus. I cannot fault him for falling prey to the beauty of our fragile Tamar.

"It was the year after her tragic death that word reached me through brother Timothy that my beloved Jeshua was in Rome. I began to call to him on the wind, knowing that my time on Earth was short. I should have known that he would find me before my passing. Has it not been wonderful to meet your grandfather and be in his great light, Gabriella? This night, he will see me through my passage just as I held the space for him when he was called to God. He will not stay with you long for he has work to do in the Far East before he joins me in the other realms. Simon will watch over you and the priestesses, as will Josephes in the future.

"I would now like to complete this, my final mission on Earth by activating the codes within you, my dear one. I see a life filled with joy for you, Gabriella. You will bear many children and the blood of the Akhus will be spread throughout this land and in Britain through your children. One of your daughters will carry the codes of light and become a priestess of Annu to continue the lineage. You will be safe and protected from all harm for this region was prepared by Jeshua, James and Simon many years ago. Know that I love you as a grandmother, a mother, and your high priestess. I leave the robes of your future with Sister Anna, who will administrate the order until you are of age. Now, lay your tired little head upon my lap, Gabriella, and surrender yourself to your destiny."

*

Mary placed her hand upon the solar disc on Gabriella's forehead and activated the codes of light within her. The child was very receptive and clear about the duties that came with the codes. Mary had been preparing her long before Gabriella had come to live with her. For Gabriella, the tragedy of her mother's illness and death had been buffered by her grandmother's wisdom and love. When Gabriella's light body was fully alive with the codes of light, Mary kissed her gently on the forehead and sent the child off to sleep. Mary stayed in her cave of solitude praying for all those she was leaving behind. She knew the boys were safe in the care of James and Simon who understood the scope of the mission and loved them dearly. She knew that the priestesses of Annu would be protected, but secrecy was yet to be their way of mastery. The new Christian sect of Paul and Peter would be hunting down the bloodline, the brotherhood, and the priestesses of Annu for they all knew the truth, and would not try to hide it.

Mary felt at peace with her life and the fulfillment of her mission. She recognized that her soul growth had come through the lessons of betrayal, separation, and persecution. Through those lessons she had arrived at union with God, trust in the Divine Plan, and the power of silence. She was an ego-less being of divine wisdom and all those around her regarded her as a saint, the Mother Goddess herself. There was no end to the love pouring forth from her heart.

She was ready to make her passage from the Earth for the last time. She loved Mother Earth for the countless lives which led to her ascension. She had always been the Mother's child. She was prepared to assist Mother Earth from the other realms, but knew that her Earth journeys were complete. She had released the planetary codes of Christ Consciousness which Jeshua continued to activate in the grid. When she had made her own journey to the heart of God, she knew that codes of divine union had opened within her light body. Her time in Gaul had given her the opportunity to attain enlightenment which made the opening of these codes possible. She knew that they would be released with her passage. Like Mir-An-Da and Lilith before her, she knew the name of God.

Her contemplation finished, she smothered the oil lamp and blew out the candles before walking down the mountain path to her humble dwelling. There she found Jeshua seated in meditation before her altar, his resplendent light filling the room. His beard and hair were long and quite gray, while his eyes had the light and spark of his youth as well as the depth of enlightenment. He was her soul twin and only love. They were quite beyond the rules of dynastic wedlock now and had passionately reunited with each other when he had arrived. This night, they would lie together in deepest love, their souls merged in oneness. He would accompany Mary on her journey to the heart of God, releasing her at the stargate to her own divine experience. His work was not yet complete upon the Earth though he was nearly seventy. He would join her after journeying to India where he had established an ashram, Shamballa, on the inner planes. He wished to open portals there for the brotherhood and the mission which would allow great avatars to enter the earth dimension in the future, on behalf of the Siriun High Council.

Some time during the night, Mary's head fell upon his shoulder as her spirit took flight. A great wind came down the mountain, the Earth rumbled and the waters within the Mother gushed forth from the hot springs flooding the lowlands as they headed toward the sea. The planet Venus pulsated in the heavens emitting a blue light that bathed the Earth. The Magda-elder had passed but the Goddess lived on in the hearts and minds of those who held the truth.

Jeshua held her body as he journeyed out with her into the universe. When she had passed through the stargate, he gently released her and walked out beneath the stars. Tears streamed down his face as he scanned the night sky sending his love and protection to his beloved. He saw the grid which had been placed around the Earth, like a web of protection and hope for the future. It was connected to Venus. He moved through the night to Simon's dwelling where he and Josephes lay, and awakened his friend and his son. They sat together under the stars outside the room where Mary's body lay until the dawn. As the sun rose, Jeshua took from his pack an alibaster jar filled with spikenard. Mary had never known that he had brought three full pounds of the sacred ointment back with him from India when they were to be married. He bathed her body and annointed her from crown to foot, wiping her feet with his long graying hair. They were as one being, ever united. She was his beloved Mary, his queen, and the twin ray to his own soul. He did for her what she had been loving enough to do for him.

Jeshua left for the east before the people began streaming to the dwelling to pay their respects to their saintly teacher. Few besides Simon, Josephes, and Gabriella knew that Jeshua had been there. Simon had prepared a tomb of alabaster for Mary's earthly vehicle and a great funeral procession brought it to its resting place. The Earth had been pulsed by the selfless love of a great being and it would forever be changed.

The Priestesses of Annu
Leah speaks

Leah and the circle of twelve women were sobbing. They held each other but could not stop the tears. They were releasing deep memories which opened them to greater light and connection to the Christed self within. Leah knew that Mary was present amongst them but said nothing. She, herself, would not have been able to continue the story of the lineage in truth and clarity if her emotional body had not released the blockages put there by the suppression of Mary's story and the fabrications about her life. The lineage was healing itself. She suggested they retire quietly and spend the next day in silence and retreat to allow the clearing to come to completion.

Replacing the sapphires within their velvet bag and, leaving the room otherwise untouched, she gathered the women together and led them from the building. The night was clear and the Moon bright. The snow on the mountain had a distinctly blue cast to it, reflecting a mysterious light in the sky. Leah looked towards Venus and saw the gentle pulsation of blue light reaching outward to the Earth. She sat by the rushing stream for a short while allowing its rhythm and sound to bring her back into her own body. Her emotions quieted and a great peace came over her. Now she could understand the magnitude of the healing which the Black Madonna had gifted them all.

Morgaine

Leah speaks

Leah's group of women was grateful for the day in silence. Most of them had been conditioned to believe that Mary Magdalen was a sinner, a prostitute or a poor wretch whom Jesus pitied and elevated to purity. Inwardly, the group was integrating truth and releasing the blanket of suppression that had kept them from knowing the real Mary. They allowed tears to flow and light to enter as they made their ways silently through the day. When evening came, they gathered in their circle holding a new level of truth and clarity. Leah saw this immediately upon entering the room. A great many codes of light had opened in the women and the frequency of the group had shifted accordingly. She was pleased, and could feel Mary's pleasure as well. Mary did not want adoration or devotion. She wanted the centuries of lies to give way to the truth. Within the workings of the Divine Plan, the time of truth was at hand. Leah's soul mission was to bring the truth forward, for the lineage of light was stepping out of the shadows to complete its mission.

Leah took her seat in the circle and opened the evening with a short prayer and meditation. With these brief introductory exercises, she brought the women from the space of introspection to that of circle and community. Sisterhood had deepened in these women through their experience the previous day. Wondering what this evening would bring, Leah removed the sapphires from their velvet bag and, once again, arranged them in a Star of David grid. She rearranged the center of the circle, changing the five-pointed star to the Star of David and placed the statue of Merlin within it.

"Good evening, Beloveds," she began, seating herself squarely upon her pillow. "Let me take a few minutes to weave last night's story together with the life of our next priestess of the lineage of light. Simon and Joseph of Arimathea watched over Mary's boys, Jeshua and Josephes. Joseph of Arimathea had remained Bishop of the New Jerusalem Church which he had founded, but finally left Jerusalem for good in 62 AD, a year before Mary's death. He was brutally stoned and excommunicated by the Sanhedrin and narrowly escaped with his life. His Nazarenes were persecuted by the Romans as were the followers of Peter and Paul in Rome. Nero, the Roman Emperor at that time, had a deep hatred for the early Christians. His brutal executions of some of them caused a revolt. Accusing them of starting the fire that burned Rome, which he had probably started himself, he had both Paul and Peter executed in 64 AD. These martyrdoms increased the fervor of the early church which remained firmly in the grip of the followers of Peter and Paul.

"Simon returned to Jerusalem in 65 AD to lead Joseph's Nazarenes east across the Jordan River to safety in old Mesopotamia. The remaining brothers at Qumran dispersed to safer monasteries in Greece, on the Mediterranean islands of Cypress and Malta, and in Egypt. The next year, open fighting began in Caesarea between the Romans and the Zealots and by 70 AD Jerusalem and Qumran had been laid to waste by the Romans. The brotherhood understood the level of darkness that was descending upon civilization. They had the vision to leave the teachings of *The Way* and the history of the community on carefully written, encoded scrolls in the caves above the Dead Sea and in the secret chambers beneath Solomon's temple in Jerusalem. The Romans burned all records and writings but never did find these scrolls. Mary's journals, which Simon kept within the Gnostic church on Cypress, were buried in the deserts of Egypt with those of others, like Thomas, who kept the truth of Jeshua's teachings alive. The Dead Sea Scrolls and the Nag Hamadi Codices now provide us with a more truthful history of the life of Jeshua, Mary and the Essene community of *The Way*.

"Simon returned to Massilia, our present day Marseilles, for a time, but, eventually, left his post as Bishop to join Joseph and the boys in Britain. He died there some years later. He was crucified and slain by the Romans. He had asked that his remains be placed next to Mary's tomb in the south of France. Joseph of Arimathea, brother of Jeshua, built the first church in Britain at Glastonbury. He began construction right after Mary's death and completed the chapel in 64 AD. Young Jeshua dedicated it to his mother and the cornerstone reads "Jesus Maria." Joseph headed a group of twelve celibate missionaries who spread the gospel throughout Britain. They were granted twelve plots of land by the Silurian King Arviragus who was the brother of the Pendragon, Caractacus. The Pendragon was Lord of the Celtic lands in Britain. These plots of land were all adjoining, giving the early church a large tract of land at Glastonbury. This was not far from a land very sacred to the Celts which later became known as Avalon. It was in this area, as well as in Scotland where Arthur's kingdom would come forth, that Jeshua, Joseph and Simon had traveled as youths to set the grids of the future and it was part of Joseph's soul mission to activate the next phase of the program there.

"After Mary's death, her son, Josephes, was made Bishop of Saraz, in the region we now call Gaza. It was when he left this post to travel to Britain to join his uncle and brother that Simon followed him from Massilia. When word reached Britain from the east that Jeshua had left this earthly world, young Jeshua was crowned king of the House of David. Josephes became the crown prince and Nazarite, assuming the role his uncle Joseph (James) had played for Jeshua. Young Jeshua married the granddaughter of Joseph's dear friend, Nicodemus, in 73 AD. She bore him a son whose name was Galains. When the crown prince, Galains, grew to be a young man, he joined his uncle's circle of twelve missionaries. He took a vow of celibacy, relinquishing the future crown to fulfill his mission. The circle became known as the brethren of Galains. His decision made Josephes the rightful heir to the throne and it was through Josephes' son, Josue, that the bloodline continued in Britain. Because Josephes was second-born, which was the position of priest rather than king, the lineage, from that time forward, became known as the fisher-kings, or the priest-kings. Josephes was the Grail child whose progeny carried the Akhu blood into the lineages that would bring forth the dream of Camelot.

"Joseph of Arimathea, died at Glastonbury, in 82 AD. It was he that had been born in the year we call 1 AD, or more correctly 0. He married a member of his congregation in Britain whose name was Anna. She bore him a daughter to whom they gave the same name. When she grew to be a young woman, Anna married Brân the Blessed, the Archdruid of the Celts. Through the entangled lineages of Anna and Josue, and a strategic conjoining with the Sicambrian lineage of the Franks, a new seed of destiny was planted in Britain. The lineage of Mary's blood carried through Gabriella found its way into the Sicambrian royal family and even-

[181]

tually to Britain in the form of Princess Argotta who married into the conjoined lineages of Josue and Anna. From this union came two lineages, one in Britain and the other in France. The lineage in Britain eventually produced the Great Bard, Taliesin. The French lineage intermarried once again with the lineage of Mary, held within the House of Acqs, bringing forth Viviane I of Avalon of the House of Acqs. Viviane, carrying the blood of Mary from two sources, married Taliesin. To them was born a girl child named Ygerna of Acqs who was the mother of both Arthur and Morgaine.

"It is not necessary to understand the details of the lineages, for they are incredibly complicated. However, it is important to know that what played out in the lives of Arthur and Morgaine, and the knights whom Arthur gathered from his relations, was the continuing story of this bloodline. The energies were set for the unfoldment of Camelot by Jesus, Simon, and James who traveled there as young men. James, as Joseph of Arimathea, nurtured the soil of the future, and the blood gathered itself once more with the brothers and the lineage of light to focus and accelerate the energies of planetary ascension. The magi had become part of the Druidic Merlin and Bard tradition. The lineage of light was embodied in the Celtic priestesses, while the bloodline of Jeshua and Mary had found its way into many of the royal families of Britain and France.

"When we look for Morgaine, as she passes the codes of light to the next high priestess of Annu, we find her in the world of fairie, what we would call the fourth dimension. It is a world that exists in the mists, not only those surrounding Avalon, the once great kingdom of the Celts, but those surrounding all places where the worlds meet. Morgaine is the High Queen of the Celts. She sits before a woman of middle years who is in the second attention, a higher state of consciousness. They are in a magic grove of oaks, with hanging moss and fairie rings surrounding them. The Sun filters through the dense canopy above them, playing patterns of light upon their gowns. Morgaine wears the black robes of the high priestess with the golden, gem-studded crown of her inheritance. Her aunt, Viviane II of Avalon, had passed the lineage of light to her before she left her body, along with the duty to be Keeper of the Celtic Mystical Tradition. Her mother, Ygerna, had given her the crown at her untimely death, a passage mourned deeply by all people of the kingdom, as she was also the mother of King Arthur and the wife of the Pendragon, Aedàn.

"Morgaine is nearing fifty years of age. In our reality, she would look worn and weathered from the turmoil brought to bear on her life, but in the world of fairie, she is radiant and lively. Her long, thick golden-red hair falls in gentle waves to her waist and her deep green eyes show the light of her mastery. A lightly freckled face has the round softness of her kinswomen as well as the glow of her own inner light. Her smile is great, yet her voice gentle and melodic as she speaks to the priestess, Clarisse, who will take her place in the third dimensional reality."

Morgaine speaks

"My dearest Clarisse, I shall not return to the world of ordinary men. There are serious distortions in their thinking which manifest as a ceaseless desire to kill one another. I could easily fall prey to their wickedness, and refuse to afford them that opportunity. There are far better ways to use my energy. I must continue on my journey through the world of fairie to the realm of love and light. I am bound to accompany the souls of Modred, my beloved son, and Arthur, my twin flame, into the reality of our unfolding work.

"I am asking you to do something seemingly extraordinary, Clarisse, though it fulfills, in every way, the mission of your soul. I pass the codes of light to you this night, ensuring the continuation of the lineage of women who have held consciousness on this planet for eons as part of the great Mission of the Akhus. You have been trained well to cross between the worlds, and so I do not worry that the lineage might be lost. I ask a greater thing of you, my friend. I pray that you agree to embody my physical form, the one Morgaine, and return with it to the world of men to complete the aspect of the mission that lies in that dimension. You will be a widowed queen, wife of the deceased Urien, and mother to Ywain who carries the royal blood of our beloved Jesus and Mary Magdalen through my lineage. More importantly, you will be grandmother to Tortolina, the girl-child of Modred. You will guide the unfoldment of her mission as the next High Queen of Avalon and Keeper of Celtic Wisdom. Do not answer my request at this time, but wait until I have finished telling you the story of the life you will be agreeing to live. Listen very closely to be well informed, should you agree. If you do not agree, I will simply disappear into the misty world of fairie bearing the bodies of my beloved king and son. I will be missed, but with understanding. I can guide Tortolina from the higher worlds and promise you that I will do this regardless of your decision.

"Now, let us begin this sacred duty certain of our intent,

[183]

The Priestesses of Annu

Clarisse. Let us reach out into those starry worlds beyond all form and link ourselves with the spirit of the lineage we carry for mankind. Let us carefully weave the next thread into the tapestry of this great Mission." With that, Morgaine withdrew a worn amulet from between her breasts and removed its delicately woven chain from around her neck. Into the amulet were woven sacred symbols, not of her Celtic heritage, but the solar symbol of the lineage on one side and the Star of David on the other. She opened the amulet and poured the six sapphires into her hand. The fairie sun caught the gems' facets and threw light magically around them. Morgaine laid out the sacred star upon the grassy floor of the oak grove in such a way that she and Clarisse were in the hexagonal center. She threw her arms upward to the heavens and called forth her power.

"I invoke the great devas of this forest and these sacred lands, the guardians of fairie and the world of men. I invoke the spirit of nature, Pan, and the spirits of the four sacred winds. I invoke the lineage of the brotherhood in all realities and through all time to guard and protect the lineage of light through this passage. I invoke the angelic beings who parallel our mission and support it from their realms. I invoke our beloved master Jesus and our sister Mary Magdalen who brought the grail codes to this part of the earth. I invoke all of the sisters of the lineage of light and especially Mir-An-Da, our mother priestess, to witness the passing of the robes and the responsibility of our legacy. I invoke Annu, the Sun, and the great central Sun behind the Sun, from which the mighty rays of creation emanate to our beloved Mother Earth. May all be blessed by our sharing today. May we stand steadfastly in our truth. Beloved masters, receive our love."

Morgaine dropped her arms slowly, and turned to face Clarisse. "You bear the solar disc upon your brow and heart, Clarisse. You are the one I am to choose as my successor. In time, you will pass this legacy to Tortolina who is still too young to assume the responsibility. It is unusual that you came to Avalon as a grown woman. I believe that God has brought you directly from the stars to take my place. You will be Avalon's high priestess, Keeper of the Celtic Wisdom, but also she who holds the lineage of light in the secret order of Annu. Outwardly, we practice the Celtic Christian tradition and, as you know, the priestesses of Avalon have long been associated with the great Moon goddess. Continue to uphold these traditions, Clarisse, for they conveniently mask our secret order and its lineage of the Sun.

"We have been hunted since the times of the master Jesus by

[184]

those who would try to hold all power externally. They misunderstood his message then, letting their jealousy of Mary Magdalen influence the way in which they founded their church. They became intimately involved with the Roman government which came to supported their wish to exterminate the bloodline of the Christ. Theirs is a great distortion of the truth, Clarisse. It is they who have turned the Motherland into the wasteland. It is they who have pitted father against son and shattered the hope that the dream of Camelot might be fulfilled in this reality. Weep not, for it is all illusion, Clarisse. Eventually, those who lust for power and control will be caught in their own web of distortion. Until that time, and it will not be soon, Camelot will not manifest again in this reality. But the dream will live on in the dimension of love and light where the building of this golden kingdom has continued, without interruption, since Jesus, James and Simon came to these lands five hundred years ago to link heaven and Earth in the Christ Consciousness grid. When that sinister grip is released on this Earth, a network of golden kingdoms will materialize from the mists through the matrix of that grid. These visions have come to me for many years. It will happen, Clarisse, but for now, the kingdom is, once again, not of this world."

Morgaine seated herself squarely in the chair of the high priestess and Queen of Avalon. She held the amulet in her hand as she began to tell her story to Clarisse. "When I was a very young girl, my grandmother, Viviane del Acqs, High Queen of Avalon, gave this amulet to me. At that time, it did not contain the sapphires. It contained nothing, and everything, for the sacred symbols of the sisterhood awakened the lineage deep within me. I was born to Viviane's youngest daughter, Ygerna del Acqs, who, eventually, inherited the crown from her. My grandmother's oldest daughter, who was also called Viviane, inherited the high priestess role of Keeper of the Celtic Wisdom. Both grandmother Viviane and Aunt Viviane held the codes of light as high priestesses in the sisterhood of Annu. With a preponderance of male offspring in our family, I, being the only girl, became the repository for both the royal crown and the high priesshood. Both of these responsibilities came to me directly through the blood of the house of Acqs which runs thickly in my veins. The house of Acqs came to Britain with Viviane I from Brittany in France. It originated from the female lineage of Mary Magdalen through her daughter Tamar and granddaughter Gabriella.

"My mother, Ygerna, had very little to do with my rearing. I was born in Carlisle, in the palace of my father, Gwyr-llew, the great warlord of Carlisle. He was at war continually. It was a loveless, political marriage for my unhappy mother and she did not want me to be party to her depression. She sent me to my grandmother in Avalon soon after I was weaned, sure that the benefits of our separation would outweigh the lacerations to my soul. Now, I can see the workings of the Divine Plan in her actions and have forgiven her completely. She had a continual sadness about our estrangement but took delight in me when I came to visit her. My grandmother's husband, and thus my grandfather, had been Taliesin, the archdruid. My grandfather died before I was born, but his blood runs in my veins as well. He carried the grail lineage in his blood through the male descendants of Jesus but also the lineage of the archdruids from the time of Brân the Blessed who married Anna, the daughter of Joseph of Arimathea. All the kings and queens in old Britain are, in one way or another, descended from our beloved master's bloodline.

"So Grandmother taught me of my bloodlines and raised me to be a queen. She kept me until I was nine years old at which time she became very ill. Unbeknownst to me at the time, she passed the codes of light to my aunt Viviane II, who took her place as high priestess of Avalon. My mother inherited the throne of Avalon at Grandmother's death. Before I left Grandmother Viviane, she promised me in marriage to Urien, King of Rheged, but not until my twentieth birthday. This was the unfortunate fate of royal children. Aunt Viviane became the guardian of the nine holy sisters of Avalon and began my training in the sisterhood.

"During my years with Grandmother, she had made room in her house for the new Merlin, Emrys Ambrosius, who had married one of my grandfather, Taliesin's, illegitimate children, Nimus. As I came to know these generous aspects of my grandmother's character, I grew to love her even more. She was not only the Queen of Avalon but the great mother to all Avalon's children. Well, the Merlin and I became fast friends and Grandmother allowed me to become completely immersed in the world of magic, medicine, and vision. That friendship continues to this day, Clarisse, and I think, in many ways, that Emrys was my true father. He taught me things that priestesses ordinarily did not know. I learned the paths of my intention through the dimensions and the universe, above and beyond the priestess training to be a dreamer. He helped me develop my masculine side which gave me power among men as well as women. As his greatest gift, he taught me the bardic art of song which drew my grandfather's filaments to me through time and space.

"I know now that Merlin holds a lineage through the brother-hood of the magi who have always been at hand to protect the priestesses of Annu and the lineage of light. It was no mistake that he was there at Grandmother's to guide my formative years. He was protecting Viviane as Taliesin had before him, for she held the lineage of light until her death. I have so many vivid memories of my experiences with Merlin, who would take me out through the dimensional doorways into universes and realms unimaginable to an ordinary child. I became a time traveler while sitting at his feet, and he would always bring me back with music and ground me into this reality with his songs. He is an incred-ibly high magician, Clarisse, and it is with his assistance that I have come to live in four worlds at once, the reality of men, the world of fairie, the higher world of love and light, and the world of symbols and magic. My vision was developed and used exten-sively during my youth to guide the priestesses and the brother-hood into the future. I did not have the childhood experiences that put limitations on perception - that imprison the soul in the world of men. Viviane and Merlin carefully guided my develop-ment as a fully awakened dimensional traveler. You might guess that I had difficulty relating to normal children, but not to the priestesses or the children raised in Avalon.

"At nine, I went to live with aunt Viviane in the house of the priestesses in Avalon. Aunt Viviane became the high priestess after Grandmother's passing and guided the priestesses of Annu, who were disguised as servants of the Moon goddess. She was the mother of the community of our women who dedicated them-selves to earthly service on behalf of the star beings. So the bal-ance of my raising was in our community, Clarisse. The experi-ence was one of discipline cloaked in softness. I was taught all the arts of the women whose lineage reached back in time to the ancient ones, with weaving, plant dying, sewing, gardening and cooking. At the same time I learned to be a healer, to mix and administer plant medicines, and to travel through the dimen-sions on the filaments of light. As I grew into a young woman, Viviane began to train me for the day I would take her place as high priestess. My own mother, I am sure, would have cared for me with the same love and tenderness as Viviane.

"Once every year, I journeyed to see my mother. Five years after I was born, she had birthed a second child by the Pendragon, Aedàn, son of Gabran, and King of the Scots. She was, at that time, still married to my father, who passed away some years later. This bastard child, my own half-brother, she called Arthur. After Father died, she married Aedàn and moved to the Scottish kingdom of Dalriada. It was clear to me that she and Aedàn were soulmates for their love was fierce and fiery. After this second marriage, which legitimized Arthur as heir to the Scottish lineage, I cherished my visits to Mother, not just because she had transformed into a vibrant, beautiful woman, but because I recognized Arthur as my own twin flame. I loved Aedàn as well. He had, within his lineage, the ancient seed of Tamar Tephi, who, legends say, carried the Akhu blood from Judah to Ireland before the time of Mary Magdalen. In truth, Emrys, the Merlin, is richer in this ancient blood than any of us. Nonetheless, when Aedàn and Ygerna conceived Arthur, the lineages of the Akhus converged within his blood. He was the king of destiny for this land, the one in whom the Grail codes planted in this land and in the consciousness of the blood by master Jesus could come to fruition.

"I saw Arthur only once a year, until he was twelve years old. Then this fair-haired, handsome boy was sent to Avalon to be prepared for his coming into manhood. The world of men prepared one to be a warrior, but the priestesses were known to prepare one for the soul's destiny. Mother knew this and Aedàn agreed that Arthur should be trained in all aspects of life before being given his kingdom. I was seventeen at the time, a completely transparent young maiden who could not mask the love I had for Arthur. We were constant companions when not in our training and Viviane allowed us to explore our feelings together. We knew we were not to be coupled in the world of men for our destinies had been forged without our consent. Royal marriages were typically arrangements of kingly alliance and not of love. However, there were other worlds in which we could openly express our love and fulfill our spiritual destiny. Viviane was also aware of the prophecies and the importance of the blood we both carried, but that part of my life was yet to unfold for me. Avalon, as you know, is, and has been, a mysterious place. This fair isle is at the center of the grid which was recognized and prepared by the beloved master Jesus, Joseph and Simon so long ago. It lies between the worlds, on filaments of light from all dimensions. When the world of men threatens us, we invoke invisibility and the cloak of dense mist rises up to mask us. When the judgments of men lash out at us, the Earth eats them up and turns them into golden apples and honey bees. It is a place of magic and Arthur was allowed to experience it fully.

During the two years of Arthur's training, we were often joined in our play by Lancelot, the son of Viviane who passed through his druidic manhood training ahead of Arthur. Lancelot was born and raised in Avalon though his father was King Ban le Benoic. Ban was called Blessed because of his descent through Faramund from the conjoined lineages of Jesus and Joseph of Arimathea. These were the true fisher-kings or priest-kings. Ban was the lover of aunt Viviane which meant that Lancelot was not legitimized, yet Viviane's blood added the female lineage through Mary Magdalen to Lancelot's blood. He was a boy filled with passion and dreams and his alignment with Arthur, a future king, was by the hand of God. We dreamed of a peaceful kingdom where love prevailed and blood was not shed. This kingdom upheld the grail codes of kingly service to the people and the land. It's inner structure was of light filaments and love frequency, bringing forth the highest ideals of the blood. Our shared reveries opened codes within me for my higher work but also for the establishment of the golden kingdom which we came to call Camelot.

"Lancelot and I were like brother and sister, whereas, Arthur and I, truly brother and sister, were more passionately attuned to each other. When together as three, the magic overtook us and we were children of destiny. Those were times in our lives to be cherished for after we entered the world of men, it became difficult to stay in truth with our destiny when their swords slashed at us. We returned to Avalon often, Lancelot and I more so than Arthur, but the world of men wears quickly upon one, Clarisse, and you see what has become of us. Forgive me, I am in the moment rather than in the telling of the past. Let me return to that magical time of our youths.

"After Lancelot came into his manhood, he left his home on the fair isle of Avalon and went to his father's kingdom to learn the manly arts of war. I wept profusely for the future of his gentle spirit for I knew he would be a great warrior, drawn deeply into the world of men. Yet, he was a son of Avalon, and no son of Avalon could be completely taken in by those who externalized power. By then, I was seventeen and he had been my companion since I was nine years of age. I grieved his departure from my everyday life.

"Arthur and I still spent much of our free time together and as he neared his time of manhood, Viviane encouraged me to expand his horizons by sharing some of the magic that I had learned from Merlin and Grandmother. Arthur knew Merlin well, but his learning time with him would come after manhood when he would be taken into the brotherhood, not as a magician but as a king. She wanted me to introduce him to the other world realms in which I was, by then, a notorious traveler and to teach him about the power of intent. On the night of the full Moon prior to the festival of Beltane when he would come into his manhood, I took his hand and led him into the forest at the edge of the sisters' gardens. As we walked further into the dense woods I worked to attune to the energies and silently called forth the fairie kingdom.

"I saw the reality bend and shift before us as we walked through an energetic gateway into the other world of fairie. Arthur was aware of nothing. I had slipped him into the fairie kingdom while he remained in his conscious state. We wandered through the forest following a rushing river strewn with great boulders that caught the water and sprayed it upwards in playful ways. He did not notice the joy-filled water sprites laughing and singing as they rode the water down the river, for he was still seeing in the other reality. Then we waded across the river to a narrow path that led up a steep embankment. He helped me climb until the path leveled out somewhat. It crossed back and forth up the side of a mountain with great fir trees reaching to the sky. At last we came to a sacred circle on the side of the hill. Pure spring water gushed out of the hill into a fountain which held it, but let it spill forth as an overflowing cup into a stream that tumbled down the hillside to the river. I led Arthur to the fountain, telling him that the water was magic, from the world of fairie. If he were to drink, it would open him more to this experience and if he were to allow the overflowing water to pulsate upon his inner eye between his brows, it would give him a sight known to few men.

"Arthur had the greatest respect for my perceptions and very much wanted to expand his awareness, so he drank long from the sweet waters. His body shook slightly as he stood upright and gazed around him. It was not so much that he saw things differently, but that he began to feel the world around him. His emotional body was opened to the impassioned ecstasy that is the fairie kingdom. Of course, it is also dangerously deceptive. One needed to master discernment to navigate in this world. I watched as he reacted to everything around him, including me. A new level of passion was awakened in both of us as he saw me in transparency and vibration. I urged him to allow the waters to open the window of his inner eye and he reluctantly took his eyes from me and knelt before the fountain in such a way that the water rushed at his forehead. When he drew back and opened his eyes, he saw the sprites sitting on the rim of the fountain laughing at him. He was shocked and excited which made them laugh even harder. When he realized how silly he must have looked, he joined them in their laughter. Arthur was now opening himself to possible realities that had only existed for him in folk tales. It was a beautiful thing to witness the awakening of so treasured a young man.

"We wandered further up the path and came to a pristine pool of water surrounded by ferns and tall trees. I walked to the edge of the pool and let my robes fall among the lush flora. I saw the look of astonishment on Arthur's face and laughed at his reaction. I dove into the water and rose up into the sunlight like a goddess. My long red hair sent streams of water down my breasts, stimulating my nipples to the fullness of passion. I was a maiden of nineteen, a virgin by law of the order, in the magical world of fairie with my brother whom I loved more than any human being. Arthur was, at that moment, fully opened sensually. It was not exactly an enchantment, but he had little choice but to join me in the water. Letting his garment fall from his strong young body, he dove into the water after me. Rising to the surface, he stroked my body from my feet to my breasts, touching me lightly upon my womanness. He kissed me deeply, sending me into waves of sexual awakening. We played with each other for hours in the water and upon the soft moss by the pool. We brought each other many times to sexual fulfillment without actually joining, for that was strictly forbidden in Avalon and we did not wish to risk entrapment in the world of fairie. It was a magical time for both of us.

"After sleeping deeply in each other's arms, replenishing ourselves completely, we journeyed onward up the hillside to find cascading waterfalls with little bridges built here and there connecting the path. We walked to the top of these waterfalls, filled with sprites and the devas of the waters, and came to a clearing in the woods where the water gushed forth from the earth. There was a quaint house built of forest materials which I knew well to be the home of the fairie queen. I blew upon her door, a traditional way in fairie world to announce oneself with power and essence. Of course, she had felt my presence as soon as I had entered fairie and had watched all of our experiences with her expanded state of consciousness from the comfort of her home. Positively gleeful, she opened the door to invite us in. She was a delicate, winged being who very much resembled a flower, although she was, and still is, a remarkable being of power and magical skill. She adored Arthur, so much so that she wanted to keep him and tempted him repeatedly to stay in fairie. It was Arthur's test, the first of many. He was quite clear and firm with her about enjoying his stay in the fairie world but returning to Avalon to follow his destiny. She offered to make him a king in fairie, to give him all of the kingdom if he desired it. He would not grow old, but would live in this fully impassioned state forever. I was in shock at her assertions. I had not seen this side of her before - tempting him with her kingdom to keep him with her.

"My dearest brother heard her to completion and then told her quite simply that he had a mission to fulfill in the world of men that was more important than his personal desires. When, at last, she was appeased, she offered us an herbal brew and little sweet cakes which we devoured. She told us both that we were welcome in the land of fairie anytime, as a respite from our everyday lives or as a safe place to hide from the wicked. She told Arthur that he did, indeed, have a great mission to accomplish but she doubted that the world of men could hold the vibration of that which he envisioned. She wished him the god's good fortune on his quest and suggested that he hold me always in his heart for I was the other half of his own bright light.

"We left the fairie queen and started along another forest path. I wished to be back in Avalon at once and drew my intent into that request with considerable energy. Reality bent suddenly. Arthur saw it this time and grabbed me around the waist as we were thrown through the gateway onto the grassy knoll above the sea just west of the huts of the Druids who had been training Arthur in the Celtic traditions. We sat up and looked at each other, stunned. Silently, we went our separate ways to contemplate the experience. When I returned to the house of the priestesses I found them in full preparation for the Beltane festival. Five days had passed in Avalon since Arthur and I had walked into the woods together. Viviane had told the priestesses not to worry over my absence for she knew we were being tested in an important way.

"We came back to the news that Arthur had been selected as the year king. What is more, because he was of the bloodline of the master Jesus, he would wear the crown of the king stag. This happened only when a new king of the messianic lineage was coming of age. It was a thrilling event for Avalon and all the Celts of Britain and the north. The excitement was so intense it kept me from thinking of the ritual of Beltane where the stag, representing the male aspect of God, coupled with the chosen queen. It kept me from dwelling on the fact that Arthur would be leaving Avalon after his journey into manhood. I, too, would be leaving

Avalon for a time to become the wife of Urien in fulfillment of the arrangement made by my grandmother. I focused my mind on the memory of our experience in fairie and helped the priestesses with the preparations. Arthur was being instructed day and night by the Druids and the Merlin to prepare him for his re-entry into the world of men and his destiny. They did not want Arthur to forget the Grail codes of kingly service and service to the land. It was the legacy and duty of his bloodline. A Grail king did not live for himself. It was a considerable duty to place upon the shoulders of a fourteen year old boy, but he was the king they had been awaiting.

"On the morning of Beltane, Viviane called me to her quarters. She did not ask me to explain my experience in the world of fairie with Arthur. I guessed that she had seen it all through her astute vision. Surprisingly, she asked me when I had last bled my menstrual blood. Attuned to all my sister priestesses, I had last bled on the full Moon. I was bleeding when Arthur and I stepped into the world of fairie, but, of course, in fairie no blood was ever lost so the entire cycle was a mystery to me that Moon. It was the best I could do for an answer and it seemed to please Viviane. She told me that it was my destiny to be the Queen of Beltane and it was good that I was fertile for Avalon awaited a child of destiny through the conjoining of the female and male lineages in myself and Arthur. I burst into tears, both in happiness that Arthur and I would have that opportunity and in shock that she could reduce something so sacred to the calculated odds of mixing blood. It took me some time to complete my reaction and pay attention to her again. She wanted me to understand that Arthur would not know it was me until the moment of our joining. It would be important for me to enchant the situation somewhat to release him from the cultural taboo of brother-sister union. She explained to me the history of the Akhus and the importance of the role of the sister-bride. This was the sacred marriage and there had been few opportunities for one so dynamic as ours in recent times.

"It was well that Viviane waited until the morning of the festival to tell me of this decision for I would not have slept until that night had passed. I spent the day in preparation, setting my intent, calling in all my power, and cleansing my body and hair with fragrant oils. My sisters helped me with the ritual baths and the preparing of my hair which was woven with spring flowers that held a heady fragrance. I was dressed in a robe of deep green which was heavily embroidered with flowers and leaves. I looked like the spirit of Mother Earth's rebirth. Just before the beginning of the event, I was given the mask of Beltane to cover my face. My identity was known only to the nine holy sisters of Annu.

"We gathered on the ridge of the western highlands of Avalon to watch the sun sink beneath the western hills that lay across the waters. When the last ray of Annu's light left our eyes, we turned and walked in procession to the sacred circle of stones where our festivals took place. These stones marked the passage of the sun across the sky throughout the year. The Avalon you know is not the one that I describe for much has been hidden, even from the priestesses, as the world of men encroaches.

"We filed into the stone circle from the west as the Druids, with Arthur, entered from the east. The bard sang several solemn songs to awaken the sleeping Earth, then the musicians began to play the great dance of Beltane. We stomped on the Earth in precise rhythms that sent messages of welcome to all awakening life. This was an old, old custom that came with the Celts from the east.

"When darkness fell upon the land, the great fire was lit and the dancing continued as passions were lit and blazed. This was the one night of the year when we broke the vows of celibacy to honor the fertility of the Earth. The children of Avalon were seeded on such nights as priestess and Druid coupled in the lush landscape of springtime. After several dances that roused the passions of sexual desire, the great energy of Mother Earth, the music of the stag king began. Arthur dashed into the circle with the antler crown upon his head. His body was bared from the waist up and he was painted with the symbols of male fertility. He was handsome beyond belief and my heart pounded as he began the dance of questing for the queen. My role in this dance was to remain elusive until the music reached a frenzied climax. It was then that I revealed myself and he fell at my feet as a profound honoring of the feminine. He rose to one knee and placed the ring with the symbol of Annu on my outstretched finger. Ordinarily it would have been the ring of the Celtic cross but Arthur was calling forth his legacy and, unbeknownst to him, my own as well. He arose and led me in the marriage dance while all our brothers and sisters clapped or kept time with their feet. When the dance was finished, we were escorted by torchlight to a magical dwelling at the edge of the woods. We bid farewell to our escorts and disappeared inside the small cottage where the marriage bed and a lavish feast were prepared for us. Our brothers and sisters feasted at the fire and danced until their passions overtook them and they crept off to make love with each other.

"Within the dimly lit cottage, Arthur led me to the soft feathery bed and began to caress my body through the thick robes. I could feel the energy of the fairie world in his intent but also the elixir given him by the Merlin to arouse his full maleness. He was on the edge of delirium and might not have reacted as I revealed myself, but I did as Viviane had recommended, and enchanted him slightly to separate him from his ingrained sexual beliefs. When I removed my mask and robes, he was surprised and more deeply aroused than he had been. Though I understood the rules of this once in our lifetime opportunity perfectly, and was in full power over my womb space, I lost my heart completely to Arthur that night, and he to me. Neither of us would ever be happy in the world of men because we could not be together. I used my visioning to look into the future for the two of us and saw that when we verged upon the worst depression, we would renew our lives together in the world of fairie. It would not cure the ache in our hearts, but it would make life bearable for both of us.

"Our love-making was ecstatic, filling the deepest places of our souls with the frequency of God's love. I truly felt a child of God, a child who carried the blood of the Akhus forward in time to the completion of the mission. When Arthur sent forth the seed of the stag king I felt the meeting and blossoming of the seed within my womb. On that treasure of a night, Modred was conceived. He was a true child of Avalon, the hope of the Celtic kindred. He was also the Grail child, holding the blood of the ancients and the male and female lineages of master Jesus. His essence sprang forth within me with all the energetic alignment of the reborn Earth. For that moment, I was fulfilled in every way."

*

Tears were streaming down Morgaine's cheeks. Wiping them away with the corner of her sleeve, she closed her eyes and rested her head against the cushioned back of the throne. She was fighting a deep exhaustion from the events of the world of men, which tested her ability to maintain emotional balance. Clarisse poured a cup of spring water for Morgaine and took a new position at the feet of her mentor. Morgaine stroked Clarisse's hair and gradually regained her balance. She was grateful for the solid presence of this woman who was to carry the light forward for the lineage. Drinking the entire cup of water to honor Clarisse's thoughtfulness in gifting it to her, she set the cup upon the arm of the throne. Her eyes took on the far away look of the time-traveler as she slipped back into her story.

*

"Forgive me, Clarisse. It is the frailty of the human heart that brings sorrow to the lives of men and I have not been able to avoid that in this life. I understand the illusion of it all, but my heart has not relinquished the pain of my unrealized love. We had that moment, and a few trysts in the world of fairie, but Arthur's mission began to unfold rapidly and I, too, was thrust into my destiny. Avalon serves its purpose as a protected place where ideals can be lived without opposition, but it is a world apart from that of ordinary men and women where lives are lived not by ideals but desires and willfulness. Perhaps the ideals that we carried into that world were like seeds planted in the spring-time. Perhaps, in time, they will take root and begin to grow. I do not know, Clarisse. It seems hopeless to me. It was clearly my undoing to be so attached to Arthur that I could not separate our love from the unfolding mission. The longing to be united with one's twin flame is overwhelming and not always in keeping with the Divine Plan. As the Divine Plan unfolds, it is like being one with a flowing river if we are in our mastery. To oppose it is fool-hardy for it creates a needless struggle that wastes our energy.

"But, let me continue. I feel the call to the other worlds and need to bring this to completion. The ritual of the stag king was the completion of Arthur's training by the Druids. He was united with the land, which is to say, with the Mother Goddess Earth whom I represented in the ritual. He left within a moon to rejoin Aedàn, the Pendragon, and our mother, Ygerna in Dalriada. Merlin and Nimus went with him, for now Arthur would begin his training in the world of men and it was Merlin's destiny to be with Arthur until the end. He would initiate him into the brotherhood and keep a watchful eye on him as the mission unfolded. Merlin was in constant contact with the Siriun High Council, the group of Akhus who were guiding the Mission on Earth. I will take you to this council before our time here is complete, Clarisse. For now, know that they exist beyond the world of light and love in the world of sacred symbol and magic. Sirius is the home of the brotherhood of magi who have been the friends and guardians of the lineage of light since the times of Zep-Tepi. Merlin is the Arch-Mage, the leader of the brothers on Earth at this time and Arthur is heir to the royal blood of the master Jesus, the House of David.

"Clarisse, you need not worry if Merlin or his successor are not always near to you as you carry the lineage forth. Though Merlin moved north to be with Arthur as he matured and came into his power, I never felt him far from me in Avalon or when I lived at Rheged with Urien. Aedàn was the cousin of Emrys, the Merlin. He had sent him to my grandmother's to gather wisdom and offer protection. I don't believe Aedàn was aware that he was acting on behalf of the lineage of light to put the brotherhood in closer proximity to us, but that is how the Divine Plan unfolds. It was also Aedàn who appointed Emrys as Arthur's official guardian. That was clearly to protect the bloodline which his son carried. I do not doubt that Mother had much to do with that decision. So Arthur was immersed in the next part of his life and I stayed within the protective cloak of Avalon to bring forth the Grail child from my womb.

"It was a joy-filled time in my life for there was a living part of Arthur developing within me. I did not hear from him during that time. In fact, I did not see him again until my wedding to Urien the summer after Modred was born. Modred was a dear baby, born on the winter solstice. All the priestesses joined in his raising. In truth, I was under Viviane's supervision and could not, in any way, direct the raising of my own son. He was the hope of Avalon and would not leave the isle until he was a man. I gradually turned his nursing over to several other young women who had also conceived at the Beltane the previous year. In the spring, I prepared myself to marry Urien, an old and unhealthy man, whose disposition was as outrageous as his appearance. Urien was the nephew of my father and was already in his thirties when I was born. I felt truly tested by this experience since it was necessary to leave my child behind and journey to an unfamiliar place in the north. I would be closer to Arthur, but that only increased the pain in my heart. Urien and I were wed at the palace in Rheged with all the royal families of Britain and Scotland in attendance. Of course, we were all related to each other in some way, so it was more a family reunion.

"Later that year, we journeyed to Dalriada, for the anointing of Aedàn as King of the Scots. It was the first time that a king of Britain was ordained by the Celtic Church and the blessed Columba, a former king himself, officiated at the ceremony. Aedàn was the Pendragon, the supreme ruler of the Celts, and everyone came to observe the ordination. Arthur, as eldest son, stood with Mother on the platform. He had matured somewhat, but his boyish good looks still attracted me. I was able to spend some quiet time with him and Mother as Urien socialized with the other territorial rulers. Mother was happy and pregnant again with another child. This boy, Eochaid, is now the only survivor of Aedàn. I have seen that he will carry the master's blood in the north which will become the land of the Scots. Arthur was happy to see me, but a bit more reserved than we had been as children. Of course, I was married to Urien at that time and Arthur was raised to be very respectful of those bonds. I felt additional separation from him, but no lessening of love.

"There is need to tell you that mine was a loveless marriage with little enthusiasm. I complied with Urien's infrequent need for love-making, but spent most of my time in the woodlands surrounding the castle communing with the fairie folk. I knew better than to make friends among my ladies for then I would be part of their dramatic plots and gossiping. More and more of my time was spent traveling to the world of sacred symbol and magic, making a solid connection with the Siriun High Council. This was important to the future of the lineage as well as the bloodline of the Akhus. They encouraged me to journey to the world of love and light where I communed, at the level of the soul, with my beloved Arthur. I found these journeys strangely satisfying and, perhaps, better than being with him in the world of men where he was learning to exercise his male side. It was after one such encounter with Arthur's soul that Urien planted his seed within me and Ywain took hold in my womb. I had not expected to bear another child. You can imagine my joy at that opportunity.

"I was pregnant with Ywain when Arthur turned sixteen. At this age, he was considered an adult, ready to exercise his manhood. He had spent two years in military training under his father's guidance, He was made the overall commander of the Guletic armies and, in addition, the anointed high king of Briton, the kingdom of the Brits who fled north when the Romans invaded their lands. We attended the ceremony, which was an easy ride north from Rheged. Arthur and I were now the king and the queen of the two western coastal kingdoms. He continued with his training, both military and brotherhood, during the years of his position in Briton. I bore Ywain and became completely engrossed in his rearing, for I wanted him to be raised aware of the feminine lineage of Mary Magdalen and not just the male lineages which he doubly inherited through those of my father and Urien. I would not relinquish this son to anyone. From the day he was born, I worked to keep his consciousness open to all the worlds. I know that he and his Beloved, Alienor, will carry the wisdom of our traditions and the truths of my lineage through to their children. Ywain is not a warrior but maintains the family lands by right relations and fairness to all. He understands my mission perfectly and will not even grieve the fact that I have chosen to leave the world of men. You will not fool him into thinking you are his mother, Clarisse, but he will support you in all your endeavors. He is a member of the brotherhood and a guardian of the lineage of light. When I felt he held the wisdom of the land, I sent him to Arthur's kingdom to train with the Merlin. He has done well.

"To return to my story, Ywain was just a lad of four when Urien took ill and died of consumption. I did what I could for him with all the medicinal skills I had mastered, but it was no use. He had abused his body all his life with over indulgence and the body would not respond to my ministries. I was left to rule Rheged, and Urien's other lands of Gowrie, alone. Thrust into the world of men, I was grateful for my training with Emrys. Arthur and I became political allies and that part of Britain grew very strong. We rekindled our childhood dream of a kingdom of peace and love, joined again by Lancelot who had become Arthur's valued assistant. It was during these years of freedom that Arthur and I would meet, on occasion, and journey to the world of fairie. There we would experience our sensual nature again and be fulfilled, to some degree, in our love.

"Then, as Arthur and Aedàn gained lands through the victories of the Guletic under Arthur's leadership, Arthur became more powerful and moved his headquarters to a beautiful area south of Carlisle where we had been born. Here he and Aedàn built a castle and Arthur gathered his many cousins and nephews around him as a circle of twelve knights. Lancelot was appointed leader of the knights and trained them. In time, my own Ywain joined his circle. It was also at this time, when Arthur was twenty-two, that Aedàn arranged a marriage for him that would forge an alliance with the French of Brittany. A maiden named Gwenhwyfar, the daughter of a lord named Leo de Grance, sailed to Britain and was wed to Arthur. In arranging the marriage, Aedàn unknowingly sowed the seeds of destruction for his own heritage. That is why I don't believe he acted consciously when aligning Grandmother and me with Emrys. I am certain it had more to do with Emrys inheritance of the great Taliesin's post with the brotherhood.

"Gwenhwyfar came with an air of superiority, sure that she had been sold to a barbarian by her father. Arthur, a truly tender man, could not please her. His efforts to do so brought nothing but harm to his kingdom. In addition to her barren womb, Gwenhwyfar brought with her the church of Rome. Arthur gave her far more power than he should have, wishing to have a wife content and fertile. She steadily influenced those in the court and even Arthur himself, until he built a chapel and established a Roman Church within his palace walls. I warned him that the Roman Church had sought our blood for centuries, and I asked him to be mindful of trickery and remember the codes of the grail - service to the people. The church of Rome did not serve the people. He did not think that religion could be so influential and told me to calm myself. I told him to be watchful of his own ego and desire for power, and begged to be left out of future political relations with him. We remained estranged for many years as a result.

"I heard of the news of Arthur's kingdom from Lancelot who visited me frequently. We often rode to Avalon, taking Ywain to see Viviane and Modred. Over time, I learned of Lancelot's love for Gwenhwyfar. It sounded very much to me like my love for Arthur. In this, Lancelot and I were kindred spirits. Not one of us was happy, but at least I was not treacherous to my tradition. As the head of the Guletic army of Aedàn, Arthur, with his Knights, was in battle often. They were generally victorious and gained much land for the kingdom. Arthur spoke often to Lancelot about the dream of Camelot and he trained his knights in service and duty to the people. He was a strong king with an unhappy wife who lusted for her beloved Lancelot. Arthur would not have interfered with their affairs, in fact, he may have encouraged them, but Gwenhwyfar's religious fanaticism crippled her with guilt and shame over her natural feelings. She would have been appalled to know of our Beltane rituals and the simple but powerful vibrations of Mother Earth's fertility. It might well have cured her barrenness to be touched in that way.

"Arthur spent more and more time with the army and his twelve loyal knights as Gwenhwyfar opened more and more doors for the church. As Ywain became a man, I often retreated to Avalon and nursed Aunt Viviane as she prepared for her passage. Much older than my mother, she was ready to make her way to the other worlds. She passed the codes of light to me from her deathbed, Clarisse, and the story she told me was both precious and unimaginable. She was a magnificent lady who had trained me well. Her strong control over Avalon was necessary for the preservation of the traditions and the protection of the lineage. My mother, the High Queen, had nothing to do with Avalon, and so it was Viviane who kept the tradition alive. I inherited that responsibility from her then and pass it on to you now.

"I was more comfortable as high priestess of Avalon than as queen of Rheged and was seldom seen in the world of men. There were times, though, when I materialized a part of myself to intervene on behalf of the tradition. Those times when I worked that magic were few, but necessary. As Arthur's dream decayed in the human drama around him, I became the voice of the truth amidst the turmoil. I appeared more than once to his round table of knights and confronted Gwenhwyfar, herself, when her plotting reached into my energetic field. I was portrayed as a witch and a harlot by the fair queen and her church. She, who lusted after another man and destroyed the good spirit of my twin flame, had turned her attention to Avalon. My appearance before her as she lay in her barren bed caused her to retract her energetic reach, but it also created an atmosphere of fear around my power. I knew she would not do further battle with me. My heart went out to Arthur, but I stayed in Avalon.

"Modred was, by that time, the archpriest of the Druids. He was twenty-two years old. When he came into his manhood at fourteen, he had been the year king. From his ritual coupling with the representative of the Mother Goddess, the priestess Lluan, Avalon received a daughter, Tortolina. Tortolina was raised by the priestesses and myself, while Modred went out into the world of men to guard the tradition of the Celts. It was in that same year that Aedàn and Arthur lead the Guletic army and the knights in the battle of Brecknock. They succeeded in driving the Irish out of Brechin but Arthur's younger brothers, Bràn and Domingart, were sacrificed. Mother never recovered from this loss and steadily declined in her health until she died. I was forty-three at the time she gave me the crown of Avalon. From that time on, I was the mother of Avalon as well as her high priestess. Those were difficult times to keep the ideals alive for the world of men pushed at our borders. More and more, I drew the mist around our holy isle, and we retreated into the other worlds.

"Arthur came to me after Mother's death and wept upon my lap. I could no longer journey with him to the world of fairie to satisfy our love, for we had entered into the wasteland ourselves. We were drawn to the completion of our mission, but it was becoming evident that it would not be in the world of men. He was dispirited and unwilling to rid himself of Gwenhwyfar though he recognized her as the core of his problems. I saw further that it was his father, Aedàn, who truly controlled the combined king-doms. Aedàn was well intentioned, but he was not a Grail king. He was the Pendragon, the supreme ruler of the Celts, a warrior and he expected the same of Arthur. Arthur's blood contained the master's codes of peace and love. You know, Clarisse, it may be that the master's blood would best be distributed far and wide, rather than held within these bloodlines. If that would happen, one day, I believe that our dream might be realized in the world of men. For now, it is too soon, and it is too late.

"Even though Arthur and Modred had little to do with each other, the blood runs thick in their veins. When Modred aligned himself with the Saxons, hoping to save the tradition, he did not know he would face his cousins, his father and grandfather in battle. He was fighting for the future of the Celtic tradition and freedom, and Arthur was supported by the church of Rome. All that was left, in the end, was their blood, spilled on the Earth like an ancient offering. Was this the intent of master Jesus or Mary Magdalen, the mother of our blood? I like to think that the codes that lie within the blood that has been spilled upon the land have somehow strengthened the Christ consciousness grid here, but, in reality, it seems an affirmation of the wasteland.

"The mortal remains of Modred and Arthur, the hope of Avalon and the bloodline of our Master, the Grail itself, lie now in the cottage of the fairie queen, Clarisse. There also, I have taken the sword Excalibur so that no mortal man can ever touch it again. May they seek invincibility in their souls, instead. Soon, I will join the fairie queen and accompany the higher forms of my beloveds to the world of love and light. There we will continue our work outside the temptations of the world of men. Our fair queen, who now finds herself a widow, will give her kingdom to the church unless Aedàn still has some warrior fight within him. He has only one son left to hold the Grail blood among the Scots. It is only blood, Clarisse. The master gave us so much more than that to guide our lives. My last act of power, before I leave this earthly life, will be to shift the order of importance in our legacy and put the truth before the blood. I will call for the dissemination of the blood to present all people with the Grail codes. That seems to be the only hope. It is my gift to Mother Earth as I finally release the codes of light which I have carried for the lineage. May God be with her and her beloved people."

*

Morgaine took Clarisse's hands within her own and blew her own power to heal within them. Then she rocked Clarisse's head toward her and blew into the crown of her head, passing her magic. The heart and the womb she had opened and empowered during her training. They stood together in the Star of David within the oak grove and merged their third eyes. Morgaine took Clarisse to the Siriun High Council to receive their wisdom and their permission to continue the mission in this way. The council confided to them that the codes of light would soon be passed through the soul lineage in such a way that consciousness of the mission would be lost. The High Council told Morgaine that an alternative plan was being enacted to carry the codes through the darkness of the wasteland. She was to journey into the fifth dimension with Arthur and Modred to actualize the golden kingdom of Camelot. When mankind would be ready to step into that frequency could not be predicted. They would all hold the intention that it would precede or coincide with the Earth's own journey into that dimension, otherwise, mankind would be lost to the wasteland and the mission would have failed.

When they returned from the journey, Clarisse agreed to take the place of Morgaine in the reality of men and in a magical transformation, she took on Morgaine's appearance exactly. When this occurred, the light within her activated and she came into the fullness of her power. Morgaine, conversely, became more and more transparent, until she was a breath of air that blew against Clarisse's cheek. Picking up the sapphires, the amulet, and the gown that lay upon the forest floor, Clarisse walked with them through the doorway of time into Avalon.

Leah speaks

Rather than an overwhelming sadness, the group of women experienced a collective wonder. There were so many interpretations in print or on film of Camelot, Arthur and Morgaine that the truth of those times was still hidden in the mists. Leah's story was refreshing and rang true, but they wanted to know more of her interpretation of it. Where was this world of love and light, and the golden kingdom. They didn't even have to voice their questions for Leah could read them all over their faces. She laughed and shifted her position by drawing one knee up under her chin.

"Well, Beloveds. That's the story of Morgaine. She was a master of all dimensions and a beautiful and sensitive spirit besides. She used her skills and power to move Arthur and Modred with the dream of Camelot into the fifth dimension. I can share with you the deep healing that I received when this truth moved through me. It was to know that the dream lived on in a reality where dreams like that can be shaped and brought to fruition. Camelot awaits us as we ascend into the new reality. All was not lost during the times of darkness and fire. These great beings returned to the Earth to complete their own cycles of ascension, which has allowed them to live in the golden kingdom while guiding those who seek them out in that dimension. The Merlin returned as our beloved St. Germain who, from his ascended state, continues to guard the lineage of light as it now regains its consciousness.

"Morgaine held the codes of consciousness for the dissemination of the blood into our veins. We all hold the grail codes of kingly service in our blood. We all are bound to the land, for the Earth is our only mother until we are released from the wheel of incarnations by our own illumination. Morgaine also held codes of consciousness for interdimensional traveling and for the right use of intent. She was a true sister and servant of the Akhus.

"What of Avalon? Avalon lost its power but did not succumb to the world of men. The great kingdom of the Celts merged with the world of fairie, but its wisdom lives on in the land of Britain, Scotland and Ireland. The doorways to the fairie world are still available to us, but the reality there must be traversed with great caution and discernment. We have journeyed there together, though you may not have been aware of it. It is called fourth dimension, the unconsious dark, interior world of shadows. It is filled with the energies of the lower centers which can pull at us and imprison us. There are doorways through that world to the fifth dimension, however, and we have used those portals to access the frequency of God."

Now much of the work the group had done with Leah over the years was making more sense to them. They entered into a lively discussion, talking far into the night about the magical worlds that could not be seen from ordinary reality.

Isabel

Leah speaks

Leah awoke in the middle of the night with a high fever. These sudden fevers had attacked her periodically since she had initiated the healing work of her soul lineage and bloodline. Usually, they left her within a day. She knew this expression of healing energy was the work of the woman who would tell her story that evening. Excusing herself from all activities, Leah centered herself to receive revelations through the release from her body of this past incarnation memory. Passing in and out of near-delirious states, she rode the waves of heat to their completion. When, in the late afternoon, the fever passed, she became filled with a bright light and increased energies. She knew that these purifications were raising her frequency and purging the wounds from all levels of her being. Refusing food, she arrived at the evening circle with a greater understanding of the importance of that lifetime and its relationship to other lives, the sisterhood, and the codes of light. A few remaining pieces of the puzzle had come into place for her and she was ready to share an unusually poignant life with her beloved sisters.

The women knew nothing of Leah's distress that day and had spent it hiking and discussing the dream of Camelot, hoping that it would still be fulfilled. Their questions, as they assembled themselves, were centered around the movement of the lineage between Britain and France and the loss of consciousness that gradually overtook the sisterhood. They were well aware of the dark forces that continually opposed the truth. With few exceptions, such as St. Clare and St. Francis in Italy, the gentle ways of the master Jesus were not evident in Europe.

The Priestesses of Annu

When they were all settled in their circle with the sapphires in place, Leah sat before them with her arms wrapped around herself, as if in protection. "I feel," she began, "that our next character will answer all the questions I see popping about this circle. Her name is Isabel and she lived between 1525 and 1550 AD in the Provence region of southern France during the latter stages of the Inquisition. We find her chained to a prison wall, counting the hours until her death. She is touching, cynical, and livid with anger at the injustice wrought upon her. I give you Isabel." Leah closed her eyes and took a deep breath, then allowed the painful voice and memory of Isabel to come forth.

Isabel speaks

"Who shall I speak to in passing these codes of light? Who will hear me? Shall I speak to these dank dungeon walls or the rings of heavy metal that cut into my tender wrists and ankles with their weight? Shall I speak to my father who betrayed me, or the women, whose fear prevented them from supporting me? Shall I speak to the beastly pig of an Inquisitor who could not bend me to his ways? Shall I speak to my mother who passed these codes to me on the way to her own execution? No, I can speak to none of these. In truth, I can speak only to my own heart which grieves this loss, and to my own soul which bears this lineage, for the codes of light shall die with me this day.

"I am Isabel de Renney. I was born in Aix-en-Provence, twenty-five years ago, on this day in 1525. Today, my birthday, I will die. I will die with my Truth and for my Truth. Ah, what more can be said, my heart? You know I am a woman of the silence. I must force myself to tell this story, not because it is so painful. I can stand the pain. I am reluctant because I see no reason to tell it. I am no one, really, simply an ordinary woman caught in extraordinary circumstances. It is senseless to waste my breath, for who will listen? However, Mother swore me to this telling as a duty. I will honor her bravery in the telling.

"My father is a Catholic and, as has been painfully revealed to me, a familiar of the Inquisitor Boulangier of Marseilles. He is a doctor of medicine in Aix-en-Provence, though I do not accept the scientific medicine he practices. My mother, Marie, pretended to be a Catholic, for to be otherwise would put her life at risk. She was from a very distinguished banking family of Provence, the de Villes. My parent's marriage was arranged to bring credibility to my father and distinction to the family of my mother. Love had nothing to do with it but that was typical of the times. Being a headstrong, romantic young woman, I wanted love more than position. I awaited my knight, but he was not able to find me in this life. I leave no children. I leave few friends for I embrace a truth that could not be revealed. I could not risk accidental disclosure through woman-talk and childish fantasy. But, I can risk it to you, dear heart and soul. To you I will disclose the entirety of my brief, humble existence.

"As the child of a Catholic familiar, an Inquisitor's spy, I was brought up within that church in a very disciplined way. After incurring my father's wrath for questioning the techniques used by Rome to suppress freedom of speech, I quickly learned to keep my opinions to myself. However, I paid a price for this because those opinions lodged within me and made me feel sour, bitter, and even a bit mean. Mother could see this happening and began to draw my opinions from me as we gathered herbs together. We were alone in the countryside when at this task. It was my favorite part of life for I deeply loved the Earth and the beauty she brought forth. I knew she was the Mother. No one had to tell me that. I loved my own mother, deeply, as well, and she seemed to understand and even share my feelings for the Earth. Mother was very guarded as she first began working with me to heal my feelings about the church and my father. She would tell stories and allow me to express my opinions. I knew better than to repeat anything to Father, so we had a mutual confidence about our conversations. As I grew older, she trained me in healing with herbs and we spent most of our summer and fall days in the fields gathering medicines. She assisted my father in his practice, but was also a respected midwife in our region of Provence.

When I was thirteen, she performed a secret ceremony with me to honor my time of bleeding. I was to tell no one that we had held this ancient ritual. We were on a journey to gather mountain herbs to the west, something we did once a year. Mother would bring back medicines from these journeys for many of the healers and medical doctors in Provence. She would always rent a stall in the fall market and earn enough from our labors to pay my tutors for the year. That is how I became well educated and wise to the world. On the journey of my thirteenth summer, she took me to a cave in the mountains of St. Baume. She asked me to help her remove the debris, from wind and wild animal, that littered the place. When the cave was clean and the Sun near setting, she took tiny candles from her bag and struck a flint to light them. Letting the wax dribble on the cave floor, she set each candle upright upon it. It was quite magical. Holding a candle, she ran her hands along the wall of the cave until her fingers detected the slightly jagged edge of rock that sealed an opening within the cave wall. She motioned me to her side. While I took the candle, she removed a small stone, the size of her hand. She asked me to move closer with the candle to illuminate a small vault within the cave wall. There were objects within the vault that she began to remove. First she withdrew an amulet of old leather hanging from a string of worked hide. It was a soft leather pouch and from it, attached to a string, she withdrew the small figure of a naked woman, an earth goddess. She allowed me to hold it in my trembling hand while I kept the candle at the level of the vault. Next, she withdrew a clear crystal wand, and then, from the back of the vault, she removed the last object, another larger leather pouch with a drawstring.

"Mother spread one of our sleeping blankets out upon the stone floor of the cave and we sat together with these treasures. Asking her how she knew of the vault, she told me that her mother had taken her to this place for exactly the reason we were here. I can remember regarding my mother as a complete mystery, and had no idea this part of her existed although I felt her tenderness and love every day. This was deep woman-mystery and it was strictly forbidden. I was excited beyond belief, and had a difficult time containing my delight. Mother asked me to remove my summer dress and the apron which protected it from the brush and sticky grasses with which we worked. I folded them neatly, setting them next to my boots which I had removed when we sat upon the blanket. She then asked that I remove my undergarments and lie naked on the blanket. It was decidedly wicked even to suggest this, which only heightened my excitement. There was no doubt that my mother's blood ran in my veins. How strongly it ran was yet to be revealed.

"From the soft pouch, she took six large, blue faceted stones. I was to learn later that they were very old sapphires. She set them in a Star of David around the blanket, then put the goddess figure around my neck. Mother took from her bag some precious oils which I had seen her purchase at market earlier that summer. She rubbed the fragrant oil into her hands and began to stroke my body with them. Though she had caressed me often as a child, no one had ever touched me in this way. I giggled, sighed, moaned, and wept. I rode on waves of bliss and knew the pleasure my body was capable of feeling. I was fully awakened as a

woman, my mother bringing the fire within me to an almost unbearable conclusion. I can still feel her delicate hands stroking
my womanness, circling my breasts, and reaching within to stimu-
late me. It was all too quick, and all too long ago. We lay, she and
I, in each other's arms that night gazing at the stars. She told me
what she would have done with the crystal wand in ancient times,
to break the seal of my virginity. In our culture, that would have
brought accusations of sinful behavior if not the practice of witchcraft. It was too much to risk. She told me stories of making love
with men and how to pleasure myself to keep my spark alive. It is
ironic, almost amusing, that now, in this women's dungeon my
arms have been chained too high by the patriarchs for me to
spark my own fire. Well, my merciless accusers, I have been
sparked by the memory of my mother who followed this way before me.

"As the years passed, Mother began speaking to me more directly about her family history. Theirs was an old family in
Provence with relations spreading north into Italy. Their facade
of Catholicism was fairly thin but they were not questioned because of their position in the world of banking. One of her ancestors was a great nobleman named Godefroi St. Omer, from Flandre,
who was chosen as one of the original knights Templar in 1118.
The knights were supported by St. Bernard of Clairvaux. Nine of
them went to Jerusalem on a mission, following the promptings
of the Cistercian Abbot, Bernard, and their grand master Hugues
de Payens, who was related to the famous Count de Champagne.
For the purposes of papal approval and public knowledge, their
work was described as the protection of the Christian pilgrims on
the bandit-ridden roads to the Holy Land. However, their real
task was the retrieval of documents and treasures from the sealed
stable beneath Solomon's temple. Well, heart and soul, you might
ask how Bernard and this elite circle of men who had avowed
poverty, chastity and obedience, knew of the existence of such
treasure. I asked Mother, incessantly, but she would not tell me.
There was a hidden past to her family that she would not reveal.
Being kept in the darkness about it did not dull my interest in the
rest of her story.

"During the time of the Templars, the family migrated from
Flandre to Provence and Languedoc. She revealed to me that the
noble part of the family had once left France to live in Britain, but
that was around the year 500. They returned to Flandre a few
hundred years later, and, during the time of the Templars, followed their original migration path back to the southern coastal

[209]

region. Something of this migration stirred in my blood when she told me, but I was not one to travel very far. I did not understand the family origins at the time. In Languedoc, our relatives support the gnostic teachings in a movement of natural spirituality. They believed that all people were created equally, male and female, Muslim and Jew, and that God could be reached without priestly intervention, elaborate churches or special words. They called themselves Gnostics and mother said they were related to a very early Gnostic sect that settled in that region after Jesus died. I told her my heart felt these people were in touch with what Jesus really said. She looked at me in a peculiar way, then looked away.

"Mother reacted sadly. She said that the Gnostics may truly have understood something that threatened Rome, something fundamentally wrong with Rome's story of Jesus. What is more, they were highly educated and discerned some deep esoteric truths that were part of the Templar legacy.

"At that time, rumors about another sect, the Cathars, flew wildly all over the region, like birds before a storm. They were said to have knowledge of Templar treasure, to participate in pagan practices and abnormal sexual rituals that were actually moon-guided methods to avoid conception. The level of fear grew, fed by the Vatican, of course and, before long, Rome had reason to slaughter them all. Thousands of people, their villages and their culture vanished in the fires. That was in 1209. Mother's relatives left that region escaping the judgment of Rome and mindless murder. The slaughter of their peaceful countrymen did not dissuade them from the beliefs that had been in their families for centuries, but they learned to be more secretive than the Cathars.

"She told me more about St. Bernard and Godefroi and the Templars. They took individual vows of poverty but the Templars became a very wealthy order within the church of Rome. Ultimately, they had so much power and wealth that Rome fabricated charges against them, and members of the entire order, which had grown considerably, were burned at the stake. The real reason was not so much the wealth but the secret knowledge which they held, taken from the documents recovered in Jerusalem - something the church did not want revealed. The wealth had been spirited away to other lands so the church never confiscated it, and the brave knights died with the secret knowledge. The last of the Templars in France, Grand Master Jaques de Molay, was burned at the stake in 1314, long after Godefroi's natural death, but our family had had knights among the Templars

[210]

throughout the two hundred years of the order's existence. They fought in the Crusades alongside Richard I and brought a sense of pride to this region of France. In life and in death, they were avowed to hold whatever level of secret knowledge was revealed to them, and not a single one succumbed to the tortures of the Inquisitors. This is our legacy, heart and soul. No wonder we are in this present situation! We are living in the ashes of my ancestors.

"Mother's family grieved the loss of the Templars, but not publicly. It was unsafe to be outspoken about the demise of this great order of noblemen. One hundred years had passed since the slaughter of the Cathars but the memory was still fresh within the bloodline when the Templars were burned. Since that time, the eyes of Rome have been sharply focused on this region for they still feel a treasure is there in the Languedoc. The Spanish Dominicans moved their Inquisition into France where regular public burnings have added to the ash. Now millions have died and it is not over. Where will this world of fear end - in the annihilation of all but the papacy? We have already lost our freedom to speak, to think, and now we women are branded witches and pagans for giving healing herbs to those in pain. It is a defilement of the natural law. How are we to remember that we are children of Mother Earth? How far we have strayed from the gentle words of Jesus? You can see, heart and soul, they have not taken away my freedom to feel," she wept.

"I must continue. Mother and I spent our summers in the fields gathering medicinal herbs. Over the years I had been apprenticed in the herbal craft with her. She was a master. It occurred to me that this way of transmission was also the way the Cathars had kept their beliefs alive until they were destroyed. My bright mind could see where this was leading, even then, and I cautioned Mother to be careful. She was openly practicing herbal medicine and assisting a doctor with healing work. The doctor was her husband and a familiar of the Inquisitor. It was a dangerous game but she could see no way to escape it. Every time we were near St. Baume, she and I would climb to the cave in the mountains where she had initiated me. Much of the history of her bloodline came through at those times. She became sentimental when we went there and did not want to leave the mountains. I felt drawn to the area as well but did not fully understand her sentiment. When I was twenty-three - heart and soul was that just two years ago? Well, when I was twenty-three, we were in St. Baume in September, gathering late mountain herbs and some special roots that we used for women's cycles. Mother was particularly watchful on that trip and careful to wait until dark before we made our way to the cave. Lighting one candle, we cleaned the cave floor as was our ritual. We had not opened the vault since my initiation so I was surprised when she asked me to try to locate it. I remember her patience and encouragement as she urged me to become completely receptive and not try to think about where the stone was situated. I ran my long, thin fingers along the rock as she stood between me and the candle, challenging my skill in the darkness. I deeply engaged the feel of the rock and linked it to my second sight which I was rapidly developing. When my fingers hit the jagged edge of the stone, my heart jumped and a feeling of deep connection ran through my slight body.

"Mother knew I had found it and brought the candle forward. We were so bonded it was difficult to keep anything from her. We were like two priestesses of old remembering the rituals that were in our blood. She told me to remove the amulet and place it around my neck, leaving the goddess inside her pouch. As I followed her instructions, she picked up my long black hair with her free hand allowing the amulet cord to lie beneath it. Next she instructed me to remove the other pouch containing the six sapphires. I spilled them out into my hand and felt the energy within my essence quicken. They were magical stones. She taught me to lay out the Star of David grid with them and we sat facing each other upon our blanket in the center. The crystal wand was left within the vault. The night was clear and a little cool. I drew a wrap around my shoulder and looked into her eyes.

"As soon as her eyes met mine, I knew I was to learn the family secret. Instead of my excited childhood reaction, I felt a churning in my stomach, a warning of danger, and a loss of any remaining innocence. She began by telling me that she had made a great mistake before our journey to St. Baume and she felt her life was in danger. She had saved the life of a mother and baby by demanding that my father stand aside while she skillfully corrected a breached position and completed the delivery. The outcome, life rather than death, was of no concern to my father whose ego was too invested in his work. Mother acted from her heart when her heart could stand no more ignorance. She stayed to soothe the mother with healing herbs and soft singing. When she returned home, Father seized her by the hair and beat her. I knew this was not the first time this had happened, but he further threatened to have her charged with witchcraft before the Inquisition. I was devastated. I knew my father was insensitive and egotistical but I did not believe he would betray a good woman who was also his wife. She told me he had been watching her for years, waiting for her to err in such a way. She was certain he had his eyes upon a younger woman and would not mind if she were removed from his life forever, it seemed.

"I had never cared for my father. I avoided him easily for Mother was his assistant and I, in assisting her, worked mostly with the herb drying and mixing. He spent his free hours at the nearby inn drinking ale with the other men of his breed. I could well imagine his seduction by the voluptuous young women who worked at the inn. I felt a sadness for my mother but she seemed to feel none for herself. She continued by telling me that there was something more important than her life at stake. I asked her what, on this Earth, could be more important than the life of my mother? Her answer was simple - the codes of light - I did not understand, but allowed her to continue. Mother explained that she was part of a lineage of women who had served the planet since ancient times. These women held codes of light that allowed humankind to elevate its consciousness toward God perfection. I did not insult her lineage by insinuating that something must have gone wrong. It was obvious that anyone practicing God-consciousness in our times was asking to be slaughtered by those who claimed they were the spokesmen of God. I found myself slipping into cynicism quite often and I cannot say that this horrible habit has left me yet.

"I heard Mother's story and many things began to make sense to me. Her lineage of light had been guarded by the Knights Templar and the Cistercians as well as other secret orders related to the Templars. She told me they were all part of a brotherhood that had watched over the women of this lineage for thousands of years. She told me all that she knew of this lineage of light, the brotherhood and the true story of Jesus and Mary Magdalen. I wept for I knew this was the truth. It shook my core essence, resonating with me fully. I could not deny it. I was a heretic. We were both heretics. I had always known that God was within my own reach, that I did not need manipulative priests to connect me to my creator. Mother did not tell me anything I did not know deep inside, except the well kept-secret.

"When the Templars were being hunted, their treasure was right under the nose of Philippe IV in Paris, but he did not find it. The brotherhood secreted it away to Scotland on a trading ship and it lies buried deep in the wall of a great monument there. It was not money. It was not gold. It was a set of tablets, the Tablets of Testimony. I could not understand why a set of tablets could be so important. Taking my hands, she blew her sweet breath upon my face. She had a luminosity that I had not seen around her before this time, and was so beautiful at that moment. A soft laugh escaped her lips and she smiled at me tenderly, lifting a hand to stroke my cheek. She told me that which she could not have risked telling me earlier. Now it was important to the lineage that I know my own identity. My mother spoke softly, but with some pride, as she told me that I was, in my maternal blood a Jew, and a soul incarnate for the lineage of light. I did not know what to say. I had always thought that I was a French Catholic. I was French Catholic on my father's side, but my mother's heritage, though carefully masked during the persecutions, was absolutely Jewish. As soon as this truth entered my core essence, I came into alignment with it and my blood ran warm with it.

"Mother continued, telling me that this lineage of light had been brought to France by Mary Magdalen soon after the crucifixion of Jesus. She told me Jesus did not die on the cross but lived many years, fathered children with Mary and spread his gentle teachings in many places before ascending. These were secrets kept in the lineage and the brotherhood as well as the bloodline of Jesus and Mary which continued to be kept secret to this day. There were many of the bloodline in France, England, Ireland and Scotland and we were two of them. I begged her to tell me more. She revealed to me that our lineage came directly from the daughter of Mary and Jesus, whose name was Tamar. We were sitting in the very cave that Mary sat in fifteen hundred years ago. It was her cave of meditation. That is why mother was so respectful of the cave and visited it yearly to maintain it. Mother was the living holder of the codes that Mary had passed on so long ago. We sat within a Star of David made with the same sapphires that Mary had used. Churches dedicated to Mary Magdalen appeared in every village in this part of France and Mother assured me that Chartres and all the great Gothic churches were dedicated to Mary Magdalen and not the mother of Jesus, for it was Mary Magdalen who carried the Grail child, Josephes, in her womb to France. I had studied the lore of King Arthur and his knights but had no idea they carried forth the legacy of the brotherhood and the bloodline of Jesus.

"Mother had me spellbound as she told the stories of Mary and Morgaine, and before them Lilith and Mir-An-Da. There were many women in this soul lineage, the priestesses of Annu, the Sun. These were the shining stars, but all of them, from the ordinary to the brilliant, were equally committed to carrying the codes of light for the Earth. I made Mother talk all night, telling me everything she knew and whatever she could intuit about these women. I wanted to know who I really was, and she birthed me into another level of my truth. We forgot all about the Inquisitors and my father. For that night we lived our heritage. We were Akhus, serving the High Council on planet Earth. I felt it. I knew it. But I could not live it. I have failed the mission. Look at me, heart and soul, an imprisoned Akhu. How have I served the Earth? Well, I will not get into grieving for myself at this moment. I am committed to the recitation of this story to its completion.

"Sometime in the middle of that memorable night, Mother brought up the great secret of the Templars and St. Bernard. She revealed to me that it was the Ark of the Covenant which the original nine Templars had removed from Solomon's stables. I could not imagine what an Ark of the Covenant was or why its whereabouts was of such great importance to the Catholic church. Within minutes, I understood. Mother revealed to me that the Ark of the Covenant was a set of stone tablets called the Tablets of Testimony. I was sure she was referring to the Ten Commandments, but she was not. According to Mother, the Ten Commandments were a covenant between Moses and his followers. The Tablets of Testimony were a covenant between the Akhus and the Divine Lineage of Kings - the Akhu lineage. These were tablets containing teachings of the star beings; sacred geometry, symbols and numbers, astronomy, and magic - all that the brotherhood held sacred. They were far older than Moses, dating to *the First Times*, what the ancients called Zep Tepi. Perhaps no one understood these tablets now, but someday, when the Akhus return, they will be found and understood. With the Tablets of Testimony were many of the Gnostic writings of Mary, Thomas, Phillop, Simon, James and Jesus and the succeeding generations of brothers and sisters of *The Way*.

"Mother had completely activated me. With the dawn, we replaced the amulet and the sapphires in the vault and carefully set the stone in place. It could not be detected. I wondered which of my sisters had first discovered the vault and thought to put Mary's sacred objects within it. The treasures had been to Camelot and back again since Mary had touched them, but I could feel her power within each sapphire as I dropped them one by one into the leather pouch. I did not sleep or take food for weeks after that night and did not suffer from deprivation. We gathered more herbs and roots than we needed to prolong our time in the mountains. Before returning to our home in Aix-en-Provence, we spent several days in the hot springs near the town, cleansing our bodies of all impurities and our minds of all fearful thoughts. That was the last time I was with my mother. We arrived home to find the Inquisitor's henchmen at our dwelling awaiting my mother. My father betrayed his own wife, my beloved mother, to the merciless Dominican, Boulangier. My father is worse than evil.

"I do not know what they did to my mother in prison. I can imagine it, for I know what they have done to me. She was imprisoned, first in Marseilles, then in Aix-en-Provence where she was brought to the stake, not in the common market, but in the central square as part of the yearly show of power by the church. We were all expected to attend these demonic events. My father forced me to attend and I did so to protect the codes of light. She was one of ten who were burned that day. I did not recognize her. She had been imprisoned for almost a year. Her round mother-body was emaciated. Her head had just been shaved before us in the square, for they feared women held the spell of witches within their hair. Her joints were too stretched from the rack to support her body so they dragged her to the stake, stripping her before tying her to the upright with coarse rope. I wept inside and held my hand to my heart to steady it. The sunken eyes of Marie de Ville looked out into the crowd, glazing over the eyes of the silent woman whose life she had saved, to rest upon the sobbing eyes of her daughter, Isabel. When our eyes met, our hearts leaped out and locked us into our truth, together. I saw her energy shift as they piled the wood around her, up to her knees. She was in her strength from that point onward. Energetically, I held the space for her as they read her name, listed her transgressions, and lit the fire that slowly consumed her. She did not cry out. She held my gaze. When her consciousness left her, I felt the touch of angels wings upon my cheeks and knew that she had passed to the light. I pray to be as brave myself, when I am brought to the square this morning.

"Sneaking back into the square that night, I gathered a portion of my mother's ashes in a small, tightly woven bag. I kept them in my room, close to a very beautiful little painting of Mary and the child Jesus. The next time my father went to Marseilles to confer with the Inquisitor, I packed up the ashes and my herb-crafting tools, and rode to St. Baume. I was careful not to be seen in the vicinity of the cave and gathered herbs and roots as I would have done with Mother during that season. When I felt acceptance as an herbalist working in the region, I found a shelter for my horse and climbed in the night to the cave. Without even thinking, I cleaned the floor of debris and laid out my blanket. After lighting one little candle near the floor, I stood facing the cave wall and began to run my hand along the rock, searching for the opening. It was frustrating, for my heart was beating fast, spoiling my concentration. After several attempts, I found the jagged edge and loosened the stone. I removed all the sacred objects, laying them out upon the blanket with the small sack of my mothers ashes.

"I visualized her there and felt something of her presence. I missed her greatly. I set the grid of the Star of David with the sapphires and knelt, naked, within it. I placed the goddess amulet around my neck, her round form nestling between my breasts. My intention was to consecrate my life to the lineage of light. I wanted clarity of purpose and a vision of the future. I did not know how to escape my father, except in the prison of a loveless marriage. Was there a chance? I wanted hope in a hopeless world. I had brought strong herbs to carry me into a trance state and took them with a long drink of water from my goat bladder. I sat in stillness until the herbs began to work, then closed my eyes and journeyed out into the world of spirit. I was guided to a beautiful star where I was met by several light beings who took me before a council of Akhus. I asked them about the purpose of my life. They told me it was truth. I was to embody truth, to become truth. If I could master this one thing, I would always be born in my truth. There was no escape from my situation and no need to escape. My lessons were to be learned in a very small space. Freedom was a universal concept and not a measure of one's boundaries upon the Earth. I understand their wisdom now but was not certain of their meaning at the time. I asked about the codes of light and what would become of them if I did not have a child. The council was patient with me for I am not, in this life, an especially enlightened representative of the lineage. The lineage was not always passed from mother to daughter or within the blood, though, they said, it had been in recent times.

"They gave me a vision. It was a vision of a candle flame. I stared at the flame and watched it diminish. It got smaller and smaller and then went out. Out of the darkness came the face of a beautiful woman. She was bronze-skinned with liquid black eyes that had a slight slant. Her hair was long, black, and braided with the subtly colored yarns of plant-dyed wool. She had a big, beautiful smile. On her back, she carried a sleeping child wrapped in a woven blanket that she had tied around her chest. She stood before green mountains where a great black bird flew in circles in the sky. In turning to look into my eyes, I could see the golden discs of the sun between her brows and on her heart. I knew I need look no further for the codes of light. The vision faded and I stood before the council of Akhus once again. My mind was at peace so they dismissed me and I found myself back within the cave of Mary Magdalen. Still entranced, I lifted the crystal wand and slid it within me. Bringing my full weight down upon it, I broke the seal of my virginity. I was a true priestess of Annu at that moment and felt full with the lineage of light. I would master my truth. It was my calling.

"When my father returned from Marseilles, he commanded that I begin assisting him as my mother had, even though I had no midwifery experience and little knowledge of disease. He claimed to know the formulation of the medicines and wished only for me to provide the medicinals, as Mother had to many medical doctors, and assist in comforting the patients. Some of his techniques were more brutal than the diseases but I did not offer my opinion. I knew that Father had been watching me since the time of my mother's arrest. He began to harass me about marriage, suggesting many of his brutish, widowed friends as husbands. Of course, they were widowed because their wives had been burned at the stake. They shared a macabre comradeship that made my blood curdle. I wondered how many of them had arranged the arrests of their tiresome wives through my father. I refused all his suggestions, telling him I was sure there was a young man for me, one who would honor my patience and purity.

"In circles of family friends, all of whom were papal loyalists, I was the well-educated daughter of a medical doctor. I counted no personal friends among them. In the market, I was a master herbalist walking in my mother's footsteps. I had friends among the women vendors in the market but confided in none of them. Leading a double life, I was lonely and was regarded as an enigma within each of my double lives for my refusal to marry and bear children. Already I was called a withered one for walking in this truth. After my mother's execution, time passed slowly for me. It seemed as if I were waiting for something to be over, some door to open into a new opportunity in my life.

"The door that opened was that of my sleeping quarters. My father returned from one of his drunken nights at the inn and barged into my room awakening me. I must have been the topic of discussion at the inn that night for he was raving about the shame I continually caused him with my snobbish tendencies and ways of my mother. Stunned, I did not act quickly enough to reach a place of safety, and he was upon me, in all his brutish ugliness. He smelled of stale ale and was slathering about the mouth. I began fighting to get out from under him, but I was a slight woman and he was a strong man, especially in his will. He threw the covers from the bed and tore at my dressing gown. Dear heart and soul, I will not recall the details for you. I have released them a hundred times over, as I have sat within this prison. To him, I was a shadow of my mother who haunted his every moment. His guilt will never set him free. He lives within his own prison and now the walls of that prison grow stronger for him. I would be his chattel still, if I had not brought myself down upon that crystal wand in the cave at St. Baume. His rage at my impurity, at my lack of virginity, far outweighed his incestuous needs. He wasted no time in summoning the henchmen of the Inquisitor, ordering them to remove the vile shadow of his wife from his home. Through all of this ordeal, no one has inquired as to how he knew to bring the charges of filth against me. Of course, that is part of their conspiracy against women. The patriarchs are faultless, but they are not guiltless.

"Seeing clearly the path of his rage, I spent the hours of freedom that still remained for me weaving sacred herbs into the deepest layers of my long black hair, close to my scalp. I would not be able to stay in my truth if I became senseless, so I wove into my hair herbs that would heal my mind of torture. Also herbs of sedation to ease the pain of my body and lastly, I wove in herbs of deep trance that would take me to the fire this day. It did not compromise my truth to stay within my power in this way.

"I was taken to the Inquisitor in Marseilles before the week was finished. They stripped me and my clothing was searched, but they did not look within the hair close to my scalp. In prison rags, I was brought before Boulangier, himself, as a scribe recorded my initial hearing. The accusations brought against me were deviant sexual practices, disobedience towards my father, and suspected witchcraft and satanic worship. I stayed in my truth during this initial inquiry and did not react emotionally. Of course, my calm gave them evidence that I was a demonic woman. They greatly feared women of power and fortunately did not sexually assault them for that reason. I denied all charges, remaining in my truth. I knew well that those women who repented, betrayed other women, or offered their bodies to save themselves, burned in fires just as hot as the women who stood in their truth. Millions of women in France and Spain had succumbed to the fires. I was not going to be an exception. My Gnostic beliefs, the great teachings of Jesus, the brotherhood and the sisterhood, lit my way through that darkness.

"Boulangier saw me once more, in an attempt to verbally extract a confession from me. He asked that I repent and place myself under the wise guidance of God's true annointed ones. I did not reply. He asked if I believed that he was divinely guided. I could not but speak my truth. Was that not the purpose of my life? I was delivered to the torturers in the prison at Aix-en-Provence that night. Here again, dear heart and soul, it is not necessary to relive my agony. I endured. The tips of my fingers and toes were slowly crushed many times until, each time I fainted. I was held under water until my lungs filled with water, then salvaged until the next drowning. My skull was slowly compressed in an evil vise until, again, I chose unconsciousness. I was stretched upon the rack until my joints gave way to freedom. I pulled the healing herbs from my hair when dragged to my chains in the darkened cell and chewed them with absolute intent. The torturers starved me, then fed me contaminated food. I refused to eat, so they forced it into me. I sat in my own defecation, picking the lice from my scalp, and unable to stop their infestation and biting within my pubic hair. It was hell, heart and soul. Through it all I held my truth. I have held it so well they saved my sliver of a life for the yearly demonstration of power in the square at Aix-en-Provence. Within the hour, exactly one year after the execution of my mother, I will be released from hell.

I do not know what to do about the pain and shock this body has endured and will suffer. Perhaps the fire will release it.

I do not know what to do about the fear and guilt that plague my emotions. I feel I am a failure to the lineage of light because the codes will be burned with me. I hold the vision of that beautiful dark-skinned woman with the solar disc between her brows, for it gives me hope that the lineage of light survives me, somehow.

I do not know what to do with my ego, for it wanted to serve the priestesses of Annu in a meaningful way. Perhaps this is a lesson for my ego.

I do not know what to do with my mind. It gives me no peace from judgment of these cruel and blind men who put the innocent to death in the name of God. I offer my life in the hope that this unholy Inquisition might end before there are no women of power left in the world.

I know what to do with my soul, for it has reached a new level of mastery. My soul has become truth and it will never incarnate on this Earth again without that truth.

I will pray for my spirit, that it might know God before this body passes.

I will pray that I die consciously in the arms of God."

*

Isabel, rested her head against the cold stone wall and entered the stillness of her prayer. She visualized herself in the meadow beneath the cave at St. Baume, gathering the bounty of the Mother. Not having seen the Earth for nearly a year, her prayers brought back to her the fragrant beauty that she longed to touch again. Moving to sit upon a flat rock, she lifted her gaze to the Sun as she prayed. The lineage of light moved through her, lighting the way through the darkness of this hour.

When she heard the guards coming for her, she deftly reached to her head, and tore from her wild hair the herbs of deep trance that she had saved for this moment. They had grown out over two inches from her scalp. She held them in her mouth, as the guards entered and jerked her to her feet. Their potent powers were absorbed into her blood as they dragged her up into the morning light. She was taken to a hanging loop of rope which was tightened around her throat to hold her upright as they stripped away her rotten garments and shaved the hair from her head and her pubis. In her consciousness, she was climbing to the sacred cave of Mary Magdalen in the mountains above her place of prayer. She found the jagged edge of the vault stone and slipped it away. Leaving the sacred objects within the vault, she removed her mother's ashes. Isabel replaced the secret stone within the vault opening, and after brushing away the accumulated debris, spread her mother's ashes upon the cave floor. She found herself sitting in this circle of ashes as they dragged her to the stake cutting her tender body with the coarse ropes as they tied her to it. The herbs began to deepen her trance whilst the wood was propped around her and the Inquisitor's henchmen read the accusations and the death sentence of Isabel de Renney.

*

"Dear heart and soul, we have been sentenced as an incorrigible witch. That is better than dying as a wench, no doubt. If I have failed to fulfill the purpose of my life, please forgive me.

The Priestesses of Annu

Perhaps God will provide another opportunity at a time when life is valued more than it is now. I look out upon this crowd with what is left of my vision and I see the faces of the women who laughed with me in the market. They are pretending not to know me. Their silence is betrayal, but I forgive them. They want to live, and I honor that. I see the face of my father and spit the bitter stems of my herbs toward him. I hear them sizzle in the growing fire beneath me. He will not look into my eyes. Dear God, I fear that I cannot forgive him for his betrayal. I can feel the heat of the fire now as it licks at my legs. I see again the cave, the earth, the ashes of my mother. The pain is unbearable. My flesh is melting but my mind will not release me.

"But now, I see the filaments of light reaching out from a point within me. They extend through the crowd into a larger matrix of light that fills the universe. Something within me shifts and the fire is gone. I feel cool. I see a Knight riding a great black stallion towards me. He is the beloved I have awaited. I am taken upon his horse between his strong legs and he rides with me out into the mountains at St. Baume. I am delivered to the sacred cave where I find the most beautiful woman sitting in meditation. She is dressed in black robes and her eyes are pools of light into which she draws me. I kneel before her and she draws my head into her lap. I release my tears. Her gentle voice is just a whisper as she says to me,

"Beloved, I am your mother, Mary.
Come into my heart to rest, my sweet Tamar."

"I am free."

Leah speaks

The women in the group were tearfully holding each other once again. It seemed that Leah's stories were becoming even more poignant and alive as she neared the present time. Leah was striking chords of remembrance which had been more recently imprinted on the collective. She knew the details of Isabel's life well for it had been her own. It was important in this life to heal Isabel's wounds. Born into fire, she had struggled and still did, to release it from her body. The wounds with that father who came again as her father in this life had been healed. At last she was able to forgive him. Leah's great healings had been the release of patterns of cynicism, betrayal, guilt, and fear of failure, which she held from that death. She knew that Isabel's memory was locked within her body, for Isabel, like so many women, found no way to release the physical and emotional pain. Holding the pattern of separation coming from Tamar, through Isabel, and then into her present life, she healed that also. Failure and separation were fabrications of the ego, she knew. Her work with the shamans had eventually elevated her consciousness beyond the ego's grasp. Therefore, when she finally spoke to the group, it was not in the first person, but the collective, the "we."

"My beloveds, not a single one of us escaped those fires. Nine million people burned in the holocausts of the Inquisition - most of them women. Mary Magdalen knew that the foundation of the church of Peter and Paul was built upon untruths, falsities and lies. Like a hideous monster, the church played games of power with kings and queens and those who would control the world. They ruthlessly hunted down the brotherhood, the sisterhood and the bloodline of Jesus and Mary. If the truth of the life of Jesus were known, the foundation of their institutions would support them no longer. To maintain their power, they hid that truth, controlled the minds of the people with lies and fear, and killed millions whom they feared might have challenged them. It was a great departure from the teachings of Jesus and the Essenes.

"Now the energies available to those in power supporting their supremacy are being withdrawn from the Earth. If we cannot live in truth in the coming times, we will perish. Institutions will perish in the name of truth. The energy behind the Inquisition, which was not limited to Europe but reached into South America as well, will be forced into balance."

Tracy, the high energy athlete of the group, looked ready to pick a fight. "Leah", she cried, "this makes me so angry. I can see that everyone here is very sad, but I am really angry. What can I do?"

"Oh Tracy, we have all been angry about the burnings. In truth, we must let go of the anger if we are to ascend into higher consciousness. Anger is such a low frequency. We have talked a lot about fire and its power of transformation. We have talked about menopausal hot flashes being cancer cell killers, for example. We have used fire to cleanse our luminous bodies. Even St. Germain works with a violet flame for purification. If we can look upon the Inquisition as the fire that is bringing women into higher consciousness we should be able let go of the painful memories carried in our bodies and souls. As the Divine Plan unfolds for the Earth, who are we to judge what is evil and unnecessary.

[223]

Does this help, Tracy?"

"It does. But Leah, what about the codes of light?"

"The codes of light died with Isabel in Europe. We have reached the end of the story of the priestesses of Annu. We are about to begin the story of the priestesses of Inti. Did you forget that the Siriuns had a backup plan?" Tracy nodded her head and allowed her shoulders to drop back into relaxation.

Leah swept the sapphires up into her hand and replaced them in the blue velvet bag. A smile crossed her face as she spoke again, "I suggest that we cool our internal fires with a short swim at the lake. Since this evening session was brief, we have time for sisterly massages and maybe some chocolate cake."

The smiles she received back meant more to her than these women would ever know. She was healed of her separation on all levels and knew that she would not fail in this life. The planetary awakening was well under way.

Mamacocha

Leah speaks

When the women came together the next evening, they found that Leah had completely changed the altar and the center of their circle. They felt the energies had also shifted to accommodate those changes. Upon the altar was a golden sun, a replica of the sun disc of the Incas. Together with Sananda, were pictures of men and women shamans and hand-carved miniature stone altars. On one of these carvings, of smooth red stone, was a hand with its thumb tucked between the index and second finger - a sign of concealed power. On another altar which was carved with glyphs, there sat a perfect six-sided generator crystal of amethyst. The third little altar held a natural emerald. Several statues carved of soft black stone stood next to lit candles. One of these statues represented Pachamama, Mother Earth, and the other was Pachakamac, Cosmic Father.

In the center of their circle, Leah had spread several colorful *tejidos* - finely woven cloths. On these lay a folded *mesa* cloth containing Leah's *quyas*, or healing stones. A ring of votive candles in gold glass cups surrounded the *mesa*. Leah entered the room dressed in black silk. A finely woven black cloth edged with deep rose and purple glyphs of Inti, the Sun, was wrapped around her shoulders to shield her from the cool air that was flowing down the mountain. The hot days and warmer nights of summer had suddenly shifted into fall-like weather as their week together had progressed. Leah loved the cool mountain nights and looked to be in her element, a shaman, head to toe. Black, the color of invisibility, was as much a part of life in the Andes as it was in the temples of Annu. She sat cross-legged on the floor and leaned forward to open the *mesa* containing her stones. She neatly folded the edges of the cloth back exposing them and picked out twelve heavy, round ones. Leah arose and placed them in a circle around the group creating a medicine wheel. Touching the floor, she invoked the devas and spirits of nature, then Mother Earth. Raising her hands upward, she summoned the lineage of light, the brotherhood of the magi, and the Siriun High Council to guide their work for the next few days. She sat down gingerly, and looked around the circle with sparkling eyes.

"My beloveds, I have put the sapphires away for now and have laid an Earth grid with the many meteorites that I was given in Peru. This will connect us to the stars, Pachamama, and all that lies between them. Isabel knew the power of the sapphires and had been careful to conceal them once again within the cave wall of Saint Baume. They have no connection to the lineage in Peru, though she was given a clear vision of the Peruvian female shaman who was carrying the codes of light when she, herself, could not fulfill her commitment to the lineage. It had helped to ease the guilt and pain she had experienced from an incomplete mission. Also it was critical to my own healing to realize that the Inquisition did not completely extinguish the light on the planet. When I discovered the bridge between the lineage in Europe and that in Peru, my heart lifted and soared with the condors. The mission had not failed. It was alive and well in the Andes.

"The codes of light had come through the European branch of the soul lineage, but there was no further conscious passage beyond Isabel. The mission of the Andean branch of the lineage was to hold the codes in preparation for re-activation as a soul group, not only bringing the passage of the codes back into consciousness, but out of secrecy. This has all occurred in the last few years as we have raised our frequency to the higher level of code activation. We have been opened, and made conscious of the mission all at once. For this to have happened any sooner, would have been dangerous to the mission. Those who are consciously carrying the codes at this time have only recently extricated themselves from the yoke of imposed beliefs that would have sabotaged the mission. As usual, the Divine Plan unfolds with precision and infinite wisdom.

"To trace the lineage back to its inception in Peru, we really need to return to the times of Aman-Ra, and the visit of Aman-Ra's son, Mak-Ma. His journey to the Andes set the stage for the later arrival of the Wiracochas, or shining beings. These, of course, were the same Akhus who birthed the lineage we have just finished discussing. When Mak-Ma, journeyed to the fertile, high plains of Peru and Bolivia, over 14,000 years ago, there were people living there who were remnants of a great civilization that existed in the Amazon near Paititi, east of Cusco. There were also people who had immigrated from the great continent of Mu in the Pacific and many mixed blood Indians from much earlier civilizations. Mu had suffered cataclysms which submerged most of the continent many thousands of years previous to the time to which I refer, but Lemuria was still above water when Mak-Ma came to the shores of Titicaca Lake. He was a master mason who knew the secrets of splitting and moving great stones with sound waves. In truth, he was the first Wiracocha who designed and built the city of Tiwanaku on the shores of the lake. The existing legends do not go back far enough into the past to include him, but the people who lived at the time of the next seeding of Akhus must have held the memory of Aman-Ra's son in their legends for they immediately accepted the new Wiracochas as their leaders and teachers.

"The Wiracochas arrived at the time of the final destruction of Lemuria and Atlantis, around 10,000 BC. By then, as a result of the cataclysms, the fertile plains around Titicaca Lake had been raised to form the present *altiplano*, or high plateau, with its unforgiving climate. Titicaca Lake overflowed, then receded leaving the city of Tiwanaku at some distance from the water. The once flourishing port city became a site of pilgrimage, but was otherwise abandoned. Many of its monolithic walls were quarried by an influx of Lemurian immigrants who arrived after the final destruction of their own continent. They were led by a great sage, Amaru Muru, who was the last of a great lineage of Akhus who were priests of Mu. The new Wiracochas found few remnant peoples after the cataclysm for most had died in the floods when Titicaca Lake spilled over the land, but there were a few left who held the teachings and the blood of Mak-Ma. Lord Muru was a spiritual leader who was in direct communication with the Siriun High Council. He was an ancient member of the brotherhood, and was aware of the need to seed the lineage of light and the brotherhood of the magi to safeguard the greater Mission of planetary ascension. He welcomed the arrival of the new starseed, a brother and sister, who came to be known as Wiracocha and Mamacocha.

"Wiracocha and Mamacocha emerged from the waters of Titicaca Lake. The translation of their names in the oldest languages of the Andes are *Foam of the Sea* and *Mother of the Sea*,

[227]

respectively. In sharp contrast to Aman-Ra who brought forth the fire of the Sun, Wiracocha and his sister, Mamacocha, brought forth the feminine power of water. Of course, they were children of Inti, the Sun, just as Mir-An-Da and Aman-Ra were children of Annu, but their origins were of the water. The feminine light ray enters the Earth at Titicaca Lake and the masculine enters in the Himalayas. I cannot tell you when those energies first entered the Earth, but it is curious that they are anchored at major points of Lemurian colonization. Mamacocha was a soul in the lineage of light. The lineage held the codes in both parts of the world which explains why many of the souls of the lineage incarnate at this time have affinities for the legends and lands of both starseedings.

"We find Mamacocha and a young priestess, Pukaya, walking through the Kalasasaya, surrounded by the ruined monolithic stone walls of Mak-Ma's astronomical palace at Tiwanaku. They move silently through the grounds, stepping in and out of the shadows cast by the fullness of the Moon, passing by the giant sculpted statue of Mak-Ma, the first Wiracocha. Soon they pass through the gates of the Kalasasaya and approach the old temple which is sunk within Pachamama. The temple, still used by the sisterhood and brotherhood for initiation and ceremony, is this night reserved for the two women who step down into the sacred space alone. The younger woman lights the oil lamps on the altar, illuminating the great golden disc of Inti, the Sun as well as the golden strands of her hair. Heads carved of stone protrude from the temple walls giving Pukaya the eerie feeling that the ancient ones are present.

"Pukaya, tall and wide-eyed, turns around to face the statue of Wiracocha, brother of Mamacocha and leader of the people of Titicaca Lake and the *altiplano*. His towering figure is flanked behind by smaller carvings of his two guardians who were never far from his side. They were called the protectors of his back. Pukaya stares up at the image of her father while Mamacocha tosses loose coca leaves on a small *mesa* cloth laid out on the temple floor. She is invoking the spirits of the coca plant and divining the meaning of the patterns they create when she tosses them down. Pukaya pretends not to be listening to her mentor as Mamacocha mumbles incantations and various exclamations of surprise, concern and hilarity. She will know the future soon enough. At last Mamacocha folds the *mesa*, tucking it in her woven bag and asks Pukaya to join her. Mamacocha is a slender, tall Akhu with the look of a wise younger woman. They sit upon folded weavings, facing one another beneath the great disc of the

Mamacocha

Sun. Mamacocha produces a *mesa* of soft woven *vicuña* and slides a very unusual stone from within it. She gives it to Pukaya to hold and begins to speak."

Mamacocha speaks

"Pukaya, my child, hold this sacred stone within your hands while I journey through my life for you, because tomorrow your father, Wiracocha, and I will return to the sea. There are many things about us, and your relationship to us, that you must know. He and I are brother and sister, having been born from the same great sea, but we are also husband and wife, seeding the Akhu blood upon the planet as part of our mission. You hold the pure Akhu blood within your veins my daughter, as do your siblings, and you bear the solar disc upon your brow and heart. You are the next high priestess in a lineage of women. This is a lineage which I have brought to this part of the Earth, and which carries the codes of light for higher consciousness on this planet. We conceived you in the human way, Pukaya, a beautiful baby born from my womb, but do not forget that you are from the stars. You and your brothers and sisters represent a blood lineage of the Shining Ones, the Wiracochas, who will guide and protect the spiritual development of the planet during some critical periods in her future. Listen carefully, my child. I want you to know of the past as well as the future.

"A long time ago, when Titicaca Lake was larger and not quite so high upon the Earth, a tall, bearded white man came here to spend some time teaching and helping the people of this area develop their culture. His name was Mak-Ma. He came from far across the sea where his father and mother began an Akhu bloodline much like ours. We are from the same star system as Mak-Ma. It is called Ak-An. You and I belong to the same soul lineage as Mak-Ma's mother, Mir-An-Da. The bloodline that they seeded is influencing a culture on the other side of the Earth. One day these two star-seedings will come together as the frequency of Earth reaches for the stars. For now, we hold an energy and a legacy of light that is important to that future. It is our task to be in the light, to remain at frequencies above the human vibration, through all possible futures. I have read the coca leaves regarding the distant future, and some of the possible futures do not look promising. I trust that good choices will be made and that the lineage will not lose the power of divination and discernment to insure that. For that reason, I have trained you well in the art

[229]

of divination, and so the higher realities are available to you.

"Your father and I were asked to come to this land by the High Council of Ak-An. This area of the Earth had been pushed up during several cataclysms as the lands of Mu sank into the sea. We came soon after the final submergence of Mu when Titicaca Lake came to its final resting place. We could have materialized anywhere, but there was a great need to anchor a more feminine energy on the planet for the distant future, so we chose to be born of the sea. We manifest the traditional bodies of our Akhu lineage, tall, blue-eyed, blond-haired and white-skinned, just like Mak-Ma. The remnant population from the older times knew well the legends of Mak-Ma, and we were honored as gods and leaders of the people from the time our feet stepped onto the shore of this magical lake. We were dressed, not as fish, though we are sometimes depicted in that way, but as priest and priestess of Inti. Your father wore the golden breast plate of Inti, and I wore the crown of gold that sent out the rays of the Sun. Our raiments were of soft white weave with gold threads spun through. You can imagine how we were received by the remnant population who had retained none of the Akhu characteristics.

"The Mission of our lineage is two-fold. Firstly, the women carry and release codes of light for the elevation of human consciousness over time, while our brothers act as guardians and activators of these codes. Secondly, we are involved in a collaborative mission with our fellow Akhus from the Pleiades, who have just suffered the consequences of their abuse of power through the destruction of the great continent in the eastern sea beyond the jungle, their major star-seeding effort on Earth. We will be assisting them, in the future, to re-create the situation of crystalline energy abuse that brought to an end their mission on Earth. If right choices can be made at the time of this re-creation, they will enter an alternative future at a higher frequency. This will also affect the Earth and her movement toward higher dimensions. Many of the survivors of that recent cataclysm, which paralleled the demise of Lemuria, will find their way to this continent and the great lands to the north where they will hold an Earth wisdom born of their great error. They will be joined by those who have survived the disasters of Mu and a merging of the red and bronze races will occur for the purpose of caretaking these lands which hold the key to the future of Earth's ascension.

"So you see, Pukaya, ours is a complicated and important mission which must be taken with the greatest seriousness. Fortunately, I have instilled in you a great sense of humor as well.

[230]

Do not lose that, my child. I know that, deep inside your heart, you have the funniest picture of your father and me emerging from Titicaca Lake. I encourage you to allow that picture to feed your sense of wonder, so that you do not fall into the trap of human illusion. You have the power to do as much as we have done. Use it wisely, my child.

"When your father and I arrived here, we were met by the remnant people and by Lord Muru and his followers from Lemuria. Lord Muru is of a different starseeding of Ak-An but he is one with Wiracocha in the brotherhood of magicians, the Amethystine Order. Muru brought this golden disc of the Sun from Lemuria and has used this temple to conduct his priestly duties since his arrival here at Titicaca Lake. Now Muru has completed a monastery for the brotherhoods in the mountains northeast of the lake. He will move the Sun disc there soon after we depart this Earth. There will come a time in the future when the brotherhoods of Ak-An will remove themselves from this reality and enter a higher dimension. They will do this to protect the truths and the mission. When the people of Earth uplift their frequency to that dimension, members of the brotherhoods will appear again to serve, educate, and continually uplift the humans.

Lord Muru has been a brother to both your father and me. When we first arrived, he gave us shelter and taught us the ways of the humans. Without such instructions, we might never have understood their behavior. Together with Muru, we have trained many of the remnant population to care for the temples and schools. There have always been a small number of people striving for enlightenment and these we have taken into the brotherhood and sisterhood to nurture and train further. Your sisters work diligently to train young women as priestesses and your brothers assist Muru and the Lemurians in the education of the young men. Now, the numbers grow in the orders and Wiracocha and I feel it is time to return home to Ak-An.

"After we adjusted to Earth life, your father began working with the remnant people to teach them the art of breeding and caring for animals. Once the wild *vicuñas* were captured, he accessed ways to work with their genes in order to breed larger animals, the alpacas which became domesticated. This was a gift from the beings of Ak-An who are masters of the genetics. When the herds were established, I taught the people to harvest their wool and spin it into thread. From the threads, I taught them to weave fine cloths into garments, blankets and bags. Later on, we experimented with designs in weaving and incorporated many of

[231]

the sacred symbols, like Inti, into the designs. The people worked diligently and made handsome garments for themselves and their families. They used the blankets to carry goods and the mothers wrapped their children in them and tied them to their backs. I really loved to participate in this way for working with the fibers is a great delight for me.

"Wiracocha improved the ways of producing food and when he began to travel to the jungle land and along the spine of the mountains, he brought back new seeds, increasing the variety of plants grown. He used methods of irrigation that tapped into the lake for crop watering. The culture soon flourished and men and women asked for ways to improve their dwellings and general way of life. Wiracocha showed them how to build stronger buildings cutting and moving huge pieces of stone with sound waves. They will not be able to do this when he is gone for he is one of two people on the planet now who have mastered sound energy, but the buildings he has helped to create will still be here thousands of years from now. He wished to extend the culture to include many whom he had visited in his travels up and down the mountain ranges, so he taught all the people of the land how to build strong roadways for ease of travel. The use of Earth's metals was also a gift that he brought. He taught them how to forge useful tools, and also the art of working with gold and silver for ornamentation and art.

"My tasks have brought different skills to the people as well. I worked with the plants and their spirits and, with my Akhu inspiration, have begun a system of healing that the priestesses are now mastering. From the harvesting of the gardens to the collecting of plants from the wild, they know the uses and formulas for the medicines that I have brought forth. Thus, they have developed healing temples throughout the land. This part of the mission integrated very well with the establishment of the sisterhood. Our beloved order of priestesses are master healers who can communicate directly with the spirits of plants. The priestesses of Inti trained midwives and herbalists in all of our villages. All of these things helped to improve the life of those who had survived the Earth changes and it made this austere land more inviting. People came from far away to live here and the population began to recover its losses. All of this took over two hundred years to accomplish, Pukaya. Your father and I have been here nearly five hundred more years completing the work we were sent to do. It hasn't seemed that long, but truly it has been nearly seven hundred years since we emerged from this high inland sea.

[232]

"After the population was stabilized, we began to teach of the simple way of living in God's light. Prior to that time, our teachings were more practical with only subtle limits of the spiritual nature, for stabilization of the people and the land was important. When we started spiritually guiding the people, they moved into harmony with each other. Arguments were few and there was no reason to hold judgments against one another. We ate good foods grown from the lands guarded by the nature spirits and we drank of sacred water running from the mountain springs. The Akhus call this a golden age, when living in the love of God is *The Way*. Well, this time of bringing forth the spiritual teachings was sacred to me, my child, and I would like to share parts of it with you to enrich your understanding of the mission."

*

Mamacocha stood up, giving Pukaya an opportunity to stretch her own legs and collect her thoughts. Her mother was quite a mystery to her, but she did not doubt that everything she said was true. The people revered her parents as gods, beings from the stars who selflessly served the Earth. She had no idea how she could walk in her mother's shoes, but she knew that when this night ended it would be so. Mamacocha was a great shaman, a wizard and the most loving being she had ever known. Her sense of loss was already upon her and she quickly brought herself back to the present, ready to reap the benefits of these last hours with her mother. Mamacocha had pulled a shallow clay dish from a niche in the wall and had filled it with dried herbs. She tipped it in front of the oil lamp and ignited the aromatic plants. Billows of fragrant, purifying smoke rose up from the dish as she circled the temple floor and her daughter, who had reseated herself. Pukaya knew these herbs well. Her mother was cleansing the space and both of their luminous bodies. She was also summoning the Apus, the spirits of the mountains, to witness their interaction. When the smoke died down, Mamacocha placed the dish before the statue of her beloved brother, Wiracocha, and took her place opposite Pukaya.

*

"Now, my child, we will talk of the sacred teachings. Some of them were given freely to the people. Such was the case with Ayni, the law of reciprocity. This law teaches that the energies

[233]

between two people or two groups of people must be in balance. For everything received, something of equal value must be given. It is a simple law but it has changed their way of life. When imbalances exist in the energies, there is no Ayni, and a weakness occurs in the individual or group. This can lead to domination and suppression or inequalities of many kinds. This law is now shared by all in the regions where Wiracocha has taught. We have also shared the teachings of the one God, and encouraged the people to work with the nature spirits and devas as they plant, grow and harvest their food, build their houses and fish and hunt. You know well that we Akhus, as well as our trained priests and priestesses, do not partake of the flesh of animals, but those who are working to sustain the communities are encouraged to eat of the flesh to strengthen their bodies.

"It was not difficult to introduce the concept of one God to a people who have recovered from devastation. However, it was a constant struggle to keep them from worshipping Wiracocha and myself as gods. When this periodic problem arose, we re-instructed the population about the Akhus, the starseedings, and the vastness of the universe. We are beings from other dimensions at higher frequencies, but we are not gods. We have opened ourselves to more gifts, greater perception, movement through the dimensions, and mastery of the elements, light, and sound. These are all things attainable by any of these people, but it will take them time to raise their vibrations, perhaps thousands of years of living *The Way*. The coca leaves show me that they will fall from *The Way* and begin fighting with each other when our lineage of pure Akhus leaves the planet. You and your brother, Tuko, will bring forth more pure Akhu children, Pukaya, but, eventually, the lineage will be diluted with the blood of the population. This is as it should be for the Akhu genes are meant to be spread, but the leadership will fail. In time, the High Council will send messengers to remind the people of their teachings. It is the way of the world, my child, and part of the unfolding plan is that humans must use their free will to discover their own divinity. The coca leaves tell me that someday they will succeed.

"We taught the people to track the seasons using the Sun and Moon in the great palace of Kalasasaya. We have followed strict schedules with the planting of crops in this way and know the dates of the great celebrations of the seasons. The greatest gathering, as you know, is the *Inti Raymi*, our festival of the Sun. We call back the Sun on this winter holiday with dancing, chanting, ceremony and meditation. The people have come to know and respect power. Inti is the giver of life. We have not taught the general population the esoteric significance of Inti, but they have learned the importance of the life giving rays of the Sun in their every day lives. The deep truths have unfolded within the sister-hood and brotherhood as they have developed and reached a level to hold the light. This you know from your own instructions in the temple, but you may not know that even two hundred years ago that which you had learned was not taught to the priest-esses. It has been the same with the brotherhood. Because both orders have reached a point where the frequency can be held, your father and I have been instructed to take our leave of the people.

"That brings me to the truths which have been imparted to those who will hold the light in the future. These are the priests and priestesses of Inti, the brothers and sisters. We have given them the deeper, esoteric teachings which are the legacy of Ak-An. I will review these with you now Pukaya, for to do so will awaken certain codes within you. We are children of the Sun for, at our best, we are pure light. The Sun is a star, generating high frequency light rays. We have taught you and the other initiates about your bodies of light and have taught you how to take the Sun into your bodies through your intention and through the practice of Sun gazing. In this way, your eyes receive the high frequency light and deliver it to your body of light, through its many dimensions. This light can be used for healing, for releas-ing stuck energies and for ascension. Ascension is the process by which the heaviness of matter is overcome and the person incor-porates more and more light into the body until the frequency shifts to a higher dimension. It is a step by step process. Our lineage of Akhus are in the sixth dimensional frequency on Ak-An. We have come here into the third dimensional frequency to assist Earth and her people to rise out of the density of form into higher dimensions. Earth is going to become a star and stars emit a very high frequency. Also important is that we not let our frequency drop, for that would defeat our purpose. It is also im-portant that we continue to initiate and guide the humans who have reached a higher vibrational level so that they can help to hold the frequency of this ascension process.

"That is why the brothers and sisters have been led to our temples and monasteries on the islands. They aspire to enlight-enment, Pukaya, and work diligently to understand the star teach-ings. Your father has re-instituted the astronomy brotherhood which Mak-Ma first established here. To study the stars is a sacred duty for the wisdom of the universe is contained within them. Our astronomers use the stones of Kalasasaya as they did in ancient times, traveling here by boat and land from their island of the Sun. The brotherhood of magicians has become very strong because your father is soul-connected to this lineage. These are the brothers who will watch over the lineage of the codes of light which you will carry forward in your work and in your offspring. These shamans have learned the ceremonies of specifically ordering the coca leaves to accelerate the movement of energy with intent after they recognize the imbalanced energies of a person. They have learned to read the coca leaves, to heal with the *quya* stones, and to speak with the spirits of the plants. The greatest of them have been touched by lightning and opened to their second sight.

"Your brother and future husband, Tuko, the next Wiracocha, is the greatest of these shaman-magicians. He will carry the lineage forward for your father. This male lineage is meant to activate the codes that are held by the women of the lineage of light which will be carried forward through the priestesses of Inti. You alone carry the codes, Pukaya, but your sisters and the women who have joined them in the sacred temple are all there to support you. You will know what to do with your energies and you will know when to leave the Earth. When that time comes, you will recognize the next in the lineage and you will pass the history to her as I am passing it to you. This will become a tradition. It will awaken her to her mission and release you from yours.

"You priestesses have been taught the medicinal arts, and the art of dreaming. You are not bound by this reality or the illusions of the world. However, you have great compassion for those who are so bound. Your sacred duty is to dream the future into existence. For this, you will journey out into the other realities and bring higher vibrational thought forms back to Earth. You will use the subtle energies to cleanse and restore the vibrational fields of the people who come to you for help. The sisters have been taught to work with the finer frequencies found in the flowers of Earth, as well as the frequencies of stars and ascended beings which can sometimes spontaneously heal. As you know, women can master subtle energy, Pukaya, and your priestesses are already very adept at that. Do all that you do with the purest intent and Spirit will be with you.

"Both the sisters and the brothers will have within their orders those who are at different levels of initiation. The criteria for these initiations has been written in the star-coded language of

[236]

the Akhus for the highest initiates to read and follow. Remember that the esoteric language and teachings are not for everyone and that even those pursuing the path of mystery must reach a frequency that will uphold and develop the teaching before it is given to them. This has always been the way of the teachings from the stars. It will, one day, be available to many, but for some ages these teachings will be passed in secrecy.

"Now, I want to talk about the Apus. The brotherhood of magicians has been trained to understand the language of Ak-An. They know that the Apus, the spirits of each mountain, provide a channel through which they can communicate with the High Council of Ak-An. In this way, the beings of Ak-An will provide wisdom to guide the people, but this will only occur at intervals of five hundred years. You can see the importance of the brotherhood, for this knowledge will be passed on flawlessly by these highly trained men to allow this continued access to the Akhus once we depart the Earth. Wherever the brothers reside in this land, they will access Ak-An through the Apus, when the brotherhood of Astronomers declare that it is time for the prophecies to be heard. Each of the masters in the brotherhood will be the guardian of a high mountain for these are the strongest Apus channels. In time, these masters will be the only people on the Earth who understand the language of the stars. The written records of these encounters with the Akhus will be kept in secrecy until such time as people will not seek to destroy them, for there will be times coming in the future ages when those who abuse power will find their way to this land. The brotherhood will see this coming and will protect the records, even if it means moving into another dimension with them.

"I have just revealed to you one of the great secrets of the brothers, Pukaya. It is your duty to be aware of their responsibilities, guide the sisters to support them, and to keep this secret to yourself. The high initiates of the women, magicians in their own way, do not need to communicate through the Apus. These women, like yourself, can journey out through the dimensions to visit the lands of Ak-An. You will be received there by the High Council and by your individual councils who will help you to guide the community, dreaming it into the future. It is your duty to insure that this art of dimensional traveling is not lost by these women of magic, the Priestesses of Inti.

"You alone carry the solar disc upon your brow and in your heart, Pukaya. Within the inheritance of your soul, you bring forth codes of light for yourself and your community. Already you have opened and released some of these codes in your intuitive development and dream work. Some are opening as we speak for I am passing the mysteries to you which awaken many of these light codes. You will use these for your own elevation of consciousness and those energies will be sent out to help support your sisters in their quest for enlightenment. Since you are an Akhu, you have very high frequency codes. These will not be of use to many, only your blood sisters, but they will inspire others to their own level of mastery. You also carry light codes for the planet, Pukaya. These are energies that will not be shared for a long time. Your soul sisters on the other side of the world are releasing these codes and will be doing so for thousands of years. They are steering a civilization there that will bring forth important blood onto the planet, the blood of a master Akhu. Unfortunately, after this happens, those who abuse power will come forward to attempt the annihilation of the brothers, the sisters and the blood of the master. This energy will cause great harm to the brothers and sisters and the mysteries will be lost or used in malevolent ways. The culmination of these abusive energies will coincide with the return of those who have recently misused their power causing the great catastrophe of sunken continents.

"At that time, the energies of the planet will be shifting again. A people who continually abuse power and destroy a planet cannot expect to return to the love of God without miraculous intervention. The Pleiadians, through the abuse of power that destroyed their continent in the eastern sea, created an impediment to their steady return to God. In the future age of Earth shifting, it is they who return to correct the error of their recent catastrophe. Remember though that they will be as unconscious as any humans incarnating on this planet. There will be the opportunity to abuse the power once again. The Akhus of Ak-An have agreed to assist the Pleiadians with the correction of their past by carrying truths forward that will awaken them to their mission. There will, at that time, be a number of Akhus from Ak-An, many of our soul lineage and other star beings incarnate on Earth to help hold the frequency necessary for the Pleiadian energy shift. It is a group effort guided by the Galactic Federation. Our lineage carries codes that will be passed until that time for their release into the collective consciousness of the planet. These codes will be carried by other soul lineages as well and when they are released, the incarnate Pleiadians will be drawn back to Pachamama to heal the wounds of the past.

"At that very critical time in Earth's future, when the ascension of the planet into the frequency of love is in jeopardy, the codes carried by our lineage of women will be activated and released upon the planet. It will draw to us the lost sisters of the lineage that work so hard right now on the other side of the world to elevate consciousness. They will be carrying the codes of light, but they will not be aware of it. They will find their way to us from the north where they will have migrated and we and the brothers will open and activate the gifts they carry for the planet. These women will journey back to their homeland with the power to activate the women around them. At first it will be the lineage of the codes of light who will become conscious of their mission through their interaction with those who led the way. Then all women will become aware of planetary ascension and be awakened to the powerful pull back into the frequency of love - of Creator Spirit.

"Pukaya, this will be a glorious time for the sisterhood, for it will mark the completion of the mission. As women elevate their consciousness towards enlightenment, the men will follow and, eventually, those who abuse power and seek to annihilate the truth will either elevate their own consciousness or leave the Earth. Earth will not tolerate low frequency after that point. It is a great gift that we carry in secrecy for the future, Pukaya. We need only pass it on in the ways that we have established through the guidance of the High Council of Ak-An.

"The stone that I have given you has much power, Pukaya. It was given to me by an old woman whose lineage had protected it since the time of Mak-Ma. She said that Mak-Ma brought the stone with him from the place of his birth. It was given to him by his mother to leave in the place of the feminine power. The stone resembles the Akhus of Ak-An and legend tells that Mak-Ma's mother received it from the stars. It has a spirit that is from the stars. Do not use this stone to heal others. It is for you alone. I give you my blessings and will not be far from you at any time. You may use the stone to contact me, my child. Pass it on to the next in our lineage for, someday, it will fulfill its own mission on the planet. Now, let me complete your activation."

*

Mamacocha asked Pukaya to lie down on her back upon the soft weavings. She cleared her etheric body and the higher levels of her field, then placed her hand upon Pukaya's third eye. She held it there, channeling star energy, until Pukaya thought she

The Priestesses of Inti

would burst into flames from the heat. Then she felt a light within her begin to expand and grow more intense. Her frequency lifted to a very high vibration until her mother removed her hand and placed it on her heart. Mamacocha filled Pukaya with the energies of Pachamama until her daughter's filaments were aligned with the grids of the Earth. Pukaya experienced a deep love and connection to all of nature, including her own body. Pachamama's energy was warm and sensual. When her daughter was completely connected to Earth and the stars, Mamacocha journeyed out with her to the High Council to complete her initiation. She was brought fully into her mission by the council before being returned to the temple at Tiwanaku. The light of the Sun had just begun to fill the sky.

The two women packed all that they had brought with them into their finely woven blankets which they flung over their backs. They glanced at each other, smiling, as they tied the ends of their blankets from left shoulder and right underarm, between their breasts. They lingered at the Kalasasaya to watch the sunrise, then walked back to the sea where their boatman waited to take them back to the island of the Sun. They were greeted by Wiracocha and Tuko who escorted them to the temples.

Wiracocha and Mamacocha called all the priests and priestesses to them that morning and spent the entire day with those who would carry on their legacy. When the day was nearing an end, they all walked down to the port where a brightly decorated reed boat awaited the two who had emerged from the sea so long ago. Many of the people of the land were floating in smaller boats upon the sea, for they knew that their beloved leaders would depart that day. Mamacocha and Wiracocha boarded their boat and sent the boatman back to the shore. They announced, like Mak-Ma, that they would return again when they were most needed and sent great waves of love to the people as Wiracocha began to pole the boat out into the sea. The Sun sank below the horizon and the magic of twilight came upon them. No one made an attempt to follow but all watched as they became smaller and smaller upon the sea. Then, there appeared a flash of light, brilliant to the naked eye, and they were gone. They had come from the sea in mystery and so it was that they departed.

Leah speaks

The group of women had been mesmerized by the ending of Mamacocha's story for it spoke so much of the present times

[240]

upon the Earth. Leah had made them aware of the Pleiadian mission to rectify the future they were already living, but those mind-boggling concepts were more difficult to comprehend than the simple words of Mamacocha. They could see that she came to the Earth, in part, to help heal the tears in the etheric field caused by the Pleiadians' destruction of Atlantis with the misuse of crystal power. Leah felt the group energy shift into deeper awareness of the great collaborative healing that was taking place.

"My beloveds, do you see that the indigenous people of many lands, including our own, and many of our generation, are returning Pleiadians who have come to honor and love the Earth that was so abused? It is interesting that our culture has reached a point similar to that of Atlantis prior to its destruction and these indigenous, incarnate Pleiadians have tried to show us how to love our Mother. At the same time, they are falling prey to patterns of self-addiction and are also using addiction of others to create wealth and power for themselves. Also, incarnate Pleiadians who have come as members of the white culture are looking to their indigenous star brothers and sisters for guidance and it isn't always clear. We who have agreed to collaborate with the Pleiadians can only project a frequency of impeccability and love, that all things will be healed and Earth will ascend.

"The codes of light carried in Mamacocha's starseed were a little different from those brought in by Mir-An-Da. They were soul sisters, to be sure, but the missions had a different timing and, therefore, a different coded energy. In Peru, the shamans have been holding a frequency. They do not need to teach us anything. We need only share this frequency with them for the codes within us to be opened and activated. Sitting in circle with the shamans, we share intention in the coca leaves and offerings to the Mother, and our filaments are woven together with their own and the Earth's, in completion of the mission. We allow the women to work with our subtle energies and those who carry the codes of light are opened to new levels of awareness and brilliance. Theirs was a more passive mission than the Egyptian starseeding, but many of us have incarnated in both lineages so that this final connection could be made with ease and deep remembrance. Do you see?"

Natalie, a slender dark-haired beauty from the east coast, cleared her throat and caught Leah's eye. "Leah, I am a little confused about the Pleiadians," she said. "I have always felt connected to that energy. You know how I love to work with crystal layouts and the grids, and how deeply connected I have felt to the indigenous elders. If my star origins are Pleiadian, what do I need to be watchful of now? Am I a returning Atlantean as I have been told, and, if so, why am I sitting in this circle with you?"

"Whoa, Natalie!" Leah laughed, raising her hand in the air. "One question at a time. All star beings are inspired by crystal energy. However, the returning Pleiadians may be tested with it and they will need to be impeccable in the choices they make using crystals, or any kind of power. My feeling is that you are on loan to the Pleiadians, as I am, and that you are in this circle because it is home."

Natalie, wiped a tear from her cheek and thanked Leah for her words. She thanked the circle of women also for the love they all shared. It really meant a lot to her. Some of the other women in the circle thanked Natalie for bringing up the questions for they had shared the thoughts she had expressed. Julia sat quietly through the group's response. Leah knew that she was holding something important in her heart space and she asked Julia to share it.

"Well, Leah, it is about the Apus," Julia began. "It seems that the spirits of the holy mountain outside this center are just like the Apus in Peru. I feel so much more connected to the mission here and so much more filled with inspiration and the frequency of God. Could you comment?"

"Very well put, Julia. What more can I add? It is not a mistake that we are sitting beneath this mountain nor that I spend as much of my free time as possible in my cabin here. I was called by this Apu to bring forth the teachings of the ascended masters. The Apus of this mountain has put me through my work as well. Living on a volcano really makes things come up for release, if you know what I mean." The group laughed, and she continued. "I used to think that the Apus were some kind of E.T.s that came to talk to the old shamans in Peru. From my experience here, I understand that it is more like a communications channel that can open those ready to reach higher dimensions. The ascended beings and the High Council don't overtly interfere with the lives of men, but will assist when called upon. Through the Apus, though, they do have direct connection with those who are ready to communicate with them. We will hear more of the Apus as our story progresses.

"I must confess that I have been unaware of time as we had been so deeply involved in the lineage of Mir-An-Da. After Isabel told her story, there was a break in the energy and I noticed that our time together has been slipping away. We have only two more days together and I have three more stories to bring forth. Would you mind if we took a short break and continue this evening?"

Everyone agreed that it would be best to go on and leave nothing out of the entire story, so they took a half-hour for herbal tea and leg-stretching before coming back to the circle. Leah could feel the energies of Mamacocha recede as the strong energies of the great messenger sent to the pre-Incan people began to move through her. Rather than socializing, she walked beneath the stars speaking to her who was the daughter of the stars.

Qoyari

The cool air of night was settling in as the women took their places once again. Leah returned to the circle refreshed and fully connected with Qoyari, whose story she would tell next. She wrapped the black weaving close around her shoulders and tossed some copal on a burning charcoal that Ellia had lit some time before. The erotic smell of the resin's smoke moved everyone into a mellow, receptive state. Leah sat with eyes closed, letting the smoke die down before she began to speak.

"Beloveds, let us move forward in time to an era well before the great Inca empire. It is around 4000 BC, a time much earlier than any archeologist or anthropologist would reckon, when the Incas were first seeded on the Earth. The original Incas were pure Akhus. The name Inca means child of the Sun - the one who shines like the Sun. These were the Shining Beings. It was, in a way, the return of the Wiracochas, but these Akhus were not the blue-eyed, blonde-haired beings of old. They took the human forms of the indigenous tribe they were to lead. They were the mother and father of the future Inca people, who were, at that time, a small tribe of Lemurian refugees settled in an isolated, fertile valley high in the Andes. Again, they were brother and sister, husband and wife for their seed brought forth a lineage of kings and queens much like those of ancient Egypt.

"Qoyari, the rising star, and her brother-husband, Inkari, ray of the Sun, did not stay a long time on the Earth as did the Akhus of the past. They came with the specific mission of reawakening forgotten mysteries in the lineages of brothers and sisters. The lineage of the codes of light and the brotherhood of the magicians had begun incarnating into the lineage of male and female shamans in this tribe when the social structure of the Titicaca tribes fell into disharmony. When the soul lineages made such changes, it was necessary to send messengers to reawaken the conscious passage of the light. Qoyari was such a messenger to the soul lineage of the codes of light. Inkari was a master magician who manifested himself on a mountain top outside the tribal village. He wore the golden solar breastplate of the kings of Inti, just like Wiracocha and Aman-Ra. His mission was the seeding of a high culture, but also the reawakening of the brotherhood lineage incarnating within the shamans of the tribe - shamans who had kept alive the ancient ceremonies and teachings of Lemuria.

"As we look back in time, we find Qoyari seated on the lowest altar of a monolithic carved stone in the courtyard of the women's temple at Machu Picchu. Much of Machu Picchu was built at Inkari's direction, though many of the dwellings and secondary temples were added later by the Incas. Qoyari is looking over the city at the highest altar, the Inti-*huatana* stone (the hitching post of the Sun), where Inkari is delivering his last messages to the master magician, the *Ylloq'e*, of the tribe. Inkari is her twin soul, the masculine aspect of herself. She is lost in the transcendent frequency of their union when a woman of middle years slips silently through the stone archway to sit before her. Qoyari senses the vibration of this priestess-shamaness, and is not startled by her arrival. Looking down at the woman, Keya, with her soft, doe-like eyes, Qoyari reaches her hand out to touch her cheek. Qoyari is the pure essence of the feminine, the divine mother in human form. Her every move is liquid love. She is an embodiment of the divine and Keya is humbled at the privilege of sitting at her feet and receiving her love. Qoyari's long black hair is held close to her head in tiny braids which are gathered in coils decorated with golden ornaments. Wearing the royal robes of a queen, Qoyari moves with the grace of her calling. Her delicate feet are adorned with golden sandals and around her neck she wears a small golden disc of the Sun. Her face has the noble bronzed look of the future Incas, but with a softness and innocence found in few women of the tribe.

"Keya, plump from years of childbearing, wears her hair in long straight braids joined together at their tips with red wool wrapped many times around them. This is the tradition of the sorcerer or midwife of the tribe. Qoyari has seen the solar disc upon her brow and heart and knows that Keya, sincere and strong,

[245]

The Priestesses of Inti

must be made conscious of her lineage. Eventually Keya will pass the codes of light to Qoyari's daughter, Maleka, but Maleka is not yet old enough to take that responsibility in a conscious way. Qoyari glances once again towards Inkari, then turns her full attention to Keya. Her eyes flash with the light of Divine Presence as she meets the God presence in the woman who will hold the energy in her absence."

Qoyari speaks

"May the great creative essence of the universe guide our meeting this evening, Keya. Inti is low in the sky. The time of our sacred duty is at hand. Open yourself to receive activation of your star-encoded mission. My love will always be with you, but Inkari and I prepare to leave the people now, so my physical presence will be gone. Know that you are a being of light, Keya, and are in service to the Divine as your mission unfolds.

"Our tribe will remain a small, isolated group of people for a long time. The secret teachings and prophetic powers are to be known only to those who seek to be masters working in service to Pachamama. The shamans with whom Inkari has worked will carry forth their lineage and you and your little group of women shamans will continue to uphold the feminine principle. You, Keya, carry codes of light within your luminous body. These codes are like the inheritance you pass on, but it is not within the blood lineage that they are passed. They are passed at the level of the soul, and tonight, I am passing the conscious responsibility for their survival to you. You need only to live in the light, Keya, striving for mastery, and your soul mission will be fulfilled. In time, when you are ready to take your leave, you will pass them to my daughter, Maleka, who is still too young to be questing for mastery. When Maleka is older, further along with her mothering, bring her into the sisterhood and teach her the ways so that she will be able to assume this responsibility and recognize the woman who will follow her.

"It is necessary, in the passing of the codes, that you hear the story of my own brief existence on Pachamama in this body. I have been of service to Pachamama before, including several lifetimes with the Lemurians, and I will come again, to bring the blessings of the divine mother to the people. One day I will birth a master who will change the vibration of the entire Earth. Inkari and I are part of a greater Mission being undertaken by the beings from the star Ak-An. When we are not incarnate, I am in residence on the star Chaska, the sister planet of Pachamama. Inkari's work is with the Akhus of Ak-An, but we are both from another star, Arcturus, which is in the distant heavens. Inkari is a member of the brotherhood of Ak-An and I am part of the lineage of the codes of light. Our Mission is the elevation of consciousness on Pachamama - to assist Pachamama in her ascension. Inkari and I are twin souls, never apart though the vastness of space may seem to separate us. Our love exists in the frequency of God, beyond human comprehension. It is eternal and knows no separation. On rare occasions, we are sent together to the Earth and have the exquisite joy of bringing that love into physical union. Maleka and her brother, Pachakutec, are the fruits of that union, Keya. Maleka is a divinely birthed child who will strengthen the sisterhood when she comes into her gifts. Pachacutec will carry forth the staff of the Incas, children of the Sun.

"I was not really birthed onto this planet, Keya, although this body was born in the human way. People believe that I am the daughter of the tribal leaders, Heka and Vonari. The child, Qoyari, came into extraordinary powers after a serious illness in which she nearly died. You must know the truth, Keya. Qoyari, really did die of her illness. I led her to the light of God for she was performing a great service for the mission. She relinquished her beautiful body to the entrance of my soul, which consciously brought the lineage forth into our tribe of Lemurian descent. The original star-seeding in the Andes at Titicaca Lake was in danger of losing the light. There were only a few old people who had any memory of the star-beings and they were not passing it on because people had ceased to seek mastery and enlightenment. They appealed to the High Council of Ak-An and Inkari and I were called forth on this mission. The child, Qoyari, died from the bite of a snake while the tribe was in the jungle lands gathering food for the winter. The tribal elders believed that she recovered from death and received her power from the snake. They can still believe that, Keya. It is for you to keep the truth alive, so that someday it will be known.

"When Qoyari's soul left her body, it was confused and frightened for she had become unconscious of her soul agreement when she was born. Such is the way of all humans, Keya. That is why I chose to come into this life the way I did. Qoyari's soul journeyed away from her body, which separated into its different vibrational layers, each with its own after-death journey. In the space of a few missed breaths, to keep her from wandering into the in-between world of spirit, I merged my soul with hers and moved my intent into the angelic realms. There I placed her soul essence in the arms of the angels who had been guarding her. She became conscious of her mission and accepted her death at once. They opened the light to her and she returned fully to her soul. She will come back to this realm again to continue her soul quest for divine embodiment on Pachamama, but, for now, she rests in the light of the Great Elders. As soon as she came into conscious awareness and acceptance of her mission, I projected my own soul into her lifeless body. Breathing life into her lungs, I gathered new etheric material to enliven her body. In doing so, I became Qoyari, the rising star, the name given for my embodiment from the time of our soul commitment to assist each other. This name honors Chaska, my home in this solar system, which was rising in the east on the morning of Qoyari's birth and on the day when I came into Qoyari's body. As I rapidly gained strength by channeling energy into the body through the etheric field, I drew in the organization of my emotional, mental and spiritual bodies. In the time it took the Sun to complete half its passage through the day sky, I was out of bed, eating and exploring the strange surroundings of my new home as well as the details of my girlish body.

"I came into the body of Qoyari when she was nine years old. Her miraculous recovery was the most important thing to happen in the tribe since they came from Lemuria. The story was enriched as I began to bring my gifts forward for the people. My mother, Heka, was so happy to have her only child returned to life that she failed to notice the obvious changes in my behavior. My father, Vonari, had not paid a great deal of attention to Qoyari anyway, since he was a very committed leader who worked day and night to ensure the tribal survival. Much of that work consisted of ensuring ways for the tribe to remain invisible to others, for it was in the prophecies, continually divined and handed down from Lemurian times, that these immigrants to the Andes held a destiny for the future of the planet that could not be jeopardized by annihilation. This is quite true, Keya, but the tribal elders had no consciousness of the actual meaning of the prophecies. They had lost the magic once possessed in Lemuria. You can see why it is important to pass on the mysteries as well as the consciousness to hold them.

"So my father and mother were, in their own ways, oblivious to the emergence of an altogether new person in the body of their daughter. This was fortunate for me, for I was continually called upon to invoke the memory of previous human experiences to behave in expected ways. I must have been a strange child to raise in every way. When I took over Qoyari's body, I was conscious of the mission and, thus, was open to my second sight. Seeing the emotional and etheric fields of those around me, I began to correlate what I saw with patterns of disease or distress. I did not speak about this for I was uncertain how it would be received. Instead, I used my intent to move the filamentous structure of their realities which allowed energies to lift from their luminous fields. There is nothing so powerful as intent, Keya. Every one of us has drawn in certain filaments of the universal to create our reality. This is one of the mysteries. For the most part, it is an unconscious activity, but it can be brought into consciousness through the use of impeccable intent. That means that realities can shift, old ways of thinking and behaving can change, and a person can begin living a completely different life. For example, some of the people who lived in our village were very unhappy. It was a choice made long ago because those around them had drawn filaments of disatisfaction to themselves. We often make choices based on what others have done before us. These people didn't realize that they could release those burdensome filaments and draw to themselves filaments of joy. I journeyed into their soul-space and asked permission to reassemble their filaments. If their soul essence agreed, I performed this little miracle for them and they became joyful.

"It was through this subtle movement of energy that the attitude of the tribe began to change to include more hope and joy. This divine love entered the people and raised the frequency of the tribe. An adept child, I reassembled the filaments of the tribe to create a very different future than they were projecting. This, the most significant work of my mission, was done in secrecy. I have since trained women shamans to move subtle energy, for women are master dreamers, experts at shaping reality. It is a feminine art, as is the art of weaving. Heka had taught Qoyari to spin the wool of the alpacas and vicuñas at a young age. Her consciousness had moved aside for mine, but her body remembered, and I was consequently very proficient in that art. When Heka taught me to weave, I began designing symbols of Inti, Pachamama, the condors and the pumas into the ordinarily plain or striped cloth. She was amazed and all the women began to copy the designs. Much later, when I trained those who had committed themselves to higher consciousness, like yourself, the designs included esoteric symbols of the tribal destiny and some of the symbolic language of Ak-An. These symbols will be passed from generation to generation, and will serve to awaken others who are connected to the mission.

"I worked closely with the shamans as I grew into a young woman, helping them formulate plant medicines to clear energies from the different layers of the luminous field. With some success, I trained them to open their second sight to see the field and watch how the medicines worked to remove dark energies. This was at my father's provocation, at a time when my gift of sight became more public. My preference, as you know, was to teach this work to women for their sight is uncluttered and they are less attached to the outcome of their treatments. This, somehow, increases the rate of successful cures. Women are natural healers for their vibration is tuned to the plant spirits and the compassionate heart needed for healing. The male shamans work well with the community vibration and the recognition of ways to bring the shadowy parts of human life into the light. Compassion is not such a necessary ingredient in that work. You will noticed that our male shamans are also guardians of the women who are carrying codes of consciousness.

"At that time in my life, before the flowering of my womanhood, I tended the alpaca herd for my parents and spent much of my time in meditation. My beloved, Inkari, was continually before me in meditation. Conscious of our mission together, I began drawing his luminous filaments to me. I knew he was not yet in body, for I had agreed to come first to shift the frequency of the tribe to accept his teachings. Sensing the time of his coming draw near, I began to prepare myself for our reunion. Mother and father talked of husbands for me but I would not hear of it. I let them know that I awaited one of dazzling brilliance and great wisdom. They thought I had lost my senses, yet they did not force their wishes on me. In my visions of Inkari, I could see him with the golden breastplate of Inti catching the sunlight, a rainbow rising up from his hand, and a puma at his side. It was powerful.

"When I first bled my menstrual blood, I was brought in from the alpaca herd to assume more womanly duties in the household. I was heartsick to be separated from the wildness of Pachamama and the alpacas whose bright spirits I cherished. Experiencing the traditional initiation with several other young women was very lovely, but my freedom became restricted for maidenhood marked the time when a woman could no longer associate with the shamans or other men without supervision. However, I kept the vivid picture of Inkari before me as I went about my household tasks. When he appeared on a high mountain holding the staff of Inca with the golden breastplate of Inti on his chest, it was in a place where I surely would have witnessed it had I been with the alpaca herd. I knew that it did not matter, but the human girl in me was disappointed that the social order prevailed over the Divine Plan.

"Born of a ray of Inti, Inkari appeared magically on the mountain outside our village. He was as you see him today, a handsome, vigorous young man, filled with the fervor that has fired the accomplishment of his mission. I laugh to think of it now, Keya, but at that time he was so singularly driven that he didn't even notice me. What could I do? As you know, it is inappropriate for a young woman to call attention to herself in front of a man. He spent a vast amount of time with my father after he first arrived. I served his meals and offered him dried fruits and he looked right through me. My mother knew that I was struggling with my emotions, and she advised me to be patient. She could see that we were intended for one another, and assured me that our union would come to pass. I was accustomed to being in my power so this situation was demoralizing. Inkari could not see my part in the mission. He was not as fully conscious as I had been, even though he had materialized himself from thin air. I wonder if the effort of that feat aligned him with the stronger male energies that can block perception and remembrance. Well, that is the story of my first encounters with the twin to my soul. My lesson was to hold my love for Inkari through his reawakening on Pachamama.

"Inkari spent a great deal of time with the shamans and with Father. He knew well the destiny of this small tribe and was anxious to awaken them to it. I am sure he was disappointed in the caliber of shamanic training and had difficulty imagining this small tribe becoming a great empire. It warmed my heart to overhear him remark about the gentle, loving nature of the people, but he never spoke of that directly to me. Father and the shamans told him of the Lemurian legends. There was a time on the old continent called a Golden Age when all beings felt the current of love running through them. The civilization made great advances during that time and all those who left Lemuria longed to recreate that Golden Age. The people emigrated in every direction before the final destruction of the continent and it was said this tribe had brothers and sisters who had traveled to the west and lived in high mountains where the masculine energy enters into Pachamama. There were stories of great queens who were like

[251]

mothers to the people. This brought forth a memory for me of earlier lives in a place of blessed peace and love. Mother and I were privy to the stories because they were told in our dwelling. She and I formed a great bond of love during those early days of Inkari's time with the tribe. The love was so great that it melted my adolescent sense of injustice about the social order.

"Those days were very sweet, in spite of Inkari not seeing me. He invited the shamans and my father to accompany him to Titicaca Lake, where he knew it was necessary to appear before the elders there for the physical passing of the mysteries to our tribal shamans. I knew it would not harm him to visit that region where the feminine energy enters Pachamama, for it might awaken in him the collaborative nature of our mission. The men packed weavings and medicines as gifts for the elders and walked off towards the south in search of the great lake at the top of the world. Inkari carried the golden staff of Inca, the child of the Sun, and wore the breastplate of his inheritance. They were accompanied by the rainbow and were guarded by the pumas as they trekked south across the mountains toward the mother water.

"Through my own visioning and the stories Inkari shared upon his return, they arrived at the edge of Titicaca Lake to find a royal boat and boatman awaiting them. The elders, who still lived there on the island of the Sun, knew that Inkari was coming to receive a great initiation. They also knew that the wisdom and mystery they were carrying would be passed to Inkari and the shamans who accompanied him. The boatmen poled, then rowed the boat out to the island where a fair number of brothers and sisters came to greet them. They were taken to the old temple of the brotherhood where a great feast and soft sleeping mats awaited them. The next day, Inkari met with the elders - both men and women. There were few old ones left who had any memory of the past, but they were in remembrance of the last reading of the prophecies which had been nearly five hundred years previous to Inkari's visit. This prophetic wisdom communicated through the Apus and the visionary skill of one old woman in the group predicted Inkari's arrival and his mission with precision. Inkari was delighted that the old ones had not lost their power of divination, but, at the same time, he saw clearly the loss of light in the rest of the community. He knew they would be sparked by his visit but that, with the natural evolution of civilization, the light waxes and wanes like the moon. It was clearly time to move the center of the mission to the mountains in the north.

"Our shamans listened to Inkari and then met with their elders. I have no knowledge of the happenings of this secret meeting, for it took place under the direction of the brotherhood. I know only that it began at the hour of power and that they exchanged histories and ceremonies until early the next day. Our shamans returned with additional ceremonies, new healing remedies and techniques, and bundles of medicinal plants that they had collected there and along the way. They also had a new light in their eyes which led me to believe that something akin to the light codes passed between brother and brother.

"Inkari had been there for over a week when the old women called him to sit with them. This was really quite a privilege and he went with a humble heart. They chewed the coca with him at the same time they threw the coca leaves onto a *mesa* cloth. The leaves told them of the future and the unfoldment of Inkari's mission. They told him of the sisterhood of Mamacocha which had been part of their own mission, and one old woman whispered to him that she held certain codes in sacred trust. They burned sacred herbs on some coals from the fire, sending clouds of smoke into the little hut. These were medicines to help align him with his mission and his own divine feminine self. Titicaca Lake is the center of Pachamama's feminine energy and there was Inkari, receiving this blessing from the old ones who carried the light of consciousness for all people.

"The woman who held the codes of light asked Inkari to kneel before her and she used the energies within her hand to force his second sight to predominate over his male vision. He said that her hand burned his head between his brows, as if she were holding a hot coal to his skin. Then, she took it away and added more herbs to the coals sending more smoke into the hut. She asked him to use his new vision to look into the smoke and know the greatest blessing of his walk on Pachamama. A shimmering light emerged from the smoke which held an image of my smiling face. He has told me that he gasped in surprise and the women cackled uncontrollably. The old one who had initiated him scolded him for being so headstrong on his male side that he would fail to recognize the co-creative aspects of his mission. How could he not see this young woman who awaited his invitation to partner with him on his journey? She whispered to him that I, too, held important codes and had many gifts to give the people of Pachamama. A warm feeling began to overtake Inkari as he understood the truth she spoke. He suddenly became anxious to return home to our village. The old one understood his reaction and rewarded him with a toothless grin. She asked the other

[253]

women to leave and reached inside a worn bag at her side. With-drawing from it an ancient mesa of fine *vicuña* wool which she treated as the fragile relic it was, she gently unfolded one corner of the mesa to reveal the polished edge of a hand-sized stone, which she cradled in her arms. She told Inkari to take the stone and mesa and present them to me when he returned to our village. The energies of the stone would connect me to the star, Ak-An, and the mission, she said. The bag would link me to the woman who brought the lineage of light to the Andes, Mamacocha.

"Inkari could feel the power of the stone and *mesa* as he wrapped them carefully and placed them in the bag he wore close to his heart. The old women had initiated him into the balance of his own masculine and feminine and they had opened his vision to the possibility that he could accomplish his mission with greater ease and balance in partnership. He found that their village and ours shared the teachings of *Ayni*, reciprocity, and so he gifted the old ones the golden breastplate of the Sun that hung around his neck. It lightened his heart to see how pleased they were. He and the other men spent several more weeks at Titicaca Lake trading with the people and then, starting home, they journeyed into the mountains to the monastery of Lord Muru. Muru was, and still is, an ageless Akhu who preserved the teachings of old Lemuria and the brotherhood in a hidden valley to the north. He is the head of the Amethystine Order of the brotherhood which is the order of magicians. The Order of the Red Hand, which he also leads from his monastery in the mountains, is the order respon-sible for the preservation of all documents and knowledge of the past, including Lemuria and earlier.

"Lord Muru allowed Inkari to see and touch the records, a privilege which unlocked further remembrances for Inkari. He saw writings from ancient Mu which his second sight could trans-late and it awakened him to our many lives in the Golden Age there. Lord Muru understood Inkari's mission and allowed him into the most secret vault of the monastery which contained records from Mu and from Titicaca Lake long before the time of Mamacocha and Wiracocha. These records were written in the language of Ak-An and Inkari was also able to translate them. They were the written word of the stars, Keya. Can you imagine? Inkari returned many times to Lord Muru's monastery to assist in translating some of these records. He is a pure channel for the Akhu energies and this experience opened him to more profound understanding of his Mission and the future. Those old tablets were left at Titicaca Lake by a giant, bearded white god named

Mak-Ma. They revealed to Inkari and thus to Lord Muru, the planetary nature of the mission. Inkari began to live his life in a more universal way from that moment onward. Lord Muru gifted him with initiation into the Order of the Red Hand and gave him a small carved hand of red stone to carry in his amulet. Curiously, the thumb of this hand protrudes between two fingers symbolizing a secret power and brotherhood.

"Inkari, Father, and the shamans returned to our village after the passage of two Moon cycles. The level of their transformation is hard to put into words, Keya. They all held a remarkable light and had acquired what could only be called wisdom, a knowledge that exists apart from human experience. Inkari appeared to me as the man I had seen in my vision, no longer the headstrong young man on his own mission. Our coming together is a very touching part of this life experience, Keya, and I want to give justice to my remembrance of that time. Why don't we break the energy of our meeting for a few moments to enter the priestess' temple and light the oil lamps. We can also wrap ourselves with heavier weavings since Inti's warmth is rapidly retreating."

*

Keya rose and entered the temple to light the oil lamps in the wall niches with the one she had brought, bringing the building to life with light and shadow. Qoyari gazed up at the heavens, drinking in the vastness of the universe like the single drop of God's love that it represents. Wrapping an elegant black cloth around her shoulders, she carefully moved her woven bag and cushion which she used to sit on, inside the temple. Then she seated herself in the place of the high priestess, a position she had held since organizing a small group of women shamans into a sisterhood. Inkari had built this high temple and beautiful terraced gardens around the great altar stone which he had carved for the women's use. It rose across the city from the high temples of the priest-shamans linking filaments of light between the two high spots of the city. Keya returned to Qoyari's feet, seating herself on a cushion she had taken from a seat near the door. When their energies were realigned, Qoyari continued her story.

*

"When Inkari and the men entered the village, we all gathered to welcome them home. I was pleased with the light they had gained and excited to hear the stories of the journey, as were all the members of the tribe. Father announced that there would be a tribal meeting at the festival grounds the next day when the entire village could become a part of their experience. He then retired to our home to rest and share his experience with Mother. I turned to walk home with Father and Mother when I heard someone whisper my name. My spine tingled and my wombspace warmed at the sound of his voice, and I turned to face Inkari. He said that he'd been given a gift for me by the old woman shaman who initiated him and he did not want to keep it from me for even the space of one more breath. I laughed at his seriousness and told him to meet me at the place where the mountain stream runs over great boulders. We took our separate ways to that secluded spot and sat upon a great stone in the middle of the stream.

"Inkari's eyes were full of light, perhaps because I had finally entered his vision. He smiled at me as he withdrew the *mesa* of *vicuña* from his bag. It was an incredibly old weaving, a little worn around the edges, but otherwise, in good condition. He placed it reverently in my hands and I felt the energy of the stars enter me immediately. In actuality, I was sitting on that rock with Inkari, holding a good-sized bundle, but I was also journeying out to Ak-An. I found myself before the High Council of Ak-An who seemed very pleased that I had finally come to them. They showed to me the entire scope of our mission, revealing events far into the future world of Pachamama, Keya. Returning to Inkari who had held me in a protective energy while I journeyed, I looked down at the *mesa* and drew back one corner then another until the stone was revealed to me. It was a carved being, like an idol, but the strangest looking creature I had ever seen. The eyes were very large and round. Inkari looked at it and said it reminded him of a statue near Titicaca Lake, at Tiwanaku, which was thought to represent the great white god, Mak-Ma who journeyed to that region a long time ago. I felt certain that it was an Akhu, not just in appearance but it had a spirit or essence that was truly alive. To be clear, I should say it was not a human spirit.

"I wrapped the being in the *mesa* again and cradled it in my arms. It seemed to evoke a mothering feeling in me. Now I realize that it awakened codes within me of the Divine Mother. I did not feel familiar with the lineage of Akhus that it represented, but I knew that it somehow linked me to the mission and the lineage of light. I thanked Inkari and asked him how he fared on the journey. He told me what he could of his experience, withholding that which he was bound to reserve in secrecy. It was very exciting to me which encouraged him to tell me more. At last, we realized that Inti was sinking quickly and we reluctantly gathered our things to return home. Before we jumped from the great boulder to the shore, Inkari touched my hand and asked if I might be his partner in this life. Tears of joy sprang from my eyes as I bowed my head and said "yes."

"We arrived back at my home to find my parents dipping bread into bowls of Mother's hearty stew. Announcing our intentions to them, the meal became a great celebration of life and love. When Father ended the tribal meeting the next day, he announced that Inkari would be his future son. The tribe voiced its approval and everyone began planning our wedding celebration. Word of Inkari's destiny had spread throughout the tribe with the storytelling of their adventures. We were honored in our marriage as Shining Beings, the new Wiracochas. The tribal mind shifted into its place of destiny and the greater Mission took root in this humble village of Lemurian descendants.

"On the day of our wedding, I was bathed by the women, dressed in the robes of an honored princess, and my hair was rubbed with fragrant oil and braided as you see it now with ornaments of gold. I spent time with my mother listening to her tales of love and marriage. She gave me little things to seed my household. My father proudly gave me to Inkari, promising to build a royal dwelling for us with the help of the tribe. Inkari and I vowed to love each other eternally and to guide the tribe toward their destiny. We let them know that we would not stay with them a long time, like the Wiracochas, but would guide them to the place of higher light from which they could continue the journey without us. Inkari placed this small golden disc of the Sun around my neck then led me out onto the grass to dance the wedding dance. It was a time of high spirits and wonderful fun, as you well remember.

"I cannot speak to you of our physical union, for to do so would betray its magic. We have had bliss in our life together that might otherwise have been missed. From our union, we have brought forth two children of Inti who will lead the tribe into the future, and we have supported each other in our individual and combined missions. I have, on many occasions, infused a particular situation or discussion with the feminine energy I hold and Inkari has done the same with the masculine for me. This has helped us achieve a balance within and without. Now that our journey comes to an end, it is good to recall what has been accomplished.

The Priestesses of Inti

"The first part of our mission together was to establish the brotherhood and the sisterhood in our own community, so that the shamans, male and female, could preserve the high teaching of the stars that we gave to them. They would guard the legacy that we began and support the leadership of our children and their heirs, who would be called Incas, children of Inti, for holding the light of the Sun. Inkari and I taught the shaman-priests and priestesses over three hundred separate *mastays*, or offerings, to Pachamama, the spirits of nature and the star beings. Some of these had been given to him by the shamans of Titicaca Lake and Lord Muru, but most of them were of his own divining. These are powerful ways to align the community or individual with the filaments of higher consciousness. The *Alto Mesayoqs* were given responsibility for the Apus and the gift of communicating with the stars to know the future. These ways must not be forgotten, Keya, for they will unlock the future to a higher consciousness. These shamans have just received the star messages through the Apus for the next five hundred years and it will be important, in the passage of the coming five hundred years, that this art is not forgotten for it could mean the failure of the greater Mission.

"I have taught the women to preserve the sacred teachings in the esoteric symbols of their families' garments. It is especially important to swaddle the newborn baby in the cloths with soul symbols and condors for that connects their filaments with their purpose and with the angelic beings. All the spinners of the tribe have been taught to spin the dual thread which weaves the filaments of balance, male and female, into the garments and cloths of all people. Women work with the subtle energies, Keya, the filaments of light. Their training has been in the mastery of moving energy, whether to heal illness, bring joy and abundance to the community, or reweave the tribal reality into the next level of consciousness. Many of the women have been able to journey into other dimensions to increase their awareness of the illusory nature of this reality.

"Inkari has gifted the people with agricultural advances by bringing the potato and maize plants into existence. These will ensure that the tribe will survive in the future when it may be very difficult to find food. We have both taught the alchemical nature of fire in cooking the food and the magic of combining certain foods for good health. Our children, the Incas, will never consume the flesh of animals for they must work with very high frequency light, but those of the tribe need this form of food to sustain a rigorous life. To this end, Inkari has worked with the inheritance of the alpaca to increase its size and quality of flesh. As a result, he has brought forth the llama as a gift to the people. These animals will be loyal and prolific friends of the tribe, providing food and warm wool for garments and blankets. All of this has been part of our mission.

"When our village was able to hold this new frequency, Inkari and I journeyed out with a few of the shamans, to find the region where he would build his first city. Following the old roads built by Wiracocha, he took the golden staff of Inca and journeyed to the west. We came, eventually, to a sacred and fertile land which sat like a bowl in a high mountain valley. We offered *mastay* to Pachamama, sending our filaments of light within her. She indicated that this was the site we were called to find. Inkari planted the staff of Inca in the soil and began our work there by using his mastery of sound to carve a flat stone on the hillside into the shape of a post. He called this Inti-*huatana*, the hitching post of the Sun. This he did in every major community he founded. Here the community was connected to Inti and the legacy of the future Incas.

"The Quechua people in this beautiful valley accepted us as the leaders they had awaited. We introduced to them much of what we had given to our tribe, but withheld the mysteries reserved for those who worked with the stars. I taught the mystery of the double spun fibers and many of the symbols which, when woven into their garments, would help them connect their filaments with the higher truth. These people were simple and loving with a great talent for working with gold and other metals. They revered us as messengers of the gods. We taught them of the one God, whose magnificence could be felt in the light of Inti. Inkari built a great temple to Inti, the Coricancha. He built waterways and many buildings for the use of leadership and sacred duty. We lived in a palace of stone with golden floors and ceilings. Inkari showed the people how to divide the community into regions for farming, for living and for sacred work. It was with attention to balance and fairness that the community began living according to his teachings. The sacredness of all things was emphasized, including the planting of crops which required the blessings of Pachamama. Festivals with sacred dance marked the turning of the seasons and the community prospered and held light.

"In time, we left the palace and journeyed into a low, long valley where a great river brought blessed water for the crops. Here we established temples and communities at either end of this valley. It was a place of great fertility and peace. I remained primarily in the community of Ollantaytambo where I found a group of tiny women who worked great magic. They were originally from a very small tribe of dwarfs who claim to have come from the planet, Chaska. These women were magnificent in their ability to gather the filaments of light and we worked together to reweave the reality of that entire region. Our intent was to align the sacred valley with the universal matrix in a way that would sustain the future of the children of Inti and protect all of their subjects from invasion and pestilence. To sustain the vibration of that reality, it would be necessary for the future Incas to rule as servants to the people. This means that the matrix of that reality will be sustained so long as personal power does not corrupt the lineage of Inti. If it does, Keya, they will be annihilated.

"You can see that, no matter what happens to the future we have seeded, and most of it will not come to fruition for a very long time, the codes of light which you and Maleka carry must never be corrupted or lost. That is why we pass them on in this way so that you are fully conscious of the importance of your duty. The brotherhood passes their responsibilities in the same way and I can assure you they will always be at the side of the priestesses of Inti to insure the success of this star Mission. You carry something that is beyond the concept of self. The codes must be carried and passed on in secrecy with no attachment to their importance. When the Mission nears completion, all secrecy will vanish from Pachamama and it will become known that this lineage of women has dedicated itself to higher consciousness, even when humanity has been lost in the dark world of survival, fear, hatred and desire. Until that time, no one is to expose the women of this lineage. I don't mean to sound harsh for I hold you in Divine Love always, but it is the way in which I would have you pass this on to Maleka - no more and no less.

"I have not mentioned the gift of motherhood that God has bestowed upon me in this life. The stone of the strange Akhu being that Inkari brought to me from Titicaca Lake opened within me the codes of the Divine Mother. Our union opened the codes of the human mother and the two combined in the ecstatic birth of my two beloved children. Pachakutec was conceived on our wedding night. He is so much like Inkari that he will not fail to develop the culture as Inkari has intended. He is strong and reliable. He has just taken his third initiation into the brotherhood of magicians and is growing in mastery everyday. Maleka was born several years later. She was conceived when Inkari and I traveled back to the village of our tribe to visit with my parents who had never met Pachacutec. Inkari and I went walking along the stream, taking it higher into the mountains. There we made love with each other and the stars, and there I buried the carved stone Akhu who had opened me to Divine Love. I knew that it would not be safe if I did not bury it myself. When I placed it in the ground, my vision expanded and I saw that it would be found one day, a long time from now. It will be given to a woman from another part of the lineage of light who, in searching for her own light, would find the legacy of her soul. It will be found when the Akhus can be understood and accepted.

"My beloved Maleka, conceived on that sacred day, is to marry her brother, Pachacutec, to preserve the star lineage in the leadership of the people. This is the Inca legacy and the way of the Akhus. We do not recommend this to the people, but rather encourage marriage with neighboring tribes, for the vibration is not strong enough to overcome the possibility of mutation. Maleka will birth the next in the line of Incas, and so it will proceed for many, many generations. Inkari has built this hidden city of Machu Picchu as the fortress of the Incas. Many of our original tribe have journeyed here to populate this great city of light. Others remain invisible in the distant valley of our people, but they will never be separate from this part of the tribe or its destiny. It is here that the codes of light and the brotherhood's magic will be preserved. It is here that the prophecies collected from the Apus of all the great mountains will be molded into a wisdom capable of guiding a people for five hundred years.

"As you know, we have just gathered for the Inti Raymi festival and the shamans who communicate with the great Apus laid their communications before Inkari. He taught them to weave the communications that came through the Apus from the stars into a tribal wisdom that will guide them for the next five hundred years. The elders saw the birth of a common philosophy that would one day meld an empire together. The next five hundred years will see the people prosper in every way. The tribes will grow in number and the valley will produce enough food to fill the storage houses to overflowing. More people will come to the valley to live from the mountains bringing their gifts and traditions. Our first community, which we have called Cusqo, will become the center of trade and culture, as well as leadership.

"Was it not fascinating to watch Inkari teach the shamans how to interpret the prophecy and how to pass that gift on to the next generation along with the count of years until the next reading? All will be well, Keya. This fortress will become a retreat for those seeking higher consciousness and our temple will welcome all women who feel called to the light. We will be a strong sisterhood.

"Now my story has come to an end. Inkari and I will go our way tomorrow, our missions complete, and our hearts filled with love. Living in this sacred place with all my brothers and sisters has been like living in the heart of God, Keya. You cannot imagine the joy it has brought me. All I can give to you now is eternal love, for sometimes I feel my heart expand to the point of bursting, which is how it feels now to be with you. Lay your head upon my lap, dear faithful Keya, you who have been with me as an older sister since our days in the tribal village. I will journey with you out among the stars to connect you with your destiny."

*

Keya, bathed in Qoyari's love, lay her head upon the folds of her royal robes and closed her eyes. Qoyari used her intent to raise Keya's frequency and released her consciousness from her body. Together, they traveled to stand before the High Council in the Great White Lodge of the Brotherhood on Ak-An. The council completed Keya's initiation as the High Priestess of the Andean branch of the lineage of light, and the two women returned to the women's temple at Machu Picchu, the city of light. They gathered their belongings together and extinguished the temple lamps. Qoyari directed Keya to hold her light before them as they made their way down from the women's temple complex. They walked through many passageways and along the side walls of the city, climbing over stones and building debris, to arrive at the great stone of Pachamama which rose like a relief of the mountains themselves from her soil. Inkari had erected this stone as an altar to the mother, and it truly held the image of twin mountains.

They climbed upon the low altar which ran the length of the monument and Qoyari asked Keya to stand with her back to the sacred stone. She then placed her hands upon the solar discs which Keya bore on her brow and heart and poured the energy of the stars within them. Keya's luminous body glowed, then sparked, sending spirals of energy out into the dark night. Qoyari knew that she was challenging Keya's light and was not surprised that she fainted, slumping into her arms. She revived her by applying sharp pressure with her fingernail just below her nose. At the same time Qoyari breathed deeply, taking the filaments of

Pachamama into her luminous field, and blew sharply into Keya's solar plexus. Keya came back into consciousness with a start, her luminous field securely gridded between Pachamama and Ak-An. The initiation completed, Qoyari took her into her arms and let her weep like a baby. In time, they found their way to Keya's quarters where Qoyari led her to her sleeping mat. Keya fell into a deep sleep.

Qoyari wandered about the grounds of the city of light allowing herself to drink in the beauty of the land on this, her last night on Pachamama. Her life had not been long, but who would measure such things. Her mission was fulfilled and Maleka was her gift to the future. All was at peace. In her wanderings, she found Inkari sitting on a seat he had carved from the stones of the wall leading up to Inti-*huatana*. From his perch he had a commanding view of the deep valley, the peak of Machu Picchu, and the city. He reached out and drew her to him. Qoyari snuggled in beside him and dosed in his arms as darkness turned to light. In the morning, they shed the heavy robes of night and walked together across the slender, hanging footbridge into the jungle land leading towards Vilcabamba, the city of gold. They were searching for the doorway to the heart of God which opened to receive them in perfect love and grace.

Leah speaks

The group was savoring the sweetness of Qoyari along with their own fond remembrances of Peru. It was a spell that Leah did not care to break with words for the love of the Divine Mother was with them all. She rose to her feet, wrapping her beautiful woven shawl around her shoulders, and left the room so quietly that no one felt her absence. It was very late when the group came fully back into the reality of their retreat. They stumbled off to their cabins and slept as hard as Keya had the night that Qoyari had put her to bed. They dreamed of the coca leaves, the burning fires of the *mastay* ceremonies, and the Princess's Bath at Ollantaytambo where they had washed their own feet. It was adjacent to the temples of the dwarf priestesses from Chaska, Earth's sister-planet Venus. They dreamed of those times when they had walked in the footsteps of Qoyari without even knowing it. Leah was aware of their dreams and the filaments of light connecting their past experience with their present knowledge. When sleep found its way to her, it brought a knowing that the filamentous weaving of the group was nearing completion.

[263]

Chuka

Leah Speaks

Early next morning, the groggy group of women piled into cars and drove to the top of the mountain road. As the sun rose, they hiked over the high ridges for over an hour, coming to a pristine meadow of wildflowers, spring fed creeks and waterfalls. One by one, they removed their clothing and submerged themselves in a pool of icy water. Screams of shock and laughter were followed by an immediate movement into a much higher frequency. They sat in a circle on the soft grass allowing the morning Sun to dry them. Leah felt very close to the masters in this sacred valley and led the women on a journey to a great amethyst temple within the mountain. There they had a profound experience with St. Germain, the ascended master who was the current leader of the brotherhood of magicians. He told them that there were very few of the brothers incarnate at that moment. Most of them were working in temples in the fifth dimension, golden cities like that of Camelot. Earth was being guided by many ascended beings. They were there to help those still in third dimensional consciousness. He invited each of the women to call upon his wisdom anytime and assured them that Sananda was also there to assist them. As they left the temple, St. Germain handed each of them a special gift which he manifested in the palm of his hand. They held it to their hearts as they returned to the grassy meadow and the rushing water around them.

Leah opened her eyes to see each one of them holding their closed hands to their hearts. Tears rolled down their cheeks as they came back into this reality. Leah sat in stillness, giving them time to integrate their experience, then she reached for her blouse as a chill wind blew down the mountain into their circle. She laughed as they all scrambled for their clothes, aware that the magic of their journey had held them in a protective warmth. Obviously, the journey was over. She explained that she had wanted them to have that experience before their time together was complete, and that St. Germain had come to her in her dreams to announce the time and place. The group laughingly forgave her for dragging them out of bed for an early morning trek. It had been well worth it.

When they gathered that evening to continue the story of the lineage, they were glowing with a joyful light. Leah could see the amethyst filaments of St. Germain in their luminous fields and she was grateful for the elevated frequency. It had been a worthwhile adventure. She also knew that everyone would be ready to sleep early that night, so she began as soon as the circle became attentive.

"Beloveds, I am happy we had such a wonderful experience with St. Germain today. I believe the timing was important to him because our story is moving into more recent times in the Andes, times in which the brotherhood became quite active in the fifth dimension preparing for the present era. We next meet the lineage of light in the year 1560 AD. Ten years before, Isabel had lost her life in southern France. In Peru, the Inca Empire no longer existed, having gone down in easy defeat to the Spanish conquistadors in 1533 AD. We find the lineage of light in the isolated and austere mountainous land of Q'ero, high above the original village of Qoyari's tribe. The village is tiny, invisible to the outside world, for the brotherhood has done everything in its power to protect the lineage of light. The brothers have entered a particularly challenging era of their mission and the women of the lineage are grateful for their protection.

"We find an ancient looking woman named Chuka poking the dung fire in a smoke-filled Q'ero hut. The lines in her dark face are as deep as the furrows of her potato field and the once-bright light in her eyes is beginning to fade. She is wearing a faded, layered black knee-length skirt that could be a rag. Her bare legs are thin but as strong as her iron poker. Woven sandals in need of mending bind her callused feet, and her upper body looks to be a bundle of worn weavings in the subtle reds and black of the Q'ero dyes. Her life has been long and difficult. Still, she cracks a smile at the younger woman, Ela, who sits across the fire from her in this little hut of the women. She looks at Ela, wondering where to begin. Ela is a young mother with a baby suckling at her breast. She could be the duplicate of Chuka except that her clothing is newer, her feet are less callused, her skin is smooth, her eyes are bright and her long, dark braids have no silver hairs. Chuka doesn't feel like wasting time. She is ready to complete her Earthwalk, so she throws more dried dung on the fire and another handful of coca leaves in her mouth before folding her arms around her waist to address Ela."

Chuka speaks

"Ela, you know I have been training you to take over my work with the mastays and the healings with subtle energies. You have done very well. I feel I have lived far longer than was necessary, in part, because you have taken so long to learn them. I do not say this to criticize you. I understand that you are young and have had a few babies to raise while you have been learning. Also, I understand that there are over three hundred of these offerings to learn, which has taken some time. I believe that you are now ready to assume my responsibilities, and I assure you I am ready to be relieved of them.

"I am sorry to be so abrupt with you. I am old, tired, and have never had too much to say. Sometimes I wondered why the great Being of Light elected me to this responsible position. I have thought that I just happened to be where I was needed at the right time, but I know it is more than that. You and I have made the same commitment for I can see upon your brow and your heart, the disc of Inti. I was very young when our shaman saw them on me. She began pulling me into the arts when I was four years old, and then, after the prophecies were read, she took me from my home and began training me in earnest. That was when I was nine. It seems to me I have lived many lifetimes since then. At the time, I resented her actions, but, later, I understood them well. Now it is appropriate for me to share our legacy with you, the one who comes next in a lineage of women who have carried light for Pachamama. It is part of the sacred rites of your awakening that I tell you the story of my life. As I tell you, your own mission will become clear.

"I will begin with my birth. It was not momentous. I was the last of ten children whom my parents loved very much. I was born in the magical fortress of Machu Picchu, the hidden city of light in the high jungle. Machu Picchu was a spiritual community, home to the brotherhood and sisterhood of light, the great shamans and priestesses of Inti. Our tribe had originally come from the valley of the sparkling river, well below this village. Ours was the tribe that Qoyari and Inkari lived with before they set off to start the empire of Inti. When they wished to move some of the spiritual people into the higher realms, they built the fortress of Machu Picchu which could not easily be found by the outside world. Inkari built roads to Machu Picchu from the sacred valley that went over very high mountain passes. Word was sent to the male and female shamans of the tribal villages, and they came to live there with their families. Machu Picchu was home to the first Incas, Qoyari and Inkari and their lineage of Inti. Legends tell us that the roofs of the dwellings were made from the feathers of hummingbirds in those times. Their blood was kept pure for many generations and those born into it held a great light for all who lived or journeyed to Machu Picchu. However, there came a time when the Incas became rulers of a vast empire and they moved to Cusqo which was not so isolated. They began to lose their light and acquire lands and power over people.

"At first, the empire was ruled with light, but over thousands of years it became like those who eventually conquered it. The true Incas were still at Machu Picchu for to be an Inca was to shine like Inti and it was the sisters and brothers of Inti who held the light. The corruption of the empire was read in the prophecies five hundred years before my birth. It was no surprise to the sisters and brothers. They let the jungle grow over the road to obscure the way into the city. They built a watchman's house with a guard always on duty should someone find their secret way through the jungle. This was the world into which I was born. We were isolated in a sacred place of very high frequency. No one voluntarily left, though some were, occasionally, banished.

"Growing up in that sacred city was very different from Q'ero, which is the only home you have known. There the days were warm and moist and the nights cool. The mountains were green with jungle plants and trees. It was a lush paradise. Well, it still is, but the jungle has encroached, taking over with the wild *salk'a* energy of Pachamama. There were many people living there who were farmers and others who herded llamas and alpacas. I have noticed that the alpacas prefer Q'ero to Machu Picchu for they love the rugged sparse life. The llamas did very well in the high jungle of that city and there was continual spinning and weaving of fine cloth. I learned dual thread spinning at an early age and helped my mother with her wool. She was an excellent weaver who sat me at a tiny loom when I was five years old. Those were very happy times for me. My brothers and sisters helped in many

[267]

ways to keep the household in abundance and our life was good.

"My father's work took him into the jungle to gather medicine plants for the shamans and healers. Some of these plants were used for medicine and some for invoking vision and clearing energy fields. He knew exactly which plants to harvest because he spoke to their spirits and could tell which of each variety held the most power. He and my brothers would be gone for half a Moon cycle each time he left, but once a year they went to the low jungle along the great river and would be gone for an entire Moon cycle. When they returned, we would all help with the plant drying or extracting, and Father would trade with many people in the market to maintain our household. My older sister was a healer who trained with the women in the temple. She was very wise in her healing ways and taught me many things as I grew older.

"One day, when I was little more than four years old, I was playing with some strange little seed pods that father had brought from the jungle. I was seated on a pile of weavings in his market booth, like most of the young children of the merchants. The pods had seeds inside that rattled and I was quite lost in the sound made by shaking them, when someone poked me in the stomach. It startled me so much that I began to cry quite loudly. I had been off stalking jaguars in the jungle, listening to the birds and monkeys. Of course I had never been to the jungle but the seed pods had taken me there. It was my first trance journey and the old woman who poked me knew it. She was Shala, the high priestess of the sisterhood of Inti. In fact, she wasn't that old but seemed so to me in my child's eyes. Looking me over quite carefully when I stopped wailing, she told my father to send Mother to the temple to meet with her. Father did as she asked and Mother went straight away to the temple early the next morning. I was far too young to care about their meeting and Mother did not tell me anything until years later when Shala was about to come for me. However, Mother began to take me to the temple for their women's meetings and services. Over time, I began to feel very comfortable with the priestesses. Shala had instructed several of them to guide me on trance journeys until I could take myself into the other realities. It was an obvious talent of mine and I must admit that, in my old age, I often don't know which reality I am in from one moment to the next.

"Well, it was right for Shala to use subtle methods to introduce me to the sisterhood, Ela, for forcing me has never been fruitful. I am sure that mother told her that. When it was time, at nine years of age, for me to enter my formal training with the priestesses I was not nearly as reluctant as I would otherwise have been. I was still upset to leave my mother, my father and his market booth, and my brothers and sisters who were still living in our home, but the priestesses were very welcoming and I entered life there quite happily. That was the year that the old shamans, the *Kuraqs*, asked the Apus for the prophecies that would lead the tribe for the next five hundred years. When they had last been read, the empire was at its height and the leaders were not yet corrupt. These prophecies predicted the loss of light in leadership and the need to isolate Machu Picchu and her people. I was aware that my people held some kind of destiny, but no one really knew what that meant.

"The *Kuraqs* journeyed out to the high mountains of the region after the rains stopped. They spoke with the Apus and waited for their communication. Then each brought his part of the prophecy back to Machu Picchu for Inti Raymi, which celebrated the return of Inti and the end of the maize harvest. The *Kuraqs* met together in secrecy with Ampuka, head of the brotherhood of Magicians, for two days. Each man put forth his communication from the stars which came through the *Apus*. They very carefully wove together a picture of the next five hundred years for the tribe and came to Inti Raymi with their prophecy.

"Inti Raymi was a great celebration in Machu Picchu. We ate no food for several days before the feast, then we prepared the very best food of the year and brought it to the great courtyard which lay between the high temples of the brothers and the sisters. The shamans and priestesses made offerings to Inti and to Pachamama, taking the best food for each. Then the elders were served great plates of food, followed by the priestesses, the shamans, and then the rest of the community. We danced all day to the music of the pan pipes and drums, until the great conch horns announced the reading of the prophecies. Everyone gathered before the shaded shelter of the elders and Ampuka stepped forward to speak to the gathering. It was the hour of power when a magical stillness came over Machu Picchu. Even at the age of nine, I recognized the serious tone of Ampuka's voice and sat up straight with attention.

"He told the people that the mountain spirits had been absolutely clear in communicating a coming danger. For the next five hundred years, life would not be easy, but they would see the fulfillment of the destiny of the tribe, the completion of the tasks put forth by Inkari and Qoyari. The crowd hummed with low whispers and everyone leaned forward to hear more clearly. I felt

[269]

my dinner churning in my stomach as codes of consciousness opened within me. At some level, I knew that what he was saying had something to do with my life and purpose. I struggled to keep my food down while I listened further.

"Ampuka announced that the misuse of power by the leadership of the empire would, as predicted, lead to its demise. The present ruling Inca would be succeeded by two sons who would divide the empire and turn on one another. For years, the rituals had turned to sacrifice, and brutality was becoming very commonplace. Following the division of the empire, there would come an army of strangers from across the sea. They would have the white skin of the Akhus but we were not to be fooled into thinking they were Akhus. On the contrary, they were evil men whose desires had no limitations. Conquering the Inca empire, they would steal all of her treasures - all except those kept at Machu Picchu and in the mountains where the brotherhood held the records. The *Kuraqs* and Ampuka could not know for sure if we would be discovered in our high jungle fortress, but the Apus' communication suggested that we would not be safe. The filaments of these evil beings were already reaching across the sea, but we had time enough to complete our work at Machu Picchu before evacuating the city of light.

"You can imagine the confusion and the questions that poured forth from the people who were in no way prepared to hear these prophecies. Running to the nearest wall of the city, I sent my dinner flying over the treetops. I think, on that day, my soul solidly connected with my body and I began to hold the energy of my destiny. It was a powerful experience for a nine year old, for I was unaware that Shala and I held codes of light for the future of Pachamama that she would awakened within me. These are the same codes I awaken in you this night, Ela. The essence of the prophecies was to secure the protection of these light codes. This meant that the priestesses carrying them were to be protected, as well as the brotherhood which has always held the truths and guarded the lineage of women carrying the codes. The mission of the tribe was being activated by the Akhus through the Apus and the *Kuraqs* who were their guardians. Every member of the tribe was taking this warning with the utmost seriousness.

"When the crowd settled down and a number of questions were asked, Ampuka revealed the final part of the prophecies. He said that by the end of this coming five hundred year cycle, the energies upon Pachamama would change. Then, the Wiracochas, the shining beings, would return and the mission of the tribe would be completed. By the time the prophecies were to be read again, these beings would come from the north following the filaments of their ancient lineages. They would sit with us in ceremony and become star-activated. Relieving us of our long-held duty, we would be free. These Akhus would use the light within them to quicken the frequency of mankind and Pachamama would take her next step in becoming a star. There would be an end to time as we know it, and all beings would be free to live as interdimensional aspects of God. Ampuka bowed his head in silence.

"The crowd cheered and began dancing as the music played again. They danced into the night. The sound of the pan pipes and drums found their way to my sleeping mat in the quarters of the young priestesses. My world had been turned inside out and I found comfort by sinking into a deep trance. Within that trance, I journeyed far into the future and saw the unfoldment of the entire five hundred years. Ampuka was quite right. Those years would not be easy, but the vision of the Wiracochas was a great blessing which I still hold deep within my heart. I believe in that distant future, Ela, and you must believe in it also. That vision will give us the strength to fulfill our mission.

"After Inti Raymi, the elders held a series of meetings with representatives of the community to develop a survival plan. Shala brought news back to the priestesses as these meetings progressed over that next year. There was sufficient time, before the arrival in our lands of invaders from across the sea, to plan an orderly withdrawal from our home. I was in the last group to leave. By that time I was thirty years old. Many messengers were sent back and forth to our original village which lay at the edge of the high jungle to the east. Eventually, delegations from Machu Picchu journeyed to that village to guide the evolution of the plan. It was decided that both communities would join together to create the villages in this land of Q'ero. Men from each community began journeying to this remote land to build the dwellings in which we now live. The villages were strung along the high mountains like the gold ornaments on the necklace of a queen. When I was at the age of my womanhood ritual, the first group of people were leaving to begin life in Q'ero. At that time, I was deeply involved in my training as a shaman-priestess.

"The community of sisters lived life as in any normal household. Spinning wool, we wove our black garments and the many blankets and clothes for use in our dwellings and the temples. We grew some of our own food on the terraces assigned to us and trading our fine weavings and the golden ornaments we made, we met the remainder of our needs. Learning to work with gold and gemstones, I created beautiful little statues for the niches in the temple walls. I loved to work with gold. It was the blood of Pachamama running deep inside her body. I was also given further instruction in healing work. We all learned to pick and dry plant medicines and to prepare them for use in healing. Father kept us supplied with plants we could not grow in our own gardens. I have missed the gardens more than anything, Ela. It was so easy to grow flowers and edible plants at Machu Picchu and there were so many growing in the wild, close to the city, that we never wanted for food. Here in the frozen lands of Q'ero we live on tiny potatoes, a few roots and grass seeds, and what we gather from the jungle in the dry months. You are young and have only known this land, Ela. I have so longed for the warmth and beauty of my former home that I am sure I will go to a similar place when I die.

"Let me get back to my story, Ela. Thoughts of the old life make me very nostalgic. The community worked to bring about a progressive evacuation while remaining in a high vibration. The priestesses remained untouched by the energies of separation. We were to be the last to leave Machu Picchu for, at that time, it was far safer to be there than in the more populous regions where factions of the empire were fighting with each other. I grew into my womanhood as the first group left the city for this land of Q'ero. My father and mother were among the first to leave since Father was so skilled in gathering food from the jungle, which would become a major part of the food supply in Q'ero. I was disappointed that Mother would not be present for my maidenhood ritual, but many of my sisters were able to attend the ceremony.

"There were three of us initiated into our womanhood that year. The priestesses took us to the hot baths at the base of the mountain near the river. We had a long walk on steep paths that wound down the mountainside. It was my first journey to this place which we held sacred for the healing powers of its water. I was wide-eyed and excited about everything that transpired. At night, the priestesses took us to pools of hot water where they had lit little oil lamps around the encroaching circle of the jungle. Disrobing, we soaked ourselves in the healing minerals. We would step out into the cooler night air occasionally, then submerge ourselves once again in the waters. After four times in the water, we three maidens were laid upon soft grasses and our bodies massaged with fragrant nut oil. Ela, I have never felt anything so mysterious and wonderful. My body came alive with feelings of love and appreciation. Mother had stroked me as a child, but this was meant to bring forth the fullness of my sexuality and womanhood. The priestesses did not marry or bear children, but they were not withered old women. We were expected to initiate the young men of the community in the art of making love and learning that art began with the priestesses that night.

"When I awoke the next morning I remember feeling I finally belonged in my body. The experience connected me more fully to Pachamama whom I have served ever since. When I was eighteen, I took the simple vows in the sisterhood, the vows to live in the light of higher consciousness and to serve in the ways taught by Qoyari. We were taken to the far side of Huana Picchu, the old mountain, to the temple of the Moon. Though our teachings were all one with Inti, we women felt the pull of the Moon within our bodies and saw how Inti was reflected from it. Women are similar to the Moon, Ela, since we are the passive recipients of male power, in the same way the Moon receives sunlight. Like the Moon, we have our own light which we send forth in discreet ways that nourish Pachamama and her children.

"In the sisterhood, women could leave and marry young men as you have done, but I chose to remain in service to the community. It was my choice, and I was supported by Shala who had a better sense of my destiny than I. She was aging and began to teach me privately after I had taken my vows, helping me develop the natural talent of time traveling which has been one way in which I have served the community. The *Kuraqs* read the prophecies once every five hundred years. The coca leaf readers can divine the future but it is limiting in its scope, like looking in a tunnel and seeing only the light at the other end while missing all that lies within. I am a dreamer, Ela, and a dreamer can see the great picture of the future without missing the details. Shala trained me so well that the shamans used my skills constantly to guide the evacuation of Machu Picchu and our journey to Q'ero.

"So it was that I spent a considerable amount of my time outside my body, flying about the jungles and mountains, entering the interior world of shadows within Pachamama and journeying to the stars to bring back the messages of the Akhus. I think I have lived so long because the community has not had another with this talent to take my place. We are in a place now where life will be hard, but we will not be touched by the dark forces that swirl around us. The Akhus will send a messenger when it is safe for us to come down from this mountain wilderness to share what we are holding with those who seek the light. Until that time, the codes of light must be held in secrecy."

*

Chuka seemed to drift off into a dream space and Ela took the opportunity to feed more dung to the fire which had burned quite low. It did not appear that Chuka could feel the cold draft continually working its way through the dwellings of Q'ero. She was piled high with every blanket and weaving she owned. On top of her head, she wore a llama fur hat. It was hard to imagine anything more bizarre, but Ela dared not laugh at the old crone. Chuka had held the light for the community, especially the women, for forty years in Q'ero, and she would be missed, for no one spoke to the stars with the same clarity.

Ela poured some mint tea for both of them and the fragrance of it brought Chuka back from her dreamtime. Looking around with a start, she let a few tears escape her eyes. Ela offered her the tea and sat back down opposite her, attentive to her every word. Chuka sipped half the cup of tea, then folder her arms over her thick waist again, and resumed her talk with Ela.

*

"I am sorry dear, Ela, I felt this strong urge to fly and was gone immediately on my flight. I was led back to the city of light which lies abandoned between the young and old mountains. It was so still that I could hear the sound of the jungle as it pushed its way into the city. The *salk'a* energy was unimaginable. I moved into the future and saw the old city would not be found for hundreds of years. After its discovery people would wonder about it for a long time and never really understand what life was like in that blessed space. We are safe here in Q'ero, Ela, but in the city of light we had few concerns to keep us from our spiritual practices and the frequency was very high. In our present villages, we have the blessings of the holy mountain, Ausangate, which sends the vibration of the Akhus to us, but the ruggedness of life is a distraction. We have managed to find the spiritual in everything we do, no matter how hard the task, and this has allowed us to hold our light. I can see the importance of having left the city, for surely it would be found if we were there gathering food in the jungle, and moving on the river with our harvests. It is best that

[274]

we are here. Forgive me if I continually drift back to the past. Telling this story brought it all rushing back to me.

"To continue my story, Shala trained me for years in the skills of high priestess and leadership of the community. Though thinking myself quite young for this training, I did not protest. I clearly had a sense of my own destiny. She asked me to lead the initiation for the young maidens, and eventually I sat beside her as the initiates took their vows. When I was nearing thirty years of age, we received the command to begin preparing for our journey here to Q'ero. We were to leave nothing behind. Those things which were too old and useless to carry such a long way were either burned or destroyed. Everything else was bundled to fit on the llamas who would carry our possessions. When our packing was complete and our departure set for the next morning, Shala called all the priestesses together in the temple. As we gathered around her, she called me forward to sit at her side. Announcing that she would not be leaving with us, because she was too old to make the journey and knew that her life was nearing an end - many signs had been telling her this - Shala informed us that I would be taking over as high priestess in her place to protect the great teachings of the Akhus and the sacred duties of the women. I was not surprised for I had seen this in my visions of the future, but I was humbled by the duty since I was clearly not a wise elder. I told them how I felt and they assured me that my vision was far more important than my age. The women were pleased with her choices - both her decision to remain behind and to appoint me as their leader. There were other old people staying behind as well. They would know when their time of death was approaching and take themselves into the jungle to die where the *salk'a* was ready to consume them.

"Shala gave final instructions and blessings to the group. She cautioned them to hold sacred the teachings of the one God, the creative force of the universe, and to keep the channels open to the stars. We were walking our destiny as a tribe and it felt right to all of us, though none of us was certain of the nature of that destiny. That last night in Machu Picchu, Shala dismissed the women and asked me to stay with her. It was then that I learned of the lineage of light and the soul agreement we had made to protect the codes until they could be reactivated in the new Wiracochas. On my journey to the High Council of Ak-An which is influencing the future of the planet, I was told that the same dark force that was about to conquer our empire wished to put out the light of higher consciousness all over Pachamama. This

[275]

force was not originally evil, but it was blinded by power, wealth, and control. At the time, it was hard for me to believe but now that I have seen the bloodthirsty behavior of our own empire, as well as its invaders, I doubt nothing.

"That night was an awakening for me, Ela. This night will be for you also. I have held the sacred duty of the codes of light for forty years, since we left Machu Picchu. Now it is time for you to know that you hold the codes as well. You are star-encoded, Ela, and you have a sacred duty to hold the connection with Ak-An. We women of Q'ero are to keep the sisterhood alive for those who come after us. Shala told me all of this. She told me of Qoyari, the great mother of our people, who came from the rising star to bring the codes of light into our tribe. She told me of Mamacocha, who came long before Qoyari, and brought the star codes to this part of Pachamama. I heard stories of Mak-Ma, the great Akhu who came before Mamacocha from a distant land in the east. You have heard these stories, Ela. I have been telling them to you during the years of your training. Do not forget them. They are our legacy. Do not forget what I have told you of the city of light. You will pass all of this on to the next high priestess. You will find the solar disc upon her brow and heart and know the time of your passing so that you can activate the codes within her.

"It was hard to leave Shala the next morning. She had sent me to bed after shooting bolts of light through my body to connect me to the mission. I slept little and was weary as we led the llamas out of the city gates into the jungle. We were a band of twenty sisters with ten brothers protecting us and twenty more young men cooking, carrying loads and clearing the way through the heavy growth along the trail. It was the dry season, the safest time to travel to the mountains. The men sent scouts ahead of us to look for signs of independent warriors and robbers and I was sent out through the dimensions to see that the way was clear. This never used to be a problem in that area, but recent unrest had developed. I believed it was a reaction to the energy that would come to us from across the sea. I saw that our empire would be following a course of self-destruction that would climax with the arrival of the invaders. It was a picture that drove me onward through the jungle and over high mountain passes as we made our way east following a course that avoided the populated areas of the sacred valley and Cusco. Sidetracking some potentially dangerous situations, we arrived in the more isolated valleys to the east of Cusco a full Moon cycle after leaving Machu Picchu.

[276]

"Free of the jungle, we began walking up toward the holy mountain, Ausangate, and the mountains of Q'ero. Finally arriving at our new village in the land of Q'ero, we were greeted by the shamans and the brothers who had left the city of light a year ahead of us. They showed us to our humble quarters which were really more than adequate compared to some of the villagers' dwellings. We had not passed through the tribe's old village since it was not on our way, but we learned that our people there would wait another year or two before coming to join us in the mountains. Until that time, they helped to provide our villages with food that we could not grow ourselves.

"Those who had come before us were not in good health. There had been many infant deaths from the cold, and that continues to be a big problem for our people, as you know. Do everything you can to strengthen the vitality of the newly born. They are the hope of the future and also the link to the Divine for they are so new to this life. It isn't good for the women to have so many children. They will lose their essence and die too young. Please work with the families to educate them in the art of breathing to increase the life force. We are living at a great height here, close to the top of the holy mountain. The air is thin, so we need more of it. Deep breathing while at work on the mountainsides will improve the overall health of our beloved tribe.

"We found ourselves using most of our energy to stay warm, herd our llamas and alpacas and grow our humble potatoes. There were wild grasses to harvest and a few edible plants, but the men still made a yearly trip into the jungle to harvest and dry fruit and plants for the harsh winter. Q'ero is not far from the high jungle which leads to the great river of the mother. Once in the jungle, it was easy to avoid danger from other men, but important for the shamans to work with the spirits of the snakes and jaguars to insure the safe journey of the group of gatherers. We women stayed in the mountains with our spinning, weaving and baby-raising. I have never left this land since we first came, Ela. I made one pilgrimage to Ausangate to ask the holy mountain to bring me my successor. That was a year before you were born and fourteen years after I came to this desolate place. I traveled to the glaciers and the sacred lagoons of the brotherhood's initiation making offerings to the Apus and Pachamama, who have always been there to guide me. The frequency on the mountain was so high I began to disappear, at times. When that happened, I was pushed back into this reality as if the Apus were telling me that I had more work to do here.

[277]

The Priestesses of Inti

"I met an old *Kuraq* of another tribe on the holy mountain who was guardian of the great Apus there. He lived in a little hut at the edge of a glacier where he held the energy for all of us. His young brothers brought food to him and dung for his fires. I was fortunate to be invited to stay with him for several days and gathered a wisdom unavailable to most of us. Cooking some tasty food for him, I gave him what bread I had left in my bag. As I prepared to leave him, a condor alighted in front of his hut and took pieces of the bread from his hand. His eyes twinkled and he asked me if I would like to fly on the wings of the condor to new heights. Never one to decline such an offer, I entered a deep trance state and merged myself with the bird. Soon we were circling over the mountain and the hut of the old *Kuraq*. I could see him so clearly that I caught the look of amusement on his face as he looked up through the dimensions to see us in flight. The condor took me over Cusco where there were men fighting and slaying each other in the city squares. We flew further, to the great sea beyond and saw the gigantic boats of the invaders landing on our shores. The energies felt black, greedy, and loveless.

"I asked the condor to take me over Titicaca Lake since I knew I would never be able to visit the home of the feminine light. Circling over the island of the Sun, I drank in the energies of Mamacocha and Wiracocha. There were reed fishing boats dotting the lake and huts floating on islands of reeds further along. The condor flew north toward the east and we observed a group of men carry a heavy load up into the mountains. I asked to fly closer to the men and the condor dove down towards them at a breathtaking speed. I clearly saw that they were transporting the great golden disc of Inti that had been in the Coricancha temple in Cusco since the times of Inkari and Qoyari. It was a legendary piece of our culture that could never be duplicated. The brotherhood had foreseen the turmoil in Cusco months before and was moving it to safety in the mountains near Titicaca Lake where they had a monastery. I was aware of the brotherhood's activity in the empire because I held the codes of light. These were the brothers of the Red Hand who were charged with the protection of all records of the past. The disc of Inti was a record of the legacy of Inkari who designed it and had it made. It contained coded messages from the stars which no one could decipher except Lord Muru. It made my heart happy to see that it was being moved to safety. I was sure that all the other treasures of the empire would be lost.

"The condor returned me to the *Kuraq's* hut where we landed clumsily in front of the old man. Suddenly, I came back into my body and opened my eyes to this reality. The old man watched me carefully to see how the experience had been integrated. He drew three coca leaves from his bag and arranged them with the leaf ends pointed up. It was the *kintu*, the great offering which Inkari brought to the shamans of our village. The three leaves symbolized love, wisdom and will. He blew onto the leaves in all directions including above and below, sending his intent out into the universal matrix. Then he drew three leaves and handed them to me, watching while I assembled the *kintu*.

"Before I focused my intent to blow through the leaves into the universal matrix, the old man stopped me. Looking deep within my eyes until I stopped everything, even the workings of my mind, he told me I had the power to bridge all realities. He had never seen anyone like me. If I practiced nothing else, he added, I would fulfill my mission to Pachamama and the sisterhood. Furthermore, I could walk from this world and take my body with me if I so intended. Of course, I am wondering why I would want to take this aged body with me, but he urged me to do even greater work between the worlds. He told me that my journey with the condor was in this reality, that everything I saw was happening as I saw it. Sitting there and taking it in like a wind running through me, I could not comment. My hand held the three coca leaves in absolute stillness. I knew what he said was true. He was telling me to be careful with my intent as this was no ordinary *kintu*.

"I had been ready to intend that the forces of evil leave the empire forever. Telling him this, he laughed at me and pointed out that the empire was as much the force of evil as the invaders, since the leaders had fallen into corrupt ways. Evil would meet evil and the evolution of the third dimension would continue. I asked him about the brothers and the disc of the Sun. He knew them well, for they were the disciples of Lord Muru, the ageless Akhu who headed the Order of the Red Hand. The disc would be safe and, if necessary, Lord Muru would move it into the higher realms. I asked him about the brotherhood of magicians and the lineage of the codes of light. The old *Kuraq* told me to believe my own vision of the future and know that the Divine Plan would unfold as Source intended. The Akhus and ascended masters were carefully watching the insane behavior of mankind. They would not let mankind destroy Pachamama. If need be, they had Akhus ready to incarnate to serve her. He had helped me to a place where it seemed permissible to intend something for my own spiritual growth. When you are dedicated to service you must be careful where you place your intent, Ela.

"Finally, I blew on the three leaves intending that I master the dimensions and leave this reality alive. I felt my filaments lock into the grid and knew that I had made a big commitment to become light. The old man told me to return to my village and the condor followed me as I concluded my pilgrimage to the holy mountain. You will make this pilgrimage too, Ela, when you are called. It will change your life.

"Returning to my village, I told the elders about the turmoil in our lands. They were expecting such news to reach them eventually. I spoke to Ampuka about the solar disc and he was relieved to know that the brothers had reached Titicaca Lake with it. The brotherhoods always acted in secrecy, Ela, so you will not repeat what I have said about this disc. There will come a time when all secrets are revealed, but now it would be most dangerous. My journey to Ausangate took place three years before your birth, Ela. When you were born, I saw the solar disc upon your brow and heart and my own heart was relieved that my successor was with me. We have a wonderful group of women, strong and reliable, but few can work with the subtle energies as I have trained you to. Be watchful of those who show that talent, for you will want to train them to become the dreamers of the future.

"I have one more vision to share with you, Ela, before we are finished tonight. One day, about ten years ago, I was watching you tend your llamas on a mountainside not far from the village. The day was bright and sunny, with a warm, humid breeze lifting up out of the jungle. Your first born son, Maki, was resting on your back, sleeping soundly. I saw the flash of your smile as you looked back at him and I entered another realm. There, I saw a young woman about your age sitting in a cave on a hillside. She was alone and in a deep trance. Tears were rolling down her face and I was deeply moved by the emotional turmoil she was experiencing. Entering her vision, I found her standing before the Akhus on Ak-An staring into a flame. I must tell you that she didn't look like you or me. Her skin was white and her dark hair fell in flowing curves to the cave floor where she sat naked and cross-legged upon Pachamama. I saw the disc of Inti upon her brow and heart and knew that she was, somehow, part of our lineage of women carrying the codes of light. As she stared at the flame, it began to grow dim, and I was overwhelmed with the feeling that you and she should somehow meet. I drew a higher aspect of yourself out of this reality and intended you to enter the candle flame. When it went out, she saw you, and it brought joy to her very unhappy heart. I do not know fully what the vision meant, Ela, but it released her from a great guilt which she carried. A greater light entered her body.

"I released the intent that had held you there and mended the crack between the worlds that the experience had created. When I returned to this reality, the condor was circling over you. His message was clear. She was part of this reality although the coming together was in the higher dimensions. It was, by far, the strangest and most moving experience of my life."

*

Chuka raised the flames with her poker and looked at Ela. The younger woman's eyes were open wide enough to fall out into the fire. Ela's mind was moving backward in time, conjuring up the memory of that day ten years before. Some part of her remembered. She found herself back on the mountainside with the llamas. She remembered a feeling of joy as she had intuitively turned to look at Maki. She saw instead the face of that beautiful white woman whom Chuka had just described. Feeling the tears run down her face, she lifted the corner of the baby's blanket to wipe them away as the vision vanished. Also, she had seen the condor and had felt, the next morning, that the great bird had been responsible for a dream she had had. Not able to recall the particulars of the dream as she excitedly spoke of it to Chuka, she could never forget the ending. The same young women, dirty and naked, was dragged into a city plaza. Her hair was cut close to her scalp in front of a crowd of people before she was tied to a post atop a huge pile of wood. A fire was lit and quickly rose up around her. Ela had awakened in horror, screaming the name Isabel. Ela looked at Chuka to know the meaning of her dream, and then she wept, finally releasing the pain and terror of that night from her body. Chuka pulled Ela to her and let her weep in her rotted old skirt.

*

"Oh, my child, we both had a powerful experience. It is a wonder we never discussed it until this day. I feel this woman was the victim of the same dark force that has swept across this land murdering all who would not become slaves to the beliefs of those in power. She was our sister for she bore the discs of Inti. It occurs to me that this dark force may be trying to find and destroy the women who hold the codes of light. I wonder why anyone would oppose the increasing of consciousness and light on Pachamama? Perhaps it threatens their power. We are fortunate that the Apus have guided us to this place which is desolate and inaccessible to most. Also, I am happy to know that our beautiful friend found her way to the Akhus of Ak-an, for they would have helped to prepare her for her sorrowful death. Isabel conquered fire, Ela. One day she will be born a shaman who will learn that the initiation of fire opens the heart to *munay*, loving power. Please, cry no longer, my child. Isabel is a master. She is the lightning. She will help to guide you as you lead our women - and so will I.

"Well my child, I never intended to talk so long or to say so much. Spirit was pushing it out of me this night so that I might complete my walk upon Pachamama. We have only a small initiation to fully activate your light and then you can go to your home. Tomorrow, when you awaken, you will be high priestess of the Q'ero sisterhood, and I will be gone. Remember your legacy, Ela. Retell the stories of Lemuria, Mak-Ma, Mamacocha and Wiracocha, Qoyari and Inkari, and our experiences at Machu Picchu. Repeat all that you know of the lineage of light only to she who will take your place, and train her to be a dreamer, for the tribal vision must not fade. If it does, we will not recognize the Akhus when they come again and Pachamama will not be served. Kneel before me now Ela, and receive your light activation."

*

Chuka transferred the power and light of her calling to Ela whose light body received it in small jolts until her emotional field cleared and she took it in fully. Her consciousness expanded to a more universal place and her frequency reached new heights. Chuka took her, in this elevated state, to Ak-An where the High Council met with Ela and reviewed her soul commitment. When they returned to the thatched stone hut in Q'ero, Ela expressed her gratitude to Chuka and gave her a beautiful stone that looked just like the holy mountain. It was for her journey home. Ela then left to return to her family home where she fell into a deep and dreamless sleep.

The old priestess rubbed out the coals of her little fire with her sandals, burning a few more layers of the fibers. She put Ela's stone in the pouch around her neck, then picked up a walking stick which she had propped against the wall by the door. Leaving the door of the women's hut open, and pulling her blankets tight around her neck, she tromped off like a bear heading north and west. She was headed for the place of power, Mistipukara. There the shamans of Q'ero went to receive their power. From Pachamama, they drew up the power left behind by those shamans who had completed their Earthwalk. She was going there, as her last pilgrimage, to release the power she still carried. After walking steadily all night and throughout the next day, she arrived at Mistipukara just before dawn the second morning. Looking down toward the jungle in the east, she could see the very first village of her tribe along the river of sparkling water. There were many people in this village now who had been influenced by the invaders. She thought of Qoyari coming into the body of the dying child there and Inkari manifesting himself on this very mountaintop, within sight of the village. It was a place of power and magic. It was also a dangerous place to be found for she might give away the location of the tribe.

Chuka seated herself on Pachamama and drew her blankets up against the wind which blew ferociously at Mistipukara. In service to the tribe, she gave all her heavy energy and painful memories to Pachamama, asking her to use it to make the potatoes grow. Then she began offering layer after layer of her soul experience, her gifts and her shamanic power to Pachamama, asking her to hold it for the next shaman who came to sit on this spot. She began to feel lighter and lighter as she did this and finally felt empty. Standing up, she asked herself what to do next. She could walk for two days and hope to make it to the chulpas, the burial tombs of the shamans, without being seen, or she could fulfill the intent of her *kintu* and leave Pachamama with her body. After pacing around in a tight circle looking rather like a small hill deciding where to plant itself, Chuka stopped and sat down on the very spot where she had released her power. Again, drawing the blankets and weavings around her, she completely buried herself inside them, her fur hat sticking out on top of the heap. No one knows how long it took her to transmute her physical body, but when the brothers came looking for her remains a week later they found the blankets and hat looking very much like a little round *chulpa*. Looking inside they found only her sandals, the layers of her black skirt, and the pouch with the stone that Ela had given her on her last night in Q'ero. They looked at each other, grinning, then sat down on that spot to gather what they could of her power.

The Priestesses of Inti

Leah speaks

The women were laughing and clapping as Leah finished the story. They had met women like Chuka high in the mountains of Peru and it was not difficult to visualize the scene at Mistipukara. Leah had taken them to that site several times with Don Carlos, the shaman they traveled with in Peru. The last time they had sat on the Earth there gathering power, they were on their way to Q'ero.

Leah went off to bed exhausted from the long day. The women caught a second wind, brewed some hot tea, and sat up most of the night telling stories of their experiences in Peru. They brought them alive again, and felt the magic of the land, the people, and their shared love. Peru was not about conquistadors and corrupt Incas for them, even though that history is written in the land. It was a magical place of rebirthing into the light, perhaps because wise ones like Chuka knew the true meaning of power and the art of detaching from it.

Francesca

Leah speaks

No one, except Leah, stirred before noon the next day. She drove
to the mineral baths for an early soak after watching the sunrise
up on the mountain. The retreat was drawing to a close and she
was pulling in filaments of light from the entire lineage to bring
forth the last of the women's stories. After dipping into the cold
creek for the last time in her round of soaks and sweats, Leah sat
naked upon a flat boulder. She felt and saw her filaments extending far beyond her into nature. The trees, the mountains, the
birds, the water, the images of the women of the lineage, and her
group all merged into an ecstatic surge that sent her spirit soar-
ing to the heart of God. Her Essence merged with all the layers of
her being and anchored itself fully in her form sitting upon the
rock.

In her vision, Leah saw before her a fork in the road. She was
being given a choice. On the road to the left she perceived that
she could soar with the eagles, pursuing her own path back to
God through personal ascension. On the road to the right she
saw herself walking with many people who were hungry for the
light. It was the Bodhisattva's path of service which she knew
was the soul commitment of the lineage. She had been given many
opportunities in her Earthwalks to soar with the eagles, but she
knew, this time, ascension was to be a collective experience. Veer-
ing to the right, instead of seeing the light of God at the end of the
road, she saw it in the eyes of all those around her. God was
everywhere she looked, including within herself.

The vision faded, but the light did not. Leah knew she had
experienced initiation on that rock. She had touched the frequency

of God. It was living within every aspect of her being, and she did not have to remind herself to hold it. The light had been anchored in her. She knew it was the final healing of her soul and blood lineages that had allowed her to hold this frequency. When the women came together for their last night beneath the mountain, Leah's light was so brilliant they were drawn into her heart space immediately. She was dressed in white - alive, present and very visible. Because she was able to hold a higher frequency, the quality of love in the room was absolutely pure. There was an excitement in the air, for Leah would surely be bringing the story of the lineage of light into present time. Her students had spent most of the night recalling individual and group experiences with the women shamans and *brujas* in Peru. Leah laughed at their excitement and moved the energy to a place where she could begin her concluding story.

"Well beloveds, we are closing our retreat tonight in a very special way. I want to tell you Francesca's story." The group applauded when they heard her name for they had all experienced her healing work in Peru. Leah continued, "You all worked with Francesca and her daughter, Angelica, when we visited the village of Pakulmaka in the mountains east of Cusco. We have known them in one way - that of visitors from a distant land seeking healing and light. Now we will know them as sisters and guardians of the codes of light.

"We find Francesca, plump and happy at the age of forty, sitting with her daughter, our beloved, Angelica, who is twenty-three and pregnant with Margarita. Francesca is still nursing her last child, Pulla, who is home sleeping with the rest of her brood and her husband, Miguel. Angelica, Francesca's first born, has four children of her own who are home with their father, Pedro. The two women have arranged this night together to speak about the past, the present and the future. Angelica is not quite sure what her mother has in mind, but is pleased to have this time alone with her. She tries to think when it was that she was last alone with her mother and cannot remember. They have spent the day planting seed potatoes on the steep slopes of their allotted farmland. Both women are sleepy but sleep can wait. They feel the importance of this night for there have been visitors to the village who awakened something deep inside Francesca.

"The night, like all nights here, is cool. They light a dung fire in the women's hut where Francesca regularly teaches the initiated women of the villages in this area. She is the most powerful shaman in the region, but her energy is so subtle she appears, as you know, no more than a simple woman. Her humble spirit is a match for her enormous heart. She has suffered much pain, lost many babies and worried quite often about her ability to serve Pachamama. Angelica is a reflection of her mother. Her high cheekbones and slightly Incan nose are softened by her smooth bronzed skin and Asian eyes. She is beautiful and her mother handsome. They both wear traditional dress with layers of knee-length black skirts edged in brightly woven wool designs. White blouses form a middle layer between gayly colored sweaters. Their embroidered black circular hats with yellow woolen fringes hanging over the edges protect them from the Sun. The hats are held in place by row upon row of white beaded ties that come together under their chins before falling to their chests. Their shiny blue-black hair is neatly braided and tied with colored yarn.

"Their names and many aspects of the village life reflect the influence of the Spanish, but these two women have lived traditional lives, staunchly refusing schooling, religion, and the Spanish language. They speak only Quechua, the language which the Inca empire spread throughout the Andes. The mother and daughter have just shared some pan, little round loaves of bread, and a traditional chuño soup, the fermented freeze-dried potatoes from the high mountains. After a little family small talk, Francesca shuts the door of the adobe hut and seats herself across the fire from Angelica."

Francesca speaks

"Angelica, daughter, there are things which I have not told you about my life and now, it is time to reveal them. The people who have come to our village to be with Don Carlos have sparked something deep inside me which I know is truth and light and I need to share it with you. This I know. I must tell you about my life for we have a common sacred duty through our lineage of women shamans, and you must be opened to it now, not when I die, but now. Time in our world is moving, Angelica, not at a predictable flow, but in a new way - very swiftly. The prophecies have spoken of a day when we will step outside of time and it is fast approaching. I can feel it. It will present the opportunity to walk through the crack between the worlds into the *hanaqpacha* (higher consciousness). I see the last of the prophecies being fulfilled as we prepare to speak once again to the *Apus*. I will speak more of that later, but first I must give you the story of my life. We are not a people who speak much of ourselves, so please, my

[287]

daughter, know that this is my duty.

"I was born further up the valley in a village higher than Pakulmaka. It had a commanding view of Ausangate, but it no longer exists. One rainy season, after I had married your father and moved to Pakulmaka, there was a terrible slide of mud that tragically buried the village. My family was lost, except for my father who was the shaman. He was visiting the villages of Q'ero at the time and came home to nothing - no wife, no children, no house. It was a great sorrow for him, but he was a master of detachment, and he did not give up on life. He walked to Pakulmaka, as you know, and lived with us until he died just two years ago. You and your grandfather were the greatest friends for each other when you were young, Angelica. Your presence in his life helped him heal the wounds of his loss.

"Mother had been the *bruja*. She taught me the craft, from plant gathering and preparing the medicines, to administering them and birthing the babies. I did not feel especially called that way and often traveled with my father as he visited the villages throughout the valley. He was a master of energy and I saw him move it with authority. When I was about nine, he asked if I would like to journey to Q'ero country with him and my brother. I was so excited, mother could not refuse my request to go. It was, and still is, most unusual for girls to travel with the men. We took food to trade for weavings and wool, and a few personal items, all packed on a sturdy little horse. Sometimes Father would put me on the horse to allow me to rest, but I was a strong girl and kept up well with both of them. Sleeping under the stars we cooked our food on small fires. I loved to be on Pachamama in that way. I felt embraced by her, our Great Mother.

"After several days walking, we came to Mistipukara, the sacred site of the shamans. I have taken you there to awaken the powers within you, Angelica, as my father did with me. We sat and prayed for a long time in an ancient circular ruin. Then Father told me to go and feel the place where I might sit down and gather my power. I did not know that he was initiating me, but went out like any nine-year old in search of energy. Mistipukara is a big place and the wind can be wild. Wrapping my blankets around me, I started circling outward from where Father sat. For some time, I had no luck, then I fell down, thinking that I had tripped on a rock by catching my sandal. I picked myself up and tried to walk back a few steps to listen more carefully to Pachamama. As soon as I lifted my foot I fell down again. Bewildered, I wondered what to do next, and looked back at Father. He motioned me to stay where I was and be with the spirits there.

"Positioning myself cross-legged, I closed my eyes, waiting for spirit to send me a message. Pachamama bumped the bottom of my spine, at first gently, then with strength. I was being bounced around like a ball until I opened myself to the energy and it began to flood into my body. It was an experience of joy that I could not describe. Within my mind's eye, I saw the face of an old, old woman. She was all wrapped up in ragged blankets and had the funniest fur hat on her head. Looking at me with her wise eyes, she told me that others had come to take her power, but she had saved the essential part of it, the feminine power, for me. In my mind I asked her if she knew me. She told me she knew me well, but not in this life. As her image was beginning to fade, she advised me to pursue the art of dreaming.

"Pachamama became silent and my vision complete. Walking back to my father, I told him what had happened. Looking very wise, he nodded his head while chewing a handful of coca leaves. He didn't really say anything to me about my experience. What could he say? I had taken in the power of that old woman, there was no doubt. The remainder of my vision was of women's work, so he would try to find someone in Q'ero who could explain the vision to me. Father was very pleased with what had happened because he secretly longed for me to follow the shamanic path and not that of the *bruja.*

"We spent the night in a valley between Q'ero and Mistipukara. The valley was out of the wind and very magical with the jungle spread before us to the east. Rising early, we arrived in the first Q'ero village before the midday meal, and were cheerfully greeted by the villagers as we made our way to the house of the shaman. We were invited to have soup and potatoes with the family. In each village of Q'ero, Father and the shamans traded medicines, healing stones and techniques. He learned more *mastays* from them every time he came to Q'ero, for it seemed the number of ways to order coca leaves for these gifts was infinite. With the other children of the household, I was invited to watch these ceremonies. In one of the villages, the shamans were joined by an old woman for such a ceremony. Her braids were gray and her skin wrinkled like a dried fruit. Her long hooked nose was from her Incan ancestors, and she had very bright eyes. She taught the men how to order the coca leaves in a ceremony they had never performed before. This *mastay* was for tranquillity and the art of dreaming. I became very attentive to every detail of this offering as she brought forth the sacred herbs, flowers and wine

[289]

that went into the *despacho* (gift).

"When the *despacho* was finished, she asked me for a piece of my clothing. Surprised, I gave her my woven belt which I used for special occasions. Producing a little waxen doll, she wrapped it in my belt, then called me to her. Wiping me down with the *despacho*, she cleansed my energetic field. She wiped me again with the doll rolled in the belt, after which I was free to sit down again. Praying over the offering, she then sent two of the shamans out to burn it. When it was completely burned, they returned to us to report the purity of the fire and the way it was received by Pachamama and the spirits. She announced to my father that I was to come back twice a year to train with her, for I was called to be a dreamer. Father and I looked at each other in disbelief, but agreed to do as the woman asked. Her name was Doña Maria Quispé, and she became my teacher in the art of dreaming. Much later, I learned that she saw the symbols of Inti on my forehead and heart while Father and I were trading in the village that day. She had asked for the ceremony to align me with my purpose and anchor the energy that I had received at Mistipukara.

"My mother was not pleased that I would be taking the path of the shaman instead of following in her footsteps as a *bruja*. I now understand that, had I remained in training to take her place, I would not be alive today. It was not part of the Divine Plan that I remain in our village. The magic that accompanied every step of my training with Doña Maria affirmed that I was on the right path. A very old woman, tougher than leather, she was the sweetest and most gentle soul I have known in my life. Her language was the old form of Quechua, the same as the Incas, so it took some time for me to get used to her dialect, but I was a child quick to learn, so it was not difficult to begin to understand her. She wanted me to be able to journey out into the other worlds, to follow the vision and fly to other places in this reality. I had heard of women who could do this, but they were, like Doña Maria, high up in the isolated mountains where their culture had not been touched by the outside world. As I grew older, I realized what an unusual woman she was and how fortunate I was to be able to train with her.

"Every time Father and I would come to Q'ero, he would leave me in her village before he made his rounds of the other ones. Then, on his return, he would take me back home. She and I would spend the days moving energy in my field, recognizing other realities, and journeying through the portals to them. I learned to warp time, expanding or contracting it as might be necessary for a healing. The most important part of what Doña Maria taught me was the right use of my intent. For everything I did, I was accountable to Source. It was, as you know, very serious work. Gradually, she opened me to my vision, and I continued to work with her for many years, even after my marriage to your father. When she was very old, I used to put coca leaves in her mouth and brew her coca tea the way she liked it. I helped her eat and put her to bed and loved her as I love my own children.

"Doña Maria had seen the seeds of unrest within me on that very first day we met. That is why she suggested the *mastay* ceremony for tranquillity, to calm and center me for the work ahead. It was a perfect choice. I was a very independent young woman who would have broken all the rules of the sisterhood following my desires. She helped me anchor my soul's purpose in this reality and make good choices for myself from that place of peace. Also, she taught me to create my reality and bring good things into my life, like your father. It was in Q'ero that I met your father because he came to train with the shamans there. An ancient wisdom was preserved there which was no longer alive in the villages further down. On the day of my puberty rites which Doña Maria insisted that I experience in Q'ero, I met Miguel. This was another magical way in which the filaments were aligned in my life. He came to Doña Maria's house to pick up sacred herbs for the men's ceremonies and I let him in the door. I was in the full bloom of maidenhood, and he delighted in that vibration. Our meeting was light-hearted and easy, but I did not think, at the time, that he would be interested in me as a wife.

"Later that night, after my ceremony was complete and I was in that beautiful place of awakened sexuality, Doña Maria and I talked of my future. She asked me to consider the possibility that Miguel had been drawn to Q'ero at that time by the power of my intent. He satisfied exactly my requirements for a good husband. I had intended a man with great light and humility who was also light-hearted. Miguel was that young man. Doña Maria was anxious to make the match for me and Miguel was quick to accept. We had a traditional Q'ero wedding with our respective teachers officiating. I was much more a part of Q'ero culture than that of my village so I was able to break tradition and move to my new husband's village, Pakulmaka, which is much closer to Q'ero than the village of my birth. Your father and I continued to journey to Q'ero together until Doña Maria passed from this world.

"Before the old one passed, she became very weak and called for me to come to her. You do not remember this, Angelica, for you were at my breast, but your father and I took you with us to Q'ero, so that I could be with her at her passing. I fed her until she would not take any more food, and brought her water and tea until she refused to drink. One night, when I thought she would refuse to breathe she sat up and told me she had to talk to me. It was then that she told me about the disc of Inti that I carried on my forehead and heart. She told me that I was part of a committed soul group that has incarnated as a lineage of women to hold higher consciousness on the planet. That is why she took me in for training, for she, too, was part of this soul group, and she told me that you carried the disc of Inti also. Angelica, this lineage of women extends back in time to the days of Mamacocha. It is ancient. Not finding any of the women in Q'ero with the disc of Inti, she had searched for me, and had used her intent to draw me in on the filaments of light.

"Doña Maria told me the story of her life in Q'ero, where she was the tribe's highest female shaman. Some called her a magician, for she had mastered the dimensions. All the women of the Q'ero villages who held the shamanic traditions had been trained by Doña Maria. There were dreamers in every Q'ero village helping to shape the future with their vision and intent. What I represented to her was an heir to this lineage of light as well as a dreamer. In telling me the story of her life, she connected me with all the women of this lineage. She initiated me at the end of the evening, activating my light body and opening me to deeper vision. Of course, I knew that you would inherit this responsibility from me for she had already seen the disc of Inti on your body, Angelica. You were with me in her humble dwelling when she passed the lineage to me and it seems to me that she passed it to you as well, for you were much more awake than most children.

"Until tonight, you have not had it in your consciousness, but it is in your soul's intent. I ask you to feel what is happening tonight and see what your dreams bring, Angelica. You are a dreamer as well and I trust that they will give us insights about what is happening in our village. To return to my story, Doña Maria passed away shortly after awakening my light. She had fulfilled her mission and was released from this realm. I saw her essence rise from the top of her head and float through the ceiling of the house. Rushing outside with you in my arms, I saw it rise above the village, then begin a fast spiral and shoot out into the stars. I went back and sat with her body, to witness the separation of all layers of her being. She was too weak to have gone to Mistipukara, so she gave her power to me during that activation of light. In gratitude, I sat there and repeated her story to her dead body. It helped me, because it sealed the lineage within my being and I think it helped her also to fully release any attachment to her life. I think that is why we wait until we are about to leave to reveal ourselves, then we can detach completely. Dreaming that night of the women, I saw their many faces - varied, and yet the same. They were sitting in dark huts around sacred fires. They were all Pachamama's face. The knowing that I was connected to that lineage of women gave me the strength to use what Doña Maria had given me.

"Your father and I returned to Pakulmaka, to the raising of our family and to village life. I began to see more and more people for shamanic healing, using the techniques to move subtle energy that Doña Maria had taught me. A few women came to me from the neighboring villages to begin learning the priestess ways that had not been well preserved, except in the high mountains. We began training and initiating our own girls so that the sisterhood lived on in a very quiet way. Doña Maria had realized that I came from the more modernized culture to act as a bridge to the old ways. The lineage wished to move out to be ready for the times to come. I have watched this village change, Angelica, like a caterpillar into a butterfly, only the other way around. Many problems plague us now that did not exist before the trucks started bringing unnatural things into our lives from Cusco. Our once rich life is eroding like the soil of a field planted without intent.

"You and I have good husbands, Angelica - be grateful for that. We will prosper in every way if we do not lose the principle by which we have always lived, which is service. The Incas brought the ideal of service to the people into their leadership and we carry those codes. When they lost that principle, they lost the empire. We are here to serve, but without suffering. It is not necessary to sacrifice one's self to serve. It is only necessary to be impeccable at all times and to avoid the energies of separation. We must always see Source in every person and not limit their potential for light with our negative thoughts. That is the secret of higher frequency, my daughter - to hold all in the light without judgment, no matter how far from the light they appear to be. Appearances can be deceiving. They are a product of our assemblage point. Everyone has the light of Source because everyone is Source. If you listen to what Jesus really said, you will hear that we are Source. We are all one. So those who are lazy and unconscious are aspects of ourselves that have those traits. If we change ourselves, they will change. These are the things Doña Maria

[293]

taught me.

"I have returned to Q'ero twice a year to work with the women there. They will not come down from the mountain to have their lives scrutinized by the western culture. So they hold their power in their isolation. You and I have held our power and our strength in secrecy. We are raising our children like any mothers, but they are receiving the subtle energies of the higher teachings. Yes, they will go to school, perhaps leave and take jobs in the city, but they will not lose their centers for they know what is their truth. A greater gift we could not give them, Angelica.

"To return to my story, your father and I were joined by my father after the loss of his home and family. He and Miguel continued to travel to Q'ero to trade and learn from the *Kuraqs*, but the shamans began coming down the mountain to visit Pakulmaka as well. Miguel and Father had many people coming to them for healing every day. When the Q'ero were in Pakulmaka, they also did healings and ceremony with the entire village. One day they brought with them a *mestizo* whom we have come to know well as Don Carlos. He came as a well educated man who had had an awakening to his tribal roots and Pachamama. Don Carlos left his home and family in Cusco and traveled everywhere in the mountains on his horse to find the way back to Pachamama. When he first came to Pakulmaka, he was studying with the Kuraq, Don Martín. Don Martín passed on ten years ago and now Don Carlos is a Kuraq himself. He loved the village of Pakulmaka and acquired an old *hacienda* up the mountain from the family who owned all of the valley before we regained our own lands. Don Carlos has been a great benefactor of our village and especially of our families, Angelica. I am now understanding that he is one of a lineage of souls who have incarnated to protect the sisterhood. It is no mistake that he found us, though it seems quite unbelievable. He does not realize that I am a shaman or of the lineage. I don't believe any of that truth has entered his consciousness yet. It is amazing that Spirit accomplishes the work even when we are not conscious of it.

"Don Carlos used to come to his *hacienda* to be in his gardens, to meditate, and to work with Miguel and my father. He has brought ease and abundance into our lives by employing our children and our husbands at his house. He would disappear for months at a time and then return to refresh himself. I learned, years later, that he would travel around Pachamama, teaching people about her, about Ayni, the Apus, and the work of the shamans. He began to bring some of the people he taught to his *hacienda.* The Q'ero would come to visit and the village shamans would join them for ceremonies that would last all night. I watched in silence to see what would come of it all.

"You grew up to be a beautiful young woman and your father and I worked the filaments to find Pedro for you to marry. Your womanhood ritual was one of the most beautiful days of my life, Angelica, and I know it was for you as well. Miguel and I instructed Pedro in the ways to please a woman and how to be a good husband and father. We wanted only happiness for you. When Don Carlos began to bring his children to the mountains, you and his daughter, Maya, became very close friends. You were lucky that she spoke Quechua for most of the modern young women in Cusco know only Spanish. What is important to my story is the time when Maya became so ill when she was here visiting. I know you remember that time. Don Carlos was crazy with fear that she might die. Carmen, the *bruja*, worked day and night to save her as her condition became more serious. You came to me in tears, Angelica, and begged me to use my power to save her. How could I refuse you, so filled with love and compassion for your friend?

" I went to the *hacienda* with Miguel while you stayed with your brothers and sisters. I took my healing herbs, *mesas*, stones, and anything I thought I might use to help Maya. Don Carlos greeted us with some surprise, but he was so distraught that he allowed me to move right past him into the house. I told him I wished to see Maya and he led me to her room. She lay on the bed in a state of delirium while her brother, Ricardo, cooled her feverish brow. I could see the remnants of the *bruja's* medicines and magic and asked Don Carlos to remove everything from the room that contained the energies of other healers or shamans. He looked at me, questioningly, and I told him that we had no time for discussions, that Maya's life was slipping away. Hurriedly, he did as I asked, and the other energies cleared from the room. I asked Ricardo to leave the room as well since his emotional body was in turmoil. Don Carlos remained, but stood by the door so as not to interfere. I touched Maya's hand and slipped into the other worlds to read her energies.

"I saw a darkness within her body. She was being consumed by this darkness that had no definition. I moved into her energetic layers trying to find its source. It was not something contagious like the diseases of children. It was not something emotional like the heart sickness of lost love. I found nothing until I entered the layer of spirit and there I saw a being. It was evil, and I knew what task lay before me, perhaps the greatest test of my

[295]

power. Coming back to this reality, I asked your father to find a pan for burning. Mixing sacred herbs, I smudged Maya and the whole room, then put the pan under the bed to smolder. Holding her hand again, I sped out to meet her spirit and confronted the being. It had been weakened somewhat and was willing to listen to me. Asking what evil it meant to cause Maya, it said, "death." I demanded to know why, and it admitted that it was a messenger. We continued to communicate in that way until I discerned that Maya was the victim of a black magician whose intent was really to hurt her father.

"I had the information I wanted, but the being had no intention of leaving Maya's field. Coming back to this reality again, I discussed what I had learned with Don Carlos. He knew the identity of the man who wished to hurt him and told us of this man in the jungle who had tried to use him to profit from the sale of medicine plants. Don Carlos could see the manipulation of the filaments very clearly and confronted the man about his impeccability. The man was very angry and threatened to harm him in some way, but Don Carlos carefully protected himself in the jungle and nothing happened. Now, it seemed that the man had found a shaman who would work with the black arts. Don Carlos was furious. I could feel his blood boiling as he paced back and forth between the window and the door with his eyes on fire. His dark face was flushed and his great mustache twitched uncontrollably. Suddenly he stopped and announced that he would perform a *kuti* to send the filaments back to his enemy through the shaman. Someone would pay for the illness and possible death of his daughter. *Kutis* were rituals which sent negative energy back to its source, but magnified it many times over. I never use this ritual. When it was first created, I think it was to return the original filaments, but later, it has been used in a way that stretches impeccability beyond limits. It is too much like sorcery.

"Don Carlos looked shocked and insulted when I told him that his suggestion would surely kill Maya. I waited until he calmed himself completely and then asked him to sit down beside me. I explained to him that there was a way to rid Maya of the evil being. I told him the being could be dissolved and the energies of it extracted in one way only, and that was with love. He lowered his eyes, and knew that I spoke the truth. He asked me what he could do. I took Maya's hand again and, with my other hand, I touched the arm of Don Carlos. Miguel guarded the door. Before slipping back into Maya's energy fields, I instructed Don Carlos to begin sending love to the man who tricked him and to the shaman who sent the dark energies. I would stay with the being and guide the process of dissolution until it was complete. At first, Don Carlos frowned, then he closed his eyes and began to bring forth the *munay* (loving power) that he knew so well.

"I moved back into the other world and out into Maya's energetic layers to the spirit. The being was still there waiting for me to return. It knew we were going to do battle. I spoke to it and asked it to make the process easier by receiving our love. The being laughed and said it would try even harder to kill Maya. I remained firm and told it to release her. Then I began to add my own *munay* to that of Don Carlos. I could feel Don Carlos struggling to keep his heart open. It would have been simple to open it to Maya, but this task was very distasteful. Eventually I saw him enter her spirit field as well, for he had amazing powers of his own. Together we poured forth love so intense that the being began to melt. Angelica, this proved to me that there is no power as great as love, no energy higher and more useful. After the being was completely dissolved, I began calling its filaments to me and, energetically, ate them. After we came back into this reality, I ran from the house and vomited them out in the garden. Miguel followed me and I asked him to cover the mess with dirt to let Pachamama eat it.

"When we returned to Maya's room, she was sitting up in bed, weak but through her crisis. Don Carlos was in tears, held in the arms of Ricardo who did not understand what had happened. I took the pan of herbs from beneath Maya's bed and told them that I would return in the morning to check on her, but felt that all would be well. Don Carlos hugged me and thanked me profusely. Then your father and I left. That was the first and last time I have been called upon to work with the forces of darkness. One time is enough. The next day I arrived to check on Maya and she was up and eating at the breakfast table. I was asked to join them for breakfast and Don Carlos served me himself. Since that time, he has honored me often and I have assisted him whenever he has called me. He understood the need for me to work in secrecy and so it has remained.

"As you grew older and married Pedro, Don Carlos was always there to help you and your family. He has been a great benefactor to us and to this village. I have watched his assemblage point shift to a new place since that healing with Maya. He has anchored his *munay* now. Before, his love was tinged with a little guilt. This was the product of his *mestizo* blood, for the offspring of the conquistadors and the subsequent land owners have taken on the filaments of guilt. Now he sees that it is not necessary to feel that way, but only to love unconditionally. If he had been unable to hold *munay* that night, Maya would not be with us now. I have seen that Don Carlos is opening codes within you Angelica, and that is another reason we are meeting tonight.

"You and I are carrying codes of light. When they are opened, they are available to the universe in accordance with the Divine Plan. They support higher consciousness. I remember when mine were opened by Don Martín. He was doing a *mastay* for universal peace in fulfillment of the prophecies, and asked me to kneel before him. He cleansed me with the *despacho* and blew into the top of my head. The sensation was similar to the time Doña Maria activated my light. That night I slept soundly and dreamed that I was flying through the starry sky. I arrived at a distant star and stood before a group of Akhus who explained to me the greater purpose of my life. It was magical. I think it was a place that Doña Maria had meant to take me, a place called Ak-An. It is the very brightest star in the heavens, Angelica - the one we call Chaska. I flew back to Pachamama and awoke to find Doña Maria standing beside my bed. She said that she had forgotten to take me to Ak-An and that it was necessary for my mission. Then I really awoke, with the realization that I had had a visitation from Doña Maria during my dream.

"Life is magical, Angelica, if we invite the magic to us. Now I realize that Don Martín had opened the codes within me and the real core of my mission began that day. The beings of Ak-An had told me that Don Carlos is a member of a very old brotherhood which has always been with the sisterhood to protect it. He is not aware of that yet, Angelica, but soon will be made aware of his lineage. I am not to tell him. This lineage of men, of which Don Martín was also a member, has the ability and the duty to open the codes of light within women. These include the codes we carry, but also codes that are more universal and intended for increasing the vibration on Pachamama. Many women in the world carry these codes, especially those in the groups Don Carlos is bringing to work with him at Pakulmaka. The Akhus told me that part of his purpose is to bring these women to our village to be opened and awakened in this way, and said that you and I would eventually have opportunities to work with them. We are to move the subtle energies within these women to awaken them to their divine feminine. Does this not sound like a joyous task, my daughter?"

*

Angelica, who had been sitting quietly through her mother's discourse, became excited. She had felt the stirring of this work within her and was feeling blessed that her mother was sharing this information. For several years, she had been helping Don Carlos by cleaning the house after the groups had left, and by working in the gardens. She felt an excitement about what was happening which she shared with her mother. Angelica poured tea for both of them and Francesca continued.

*

"You are closer to these people than I am, Angelica. I have purposely stayed away and Don Carlos has respected my need for secrecy. It is thrilling, my daughter, because the prophecies are being fulfilled, and two years from now, those for the next five hundred years will be divined. Five hundred years ago, it was said that at the end of this cycle, the nature of time would change. Consciousness would expand to include the many realities previously known only to shamans. I feel this time of change upon us, Angelica. It was said that the new Wiracochas would come from afar to this land and that we would, at last, pass the responsibility of conscious ascension to them. Imagining this at first was not easy, but now I see how it will happen. The Akhus told me that you and I were to act as a bridge for this great blessing to occur. Angelica, this is a mission that began in Peru with Mamacocha. Qoyari enlivened and infused it with more truth and wisdom. What a great honor it is to be the last of the Andean lineage, and to fulfill the mission of all the women who have come before us. It brings tears to my eyes to speak of it.

"We will have many interactions with the new Wiracochas in the near future, my daughter. There is a Divine Plan unfolding for all of us. However, I did not know how to put the last pieces of this puzzle together until this morning. Don Carlos asked me to come to the *hacienda* for breakfast. A small group of women are visiting him now from the United States. He said that he had a powerful dream last night in which Don Martín and he shared a casual bottle of wine. At one point in the dream, Don Martín leaned towards him and told him to introduce his group of women to me. He awoke and devised a plan that would be very simple. He asked Miguel to come to breakfast to speak of shamanism and I was to accompany your father as his wife.

"I sat quietly and observed the group while sipping tea and

eating buttered pan. One woman whose light was noticeable appeared to be the leader of the group. The other women had very good light too, in fact extraordinarily so, but this woman was more open and she intrigued me. While she was engaged in a discussion with Don Carlos and Miguel, I moved into trance state and entered her field. Angelica, she bore the disc of Inti on her forehead and her heart. She is a sister from a far away land, and she looks like the Akhus of legend with her blonde hair and blue eyes. I saw that our hearts formed a bridge to each other and it was hard not to weep. Don Carlos assured me that she would return many times to Pakulmaka and I became content to allow the unfoldment of the Divine Plan. I know now how Doña Maria felt when she saw the disc of Inti on my forehead.

"It is different for you and me, my daughter. I do not have to wait until I die to pass the lineage on to you. We are to work as a team and pass back the lineage to those who have finally found us. It will not occur overnight for this woman has healing to accomplish within herself before she can assume the mission which awaits her. In time, the opportunties will arise to work with her and move the subtle energy. For now, her work is with Don Carlos who understands her importance to the mission. She will help Don Carlos understand his own lineage, for when she finally does open to her light, her vision will be as vast as the starry night.

"Now my Angelica, I wish to complete my sacred duty to you and awaken your light completely. Your work will unfold quickly then, and I will help you in every possible way. Come to me, my beloved daughter, and I will complete our work tonight."

*

Francesca asked her daughter to sit quietly next to her. She placed her hand upon her brow and sent energy within to activate Angelica's light body. There was not so much a shower of sparks and light, but more the glow of a star shining as her power came forth in a process not unlike birth. It was strong light, filled with *munay*. Francesca was careful not to embrace her daughter for she wanted the filaments of light to fully connect with Pachamama. She asked Angelica to sleep for several hours, if not the entire night, in the women's hut so the filaments would not be disturbed. Angelica did as she was told, lying down on a sleeping mat kept in a corner of the room for healings. Francesca built up the dung fire before emerging out under the night sky. As she made her way back to her own home, she kept her eyes on Chaska, the brightest star in the sky, and thanked the Akhus for sending the dream to Don Carlos. That night Angelica dreamed of women - circles of women sitting in dark huts around a fire. They were ancient women with discs of the Sun on their foreheads. They were dark-skinned and light-skinned, dark-haired and light-haired, dark-eyed and light-eyed. They were all beautiful.

Leah speaks

Magic was thick in the room as Leah finished her story and emerged from the light trance she had used to bring Francesca through her. She pulled towards her a woven bag that Don Carlos had given her several years earlier. Careful to work silently, without disturbing the group energy she removed an old weaving from the bag. She held the bundle briefly to her heart and then arose. She circled the back of the group using the bundle to weave and uplift the filaments even further. Returning to her place in the circle, she held the bundle in her arms and spoke in a whisper.

"Beloveds, our time is complete. It is not appropriate for me to speak of my own life now. I know you will understand and forgive me, for your hearts are so big. When we meet again next summer, we will continue this work together. For now, I leave you with a little mystery. I surround you with my own love and ask beloved Sananda to guide each of you in your work. You are the new Wiracochas. Be in God's grace. I love you so much."

The circle of women were tearful as Leah bowed her head and began gently pulling the old weaving away from that which lay within the bundle. They saw the smooth edge of a large stone emerge as she folded one corner of the cloth beneath it. She rocked the bundle in her arms for a moment, then picked it up and kissed the stone. Setting it in her lap, she pulled back the cloth from the left, the right and finally below the stone, exposing it. Tears fell from her eyes upon the stone as she picked it up and turned it to face the group. The women gasped and held each other. It was the Akhu, the very stone brought from Mir-An-Da to Titicaca Lake by Mak-Ma. The very stone Qoyari buried above her village. Leah cradled it in her arms again and then handed it to Katy on her left, who received it as she would a newborn. Leah pushed her heart energy out to the women and spun them into a magical cocoon of light. "My beloveds," she concluded, "each of you take a turn holding this being to your heart. Allow the Divine Mother within you to come forth in ecstasy. Allow the codes of deep re-membrance to open, and never forget that you are from the stars."

About Jessie E. Ayani, PhD

A scientist turned shaman, Jessie travels internationally training women and men to awaken their true power - the power of a
focused heart. She was awakened by the Andean Elders, the open-
hearted people of Peru, and the Ascended Masters. Jessie is the
author of *The Lineage of the Codes of Light* and *The Brotherhood
of the Magi*, as well as *Awakening and Healing the Rainbow Body*,
a personal guide to enlightenment. She has recorded two audio
CDs to support the healing of the rainbow body with a third CD
and a workbook planned for 2006.

Jessie leads sacred journeys to places of activation and
healing each year for those who have studied in circle with her.
For information about working in circle with Jessie, travel opportunities, her annual Mount Shasta Retreat, and current publica-
tions, visit our website. If you would like to sponsor a circle, email
inquiries to info@heartofthesun.com.

HEART OF THE SUN
http://www.heartofthesun.com

ORDER FORM

Please send:

_____ *copies of* The Lineage of the Codes of Light

_____ *copies of* The Brotherhood of the Magi

_____ *copies of* Awakening and Healing the Rainbow Body

_____ CDs, Deep Trance Shamanic Journey, Volume I
Pachamama's Child
_____ CDs, Deep Trance Shamanic Journey, Volume II
Right Relationship

Name: _____

Address: _____

City: _____ State:____ Zip: _____

email: _____

I ENCLOSE THE FOLLOWING PAYMENT:

Lineage $18.00 X _____(# of copies) = $_____

Magi $18.00 X _____(# of copies) = $_____

Awakening $16.00 X _____(# of copies) = $_____

CDs $16.00 X _____(# of copies) = $_____

CA residents add sales tax of 7.25% $_____

Shipping and handling (1st item $3, add'l items $1 each) $_____

Total enclosed $_____

MAKE CHECKS PAYABLE TO:

Heart of the Sun, P.O. Box 495, Mount Shasta, CA 96067.

To use credit cards for shipped books, order from Village Books in Mt. Shasta (linked to our website or 530-926-1678) or Amazon.com.